W0252601

STARK

ABITUR
2011

Prüfungsaufgaben
mit Lösungen

Englisch

Grundkurs
3. Prüfungsfach und Colloquium
Gymnasium
Bayern
2000–2010

STARK

ISBN 978-3-89449-090-4

© 2010 by Stark Verlagsgesellschaft mbH & Co. KG
33. ergänzte Auflage
www.stark-verlag.de

Das Werk und alle seine Bestandteile sind urheberrechtlich geschützt. Jede vollständige oder teilweise Vervielfältigung, Verbreitung und Veröffentlichung bedarf der ausdrücklichen Genehmigung des Verlages.

Inhalt

Hinweise
Stichwortverzeichnis

Hinweise und Tipps zur Textbearbeitung

Figures of Speech I
Tips for Composition V
Tips for Questions on the Text IX
Tips for Translation XI
Tips for the Exam XV

Colloquiumsprüfung

I. Allgemeines zum Prüfungsablauf und zu den angeführten Beispielen 1
II. Referat zum Schwerpunktthema und weiterführende Fragen 1
III. Bewertung 2
IV. Beispiele 3
– Lord of the Flies 3
– Home-schooling 5
– US Immigration 7

Abiturprüfung 2000

Aufgabe I: Do Parents Know Their Kids? 2000-1
Aufgabe II: From: Anne Tyler, *Searching for Caleb*, 1975 2000-7

Abiturprüfung 2001

Aufgabe I: A Princely Pioneer 2001-1
Aufgabe II: From: Nick Hornby, *About a Boy*, 1998 2001-7

Abiturprüfung 2002

Aufgabe I: What the Internet cannot do 2002-1
Aufgabe II: From: Roddy Doyle, *The Dinner*, 2001 2002-7

Abiturprüfung 2003

Aufgabe I: Kings of Spray 2003-1
Aufgabe II: From: Barbara Kingsolver, *The Bean Trees*, 1988 2003-8

Abiturprüfung 2004

Aufgabe I: Must the Backpackers Stay Home? 2004-1
Aufgabe II: From: Hanif Kureishi, *Love in a Blue Time*, 1997 2004-7

Fortsetzung siehe nächste Seite

Abiturprüfung 2005

Aufgabe I: Pay up! Pay up! And play the game! 2005-1
Aufgabe II: From: Gore Vidal, *The City and the Pillar,* 1948 2005-9

Abiturprüfung 2006

Aufgabe I: A New Irish Migration 2006-1
Aufgabe II: From: Charlie Higson, *The Red Line*, 1993 2006-8

Abiturprüfung 2007

Aufgabe I: Fill Notebooks, And Then A Few Bellies 2007-1
Aufgabe II: From: Jonathan Safran Foer,
Extremely Loud and Incredibly Close, 2005 2007-8

Abiturprüfung 2008

Aufgabe I: Minding about the gap 2008-1
Aufgabe II: From: Paul Auster, *The Locked Room*, 2004 2008-9

Abiturprüfung 2009

Aufgabe I: Britons are leaving the gym 2009-1
Aufgabe II: From: Frank McCourt, *Tis – A Memoir*, 1999 2009-8

Abiturprüfung 2010

Aufgabe I: Caterpillars and Cookie Dough 2010-1
Aufgabe II: From: Alan Bennet, *The Uncommon Reader*, 2007 2010-8

Jeweils im Herbst erscheinen die neuen Ausgaben
der Abiturprüfungsaufgaben mit Lösungen.

Lösungen der Aufgaben:

2010: Jürgen Naumann und Christoph Neuerer
2007–2009: Dieter Hannack und Jürgen Naumann
2000–2006: Dieter Hannack und Klaus Reitemeier

Hinweise

In Bayern werden die schriftlichen Abituraufgaben zentral vom Kultusministerium gestellt. Beim Grundkurs Englisch stehen zwei Texte zur Auswahl (Aufgabe I: Sachtext/Aufgabe II: literarischer Text), von denen der Schüler einen auswählt.

Die Arbeitszeit beträgt im Grundkurs 210 Minuten, einschließlich 30 Minuten Einlesezeit.

Die maximale Zahl der Bewertungseinheiten (BE) pro Textaufgabe beträgt in der Regel für den Grundkurs 160 BE. Je nach den spezifischen Eigenheiten des zugrunde liegenden Textes bieten sich unterschiedliche Gewichtungen der einzelnen Aufgabenteile an, die sich jedoch in folgendem Rahmen bewegen sollen:

Textverständnis und Textanalyse:	50 %
textübergreifende Aufgabe(n):	25 %
Version:	25 %

Bei den Aufgaben zum **Textverständnis bzw. zur Textanalyse** ist die **inhaltliche Leistung** folgenden BE-Stufen zuzuordnen:

5 BE voll text- und sachbezogen; überzeugend dargestellt
4 BE im Wesentlichen text- und sachbezogen und folgerichtig dargestellt
3 BE einzelne Mängel in Text- und Sachbezug; z. T. Lücken in der Darstellung, aber noch klar *

---

2 BE gravierende Mängel in Text- und Sachbezug; Darstellung wiederholt nicht folgerichtig
1 BE Text- und Sachbezug kaum erkennbar; unübersichtliche Darstellung
0 BE völliges Missverstehen bzw. Themaverfehlung; wirre Darstellung

Für die **sprachliche Leistung** ergibt sich entsprechend folgender Zuordnungsvorschlag:

5 BE sprachlich und stilistisch überzeugend; eigenständige Formulierungen
4 BE sprachlich und stilistisch überwiegend korrekt; meist eigenständige Formulierungen
3 BE sprachliche und stilistische Mängel; z. T. längere Übernahmen aus der Textvorlage *

---

2 BE Teile der Aussage wegen gravierender Mängel schwer verständlich bzw. wenig eigenständige Formulierungen
1 BE wegen einer Vielzahl gravierender sprachlicher Mängel insgesamt kaum verständlich bzw. im Wesentlichen Übernahme der Textvorlage
0 BE insgesamt unverständlich bzw. keinerlei eigenständige Textproduktion

* Die Linie kennzeichnet die Schwelle zwischen noch ausreichenden und nicht mehr ausreichenden Leistungen

Bei den **textübergreifenden Aufgaben** gilt zur Einstufung der **inhaltlichen Leistung** folgendes Schema:

4 BE differenzierte und sachbezogene Argumentation; überzeugende Darstellung
3 BE im Wesentlichen differenzierte und sachbezogene Argumentation; meist folgerichtige Darstellung
2 BE nur zum Teil differenzierte und sachfremde Argumentation; Darstellung teilweise nicht folgerichtig *

---

1 BE mehrfache Abweichungen vom Thema; unübersichtliche Darstellung
0 BE Themaverfehlung; wirre Darstellung

Für die **sprachliche Leistung** wird folgender Zuordnungsvorschlag empfohlen:

6 BE sprachlich und stilistisch hervorragend; großer Abwechslungsreichtum in den Bereichen Wortschatz, grammatische Strukturen und sprachliche Textstrukturierung
5 BE sprachlich und stilistisch ansprechend; Bemühen um Abwechslungsreichtum in den Bereichen Wortschatz, grammatische Strukturen und sprachliche Textstrukturierung deutlich erkennbar
4 BE sprachlich und stilistisch nicht immer korrekt und treffsicher; Neigung zu einfacherem Wortschatz, einfacherem Ausdruck und einfacheren Strukturen; wenige textstrukturierende Elemente
3 BE sprachliche und stilistische Mängel; Verwendung von einfachem Wortschatz, einfachen Strukturen; kaum textstrukturierende Elemente *

---

2 BE wegen gravierender Mängel Teile der Aussage schwer verständlich; deutlich begrenzter Wortschatz; einfachste syntaktische Mittel und Strukturen; keine textstrukturierenden Elemente
1 BE wegen einer Vielzahl gravierender Mängel insgesamt kaum verständlich; unzulängliche Verwendung von angemessenem Wortschatz und entsprechenden Strukturen
0 BE sprachlich völlig unbrauchbar und insgesamt unverständlich

Es gelten folgende **Sperrklauseln:**

1. Wird im Beurteilungsbereich *Sprache* bzw. *Inhalt* nur weniger als die Hälfte der maximal erreichbaren BE zuerkannt, so kann die Gesamtleistung bestenfalls mit „noch ausreichend“ bewertet werden.
2. Entfallen auf den Bereich *Sprache* bzw. *Inhalt* 0 BE, so kann für den jeweils anderen Bereich nur weniger als die Hälfte der maximal erreichbaren BE vergeben werden.)

Für die Bewertung der **Version** bei einer Maximalpunktzahl von 40 BE wird folgendes Beispiel gegeben:

Fehlersprung	Note	BE-Spanne bei max. 40 BE
bis 3 F	1	40–36 BE
bis 6 F	2	35–31 BE
bis 9 F	3	30–26 BE
bis 12 F	4	25–20 BE
bis 15 F	5	19–13 BE
ab 16 F	6	12–0 BE
ab 22 F	6	0 BE

Für die Ermittlung der Notenpunkte gilt (bei einer Gesamtpunktzahl von 160):

Bewertungs-einheiten	**Noten-stufen**	**Noten-punkte**
0–52	6	0
53–61	5–	1
62–70	5	2
71–79	5+	3
80–84	4–	4
85–89	4	5
90–95	4+	6
96–100	3–	7
101–105	3	8
106–111	3+	9
112–119	2–	10
120–127	2	11
128–135	2+	12
136–143	1–	13
144–151	1	14
152–160	1+	15

Bei anderen Gesamtpunktzahlen muss
das Schema entsprechend umgerechnet werden.

Sollten nach Erscheinen dieses Bandes noch wichtige Änderungen in der Abitur-Prüfung 2011 vom Kultusministerium bekannt gegeben werden, finden Sie aktuelle Informationen dazu im Internet unter:
www.stark-verlag.de/info.asp?zentrale-pruefung-aktuell

Stichwortverzeichnis

I. Points of Special Interest

adoption 07-3
adventure holidays 04-5
American Dream 08-5 f.
art 03-5 f.
art exhibition (cartoon) 03-3

backpacking 04-1 ff.
British identity 04-9
bullying 04-11
Bush, George W. (US President) 01-5

career 00-11
– choice of ~ 00-7
Celtic Tiger (Irish economic boom) 06-1 f.
childhood 08-13
children and parents 03-12
city planning 01-1 ff.
class 08-1 ff.; 09-10
Clinton, Bill 06-1
computer freaks 02-5
courage 09-12 f.

digital divide 02-4
Delaney, J. J. 06-1

ecological problems 01-5
education 00-1 f.; 00-5; 05-1 ff.; 08-6; Coll. 5
eleven plus (11+) exam 05-1
emigration 06-1, 4
energy problems 01-5
environment 01-5
Eton College 05-3
European Union 06-1 ff.

family 05-12 ff.
family relationships 08-14
farming (organic) 01-1 ff.; 03-14; 10-1 ff.
fitness 09-1 f.
Fitz Gerald, Garret 06-1
food 10-1 ff.
friends 07-9
fulfilment 00-11
fun society 06-12 f.

gender roles 08-3
genetic engineering 03-13
Golden, Harry 06-3
graffiti art 03-1 ff.

Harrow School 05-7
Hispanics (c.f. Latinos) Coll. 7 f.
home-schooling Coll. 5 f.

immigration 02-9; 06-1 ff.; Coll. 7 f.
– ~illegal Coll. 7 f.
information, amount of 00-5
Internet 00-5; 02-1 ff.
Ireland 06-1 ff.

journalism and ethics 07-1 ff.
juvenile problems 00-1 ff.

Kennedy, J. F. 06-1
Kilkenny Castle 06-1, 4

Latinos (c.f. Hispanics) Coll. 7 f.
liberty 07-13 f.
Lonely Planet (guidebooks) 04-5 f.
London (growth) 06-10

marriage
– racially mixed 04-9
Mexican immigrants 06-5
migration 06-1 ff.
mobility 05-4; 08-1 ff.
money 00-11; 05-7; 08-5
Mulroney, Brian 06-1

parents 05-14
personality, analysis of 09-12
potato famine 06-1, 4
Poundbury (model township) 01-1 ff.
prejudice 04-11
Prince Charles (Prince of Wales) 01-1 ff.
Princess Diana 01-1 ff.
public schools (Eton) 05-3

Queen Elizabeth II 10-8 ff.

racial prejudice 02-11
reading 10-8 ff.
Reagan, Ronald 06-1
rights, defending your 02-11
role models (c.f. idols) 01-9
Royal Family (British) 05-7

school exchange 06-6
schools (state and private) 05-1 ff.
school systems (Bavarian) 06-6
school uniform 01-8

September 11th 07-8 f., 14
social class 05-1 ff.; 08-1
social skills 01-10; 07-6
sport 09-5 f.
state schools 05-1 ff.

teachers 05-6
teenagers 00-1 ff., 5
terrorism 04-1 ff.
tourism 04-1 ff.
travelling 04-1 ff.; 06-13

TV (television) 00-5

university admission 05-1 ff.
urban problems 01-5

videoclips 03-5 f.
violence (at school) 00-3; 00-9

workaholics 00-11 f.
World Trade Center (9/11) 07-8 f., 14

youth 00-1 ff.

II. Literature, Film

Auster, Paul: The Locked Room 08-9
Bennet, Alan: The Uncommon Reader 10-8 f.
Cry Freedom 09-12 f.
Doyle, Roddy: The Dinner 02-7 f.
Dreiser, Theodore: Sister Carrie 01-5
Fitzgerald, F. Scott: The Great Gatsby 08-5 f.
Foer, Jonathan: Extremely Loud and Incredibly Close 07-8 f.
Golding, William: Lord of the Flies Coll. 3 f.
Higson, Charlie: The Red Line 06-8 f.
Hornby, Nick: About a boy 01-7
Kingsolver, Barbara: The Bean Trees 03-8 ff.
Kureishi, Hanif: Love in a Blue Time 04-7 f.
McCourt, Frank: Tis – A Memoir 09-8 ff.
Sinclair, Upton: The Jungle 01-5
Tyler, Anne: Searching fo Caleb 00-7 ff.
Vidal, Gore: The City and the Pillar 05-9 f.

III. Stylistic Devices and Composition

antithetical structure 02-7
attitude of the author 01-4; 03-4 f.; 05-6; 06-4, 5

cartoon, analysis of 03-3, 6; 05-3, 7, 15; 07-14; 08-6; 08-14; 09-6, 10,13; 10-7, 13 f.
characterization 01-9
– language 04-10
choice of words 01-4; 02-5; 06-4; 08-13

effect 01-9 f.
email 10-12 f.
exaggeration 05-6; 09-5
expository (text) 01-4; 06-5

factual information 06-5
fairy tale 01-4 f.; 08-11
figures (function) 06-5

headline (effect) 00-4; 03-4, 10-11 f.
– subject matter 02-4
humour 10-12

imagery 06-4; 08-12
Internet forum 08-13
introduction, function of 01-4 f.
irony 05-6, 14

language, use of 05-13; 07-13; 10-5, 12
letter-writing
– formal letter 03-14
– letter of complaint 04-5 f.
– letter to a friend 95-10; 06-13
– letter to the editor 07-6 f.

metaphor 00-4, 11; 07-5; 08-12; 09-5; 10-6, 12
mode of presentation 03-12

narrative (text) 06-5

outline (c.f. summary)

personification 09-5
perspective 01-9 f.; 06-12; 08-13; 09-12
point of view 03-4 f.; 06-12

questions
– real/rhetorical 07-5
quotations
– function 00-4; 01-4; 02-4; 06-4, 5

reader's
– interest (arousing of) 00-4
– feelings 02-10

short sentences 07-5
simile 00-4
statement (function) 04-4
style 03-12; 06-5
summary Coll. 3 f., 6, 9, 12
surveys 00-4

text type 06-5; 08-5

writer's attitude (see attitude of the author)

Hinweise und Tipps zur Textbearbeitung

Figures of Speech

Glossary

In the "Questions on the text" assignments you are sometimes asked to identify and analyse figures of speech (stylistic devices). These are expressions and phrases which are different from normal usage or sentence construction. Their aim is to make language more beautiful and/or to achieve certain effects. As the texts used for the Abitur exams are rarely very poetical, nor the questions about figures of speech very numerous, we will not give you the complete list of these devices but concentrate on the usual ones and the ones that have already occurred in previous Abitur texts.

Accumulation: A string of similar expressions one after the other. When they increase in importance → climax, when they decrease → anticlimax
Example: He moved the whole company*, lock, stock, and barrel*, to Mexico. (Dictionary of Contemporary English, DCE)
Effect: Emphasis

Alliteration: Words beginning with the same sound
Example: Learn to say before you sing. (Proverb)
Effect: Emphasis, force, rhythm of language

Antithesis: Showing the exact opposite in parallel words, phrases or grammatical structures
Example: Poor men seek meat for their stomach, rich men stomach for their meat. (Proverb)
Effect: Emphasis of content through contrast in form

Climax: A series of statements or ideas starting with the weakest and ending in the strongest
Example: Friends, Romans, *countrymen*! (Shakespeare, Julius Caesar)
Effect: Emphasis, surprise

Anticlimax: The opposite of climax: a sequence of expressions that decrease in importance or value
Example: For God, for country, and *for Yale.*
Effect: Humour, satirical

Ellipsis: One or more words necessary for the grammatical structure are left out on purpose
Example: In Essex he could go anywhere he pleased. Alone. (Instead of: He could go alone.) (L. L. Rice, Southern Exposure)
Effect: Showing emotion, emphasis

Emphasis: Stressing the importance of a statement, usually by using the *to do*-structure in positive sentences
Example: He *does go* to school …
(B. Vine, King Solomon's Carpet)
Effect: Of course: emphasis!

Euphemism: The use of more polite expressions for something the writer considers shocking or unpleasant
Example: rest room, for: toilet; to pass away, for: to die
Effect: The tone (or the writer) is shown as mild, inoffensive, or prudish

Exaggeration: (Also: overstatement, hyperbole): To make something greater or bigger than it really is (This is also a form of → irony). See also the opposite: → understatement
Example: They advertise in about a thousand magazines.
(Salinger, Catcher in the Rye)
Effect: Emphasis, humour

Irony: Expressing the opposite of one's real opinion. This only works if it is clear that the speaker doesn't mean what he says.
→ Sarcasm and cynicism (the bitterest) are stronger and more negative forms of irony.
Example: I was the goddam manager of the fencing team. Very big deal. (Salinger, Catcher in the Rye)
Effect: Humour, criticism, (shows the speaker's wit and superiority, underlines the real meaning)

Metaphor: A poetical comparison that does not use *like* or *as*. It indicates resemblance but does not express it directly.
Example: All the world's a stage … (Not: … is *like* a stage …)
(Shakespeare, As You Like It)
Life's but a walking shadow …
(Shakespeare, Macbeth)
Effect: Poetical, vividness

Paradox: A statement that seems impossible at first glance as it contains two contradictory or strange assertions, but is intended to be true all the same
Example: Divorces are made in heaven.
(Wilde, The Importance of Being Earnest)
Fair is foul and foul is fair …
(Shakespeare, Macbeth)
Effect: Surprise, amusement, makes the reader think

Parallelism: The use of corresponding grammatical forms and structures in a sequence
Example: What a day may bring, a day may take away. (Proverb)
Effect: Emphasis

Personification: Things, animals, or abstractions are given human qualities or are presented as persons (can also be considered as a → metaphor – it compares indirectly)
Example: The day has eyes, the night has ears. (Proverb)
Effect: Poetical, vividness

Pun: A play on words: sometimes on different meanings of the same word (homonyms: the bear – to bear), sometimes on the same sound of two words (homophones: new – knew)
Example: Seven days without water makes one *weak*. (DCE) homophone*: week*
Effect: Humour

Repetition: Mentioning the same word or phrase several times
Example: Tomorrow and tomorrow and tomorrow… (Shakespeare, Macbeth)
Effect: Intensification, poetical

Rhetorical question: A question to which no answer is expected, as the answer is believed to be too obvious
Example: Who is here so base, that would be a bondman? (Shakespeare, Julius Caesar)
Effect: Emphasis; makes the listener feel he himself has found the answer and thus agree with the speaker. Often used in political speech

Sarcasm: A form of → irony which is mocking, contemptuous, or aggressive
Example: Protesting can be fun – particularly if the weather is good. (The Guardian Weekly)
Effect: Shows the author's anger or contempt

Simile: A poetical comparison using the words *like* or *as* (unlike the → metaphor)
Example: My love is like a red, red rose. (Robert Burns)
Effect: Poetical, graphic power

Symbol: A word which represents or is associated with an idea, a sign of something
Example: *Dove* standing for *peace*, the *sword* representing *force*
Effect: Poetical

Understatement: (Also: Litotes): Expressing oneself in a way to make something appear less important than it really is. Also a form of → irony, as it usually means the opposite
Example: The Queen was not amused. (She was very angry!)
Effect: Emphasis through apparent lack of emphasis

Practice

The following examples all contain figures of speech. Try and identify them. The solutions are given at the end.

1. You look as if your name was Ernest. You are the most earnest looking person I ever saw. (Wilde, The Importance of Being Earnest)
2. [A diary] is simply a very young girl's record of her own thoughts and impressions, and consequently meant for publication. (Wilde)
3. … the way you flirt with Gwendolyn is perfectly disgraceful. It is almost as bad as the way Gwendolyn flirts with you. (Wilde)
4. If I am occasionally a little over-dressed, I make up for it by being always immensely over-educated. (Wilde)
5. Your vanity is ridiculous, your conduct an outrage, and your presence in my garden utterly absurd. (Wilde)

6. … Edgar, who has seen me buy white paper about 36,987 times (Newsweek 2002)
7. I have dared to love you wildly, passionately, devotedly, hopelessly. (Wilde)
8. Today I broke off my engagement with Ernest … the weather still continues charming. (Wilde)
9. Oh, do let me read them, Cecily! (Wilde)
10. Did this in Caesar seem ambitious, … was this ambition? (Shakespeare, Julius Caesar)
11. There is tears for his love, joy for his fortune, honour for his valour, and death for his ambition. (Shakespeare)
12. … believe me for mine honour, and have respect to mine honour. (Shakespeare)
13. … drive the scourge of slavery from our soil. (Barack Obama)
14. … after the last glass of Pommard with blue cheese, it is not wise to rise too rapidly from the chair. That might be too strenuous. (TIME, 1968)
15. (The House of Lords) has given the impression of being preserved somehow in aspic. (The Observer)
16. I think my father is like the Holy Trinity … (Frank McCourt, Angela's Ashes)
17. The stove showed what importance every one of us held in the classroom. (LK 96, adapted)
18. Familiarity breeds contempt. (Proverb)
19. Death pays all debts. (Proverb)
20. It is an outrage to bind a Roman citizen; it is a crime to scourge him; it is almost parricide to kill him, but to crucify him …? (Cicero)

Solutions

1. Pun 2. Paradox 3. Antithesis 4. Parallelism 5. Accumulation 6. Exaggeration 7. Accumulation 8. Anticlimax 9. Emphasis 10. Rhetorical question 11. Anticlimax 12. Repetition 13. Metaphor 14. Irony 15. Sarcasm 16. Simile 17. Symbol 18. Cynicism 19. Personification 20. Climax

Tips for Composition

1. Comment

Before you begin it is recommendable to get into the topic by brainstorming, for example by drawing a mind map, starting with a key word and branching off further ideas in topical or logical order.
In the classic **argumentative type** you have to weigh some pros and cons. The structure is quite easy:

A. Introduction referring to the topic

Here are some ways of introducing your composition. Remember to keep it short, though.

- a **quotation** (from an expert, a song-line, a proverb or other saying, what your parents always say, etc. They don't have to be literal quotes.)
- a **definition** of the key words in the question (e. g. What is society, what is misbehaviour?) It is recommendable to consult the dictionary, even when you don't want to define your key-words: you will understand exactly what they mean, you get paraphrases you can use later in the text, you find related words, you will see what the corresponding prepositions are.
- an **example** from a book or film, an article you read
- a **personal experience** with the theme
- a **commonplace** like: The older generation always lament the decline of manners …
- a **provocative question** or statement
- a **current** or **historical event**

B. Topic sentence introducing the pros (or cons)

1, 2, (3): Arguments, views and examples

C. Topic sentence introducing the cons (or pros)

1, 2, (3): Arguments, views and examples

You should first present the views you oppose (B) and then the arguments that support your own opinion (C).
For a greater variety in enumerating and connecting sentences or arguments you can use some of the following expressions:

- *First(ly), second(ly), third(ly)*
- *First of all; in the first place, in the second place; on the one hand, on the other hand*
- *Moreover, furthermore, in addition to that, similarly*

To express contrary or qualifying ideas you can write:

- *Although, however, yet, nevertheless, even so, whereas, contrary to*

D. Conclusion (your own position)

To round off your composition:
- *In short, to sum up, in conclusion, all in all, as far as I am concerned, taking everything into consideration, personally, it seems to me*
- return to the title
- show consequences
- present a view to the future

The **expository composition** is similar in introduction and conclusion, only in the main part one argument follows the other, with the strongest one put forward at the end. You should always and clearly stick to the basic structure of introduction, main part and conclusion, and use concrete examples to avoid being too theoretical.
Most students don't take the trouble to write rough drafts, to save time. This is quite OK but you should at least group your ideas in an outline, which you can stick to while you are writing.
When you are done read everything again carefully checking for mistakes in spelling, grammar and expression. Consult your dictionary as much as possible.
Don't add new arguments.

2. Commenting on a cartoon

When asked to analyse a cartoon, you should first describe the scene, the persons, objects and the action portrayed in the picture. Then you should identify the title or/and caption of the cartoon and relate it to the picture.
As a next step you should recognise and decipher the symbols and icons used in the cartoon, e.g. a dove stands for peace, chains for bondage, scales for justice, etc.
Then you should be able to relate the cartoon to the political or social situation to which it refers and you must try and explain the message (what/who does the cartoonist want to criticise, which current problem does he refer to, who does he side with/against, etc.). Finally you may say, from your own experience and with your own arguments, whether you agree or disagree with the cartoonist.

3. Letter-writing

A. Personal letter (Letter to a friend)

Writer's address Date My/dear/Dear/Dearest, Capital letter … … … Love, kind regards, best wishes, First name PS …	Paragraphs – Reason, thanks, excuse – Subject – Conclusion (wish, hope, looking forward to) Colloquial but correct and good style

Example: Try to explain your behaviour to a friend. (gk 2006 II)

B. Letter to the editor

Writer's address Date Name and address of recipient: The Editor Newsweek Inc. 251 West 57th St New York, NY 10019 Reference Re: Your article on … Dear Sir or Madam … Yours faithfully, Writer's full name	Structure: – Refer to the particular article/letter (opinion, appreciate, protest, suggest) – State your concern, with arguments Formal language Polite and logical

Example: Point out why you are appalled by a particular picture. (gk 2007 I)

C. Letter of complaint

Writer's name, address, phone, fax, email Date Recipient's address Reference (Re: …) Dear Sir or Madam … Yours sincerely, (Or: Yours faithfully,) Full name	Structure: – Your complaint – Details – Suggestions for settlement of the matter – Express hope for favourable reply – Set time limit, threaten further action Formal language Polite but firm

Example: Complain about a disastrous holiday. (gk 2004 I)

D. Letter of application

Form: see B and C

Structure: – How you heard about the post – Info about yourself (age, education, career) – Why you are interested/qualified – Readiness for interview – Inclusion of C. V., certificates, testimonials, stamped addressed envelope Tone: Formal, enthusiastic **Don't:** boast, flatter, make demands, complain about your present employer, show how much you need the job

4. Speech

- Structure your arguments clearly
- Address and welcome the audience
- Use stylistic devices like
  - rhetorical questions
  - repetition
  - alliteration
  - metaphor
  - irony
- Integrate the audience *(As responsible citizens, consumers, parents, etc., we ...)*
- End forcefully, with an appeal, a call for action

Examples: A speech at a school meeting (gk 2004 II)
A farewell speech at a school assembly (gk 2006 I)

5. Interview or dialogue

- Don't just write along what comes to your mind but structure your points in advance
- Introduce the situation or subject; save the stronger parts for the second half
- Conclude with thanks and good wishes
- Pay attention to the stylistic levels (formal, colloquial) of each partner

So far this type of task has only been tested in Leistungskurs exams.

Examples: An interview with an animal rights activist (LK 2003 I)
An interview with an athlete who has tested positive (LK 2004 I)
An interview with the Minister of Education (LK 2005 II)

Tips for Questions on the Text

It is wise to answer them in the given order.

Begin by reading the first question carefully and find out **how many parts** it includes. Then go through the text with a **text marker** and highlight every passage that refers to the question.
Employ the same technique in the following questions with different markers. You may discover parts of the text which you have overlooked previously.
Now work on the questions by **using and connecting** the underlined quotes. Try to use your own words – the dictionary can help you to find suitable paraphrases. If you decide to use a passage, make sure to **quote it properly**.
The following **question-types** have often been used:

– **How does the author arouse the reader's interest?**

Hints for your answer:
- headline, introduction, first paragraph
- personal approach, personal experience, human interest
- tone (humour, irony)
- direct speech
- examples, quotes, facts
- surprise (unexpected turns, statements)
- figures of speech (rhetorical questions, comparisons, metaphors, parallelisms, climax, anticlimax)
- unusual structure

– **What is the function of the first paragraph?**

Hints for your answer:
- arouses the reader's interest
- states important opinions, raises questions
- introduces the issue

– **How does the author make his article appear objective?**

Hints for your answer:
- avoids personal opinion and judgement
- states facts and figures
- quotations
- refers to scientific studies
- uses controlled language

– **What is the author's tone?**

Hints for your answer: Tone refers to the author's mood or attitude, which can usually be described by the corresponding adjectives, e. g.
- ironical
- sarcastic
- cynical
- humorous
- earnest, solemn
- detached
- angry
- provocative.

Another possibility is understatement or exaggeration.
Don't forget to support with <u>evidence from the text</u>.

- **Characterize a person**

  Hints for your answer:
  - direct (explicit) characterization: author, narrator, or persons tell the reader about somebody's character. Look for examples!
  - indirect (implicit) characterization: the narrator gives clues from a person's actions, opinions, or choice of words what to think about him/her. Find these examples and draw your conclusions!

  (s. Stichwortverzeichnis III: characterization)

- **What kind of reader is the text intended for?**

  Hints for your answer:
  - The source: TIME, Newsweek etc.
  - The content: non-fictional reports, comments, descriptions, criticism, allusions to general knowledge
  - The structure: expository, argumentative, coherently organised
  - Style and language: figures of speech, expressions derived from Latin, formal (colloquial, slang?), educated words, objective (emotional?), complex sentence structure

  Usually the criteria above appeal to politically and culturally interested readers.

- **Analyse the perspective/point of view**

  Hints for your answer:
  - **First-person-narrator:** He tells the story from his personal perspective and shares his ideas and feelings with the reader (strong identification). Problem: he may not be reliable.
  - **3rd-person-narrator:** He may be omniscient about all characters' thoughts and feelings, which leaves little room for the readers' own interpretation. His point-of-view may be limited, so he will tell what only he knows and feels. The reader will also identify with him, but not as strongly as with the first-person-narrator. The reader can only speculate on the motives of other characters.

    The observer-narrator strictly observes, like a camera, and doesn't draw conclusions or speculate on feelings, so that his narration appears trustworthy and objective.

    Stream-of-consciousness-technique: The reader is allowed to read the character's unfiltered thoughts (which are neither organized, nor interpreted) and can make his own analysis.

    Interior monologue: Events and feelings are presented through the mind of one character, without interruption, as if he is speaking to himself. Usually the first person is used.

    Reported thought: It informs the reader, in a coherent way, without discourse markers like "he thought," about what the narrator thinks or feels.

  (s. Stichwortverzeichnis III: point of view)

– **Characterize the stylistic level**

Hints for your answer:
- choice of words (register): colloquial, formal, scientific
- tone: humor, irony, matter-of-fact
- sentence structure: simple, complex
- text type: expository, descriptive, argumentative, narrative

Tips for Translation

Die Übersetzung nimmt in der bayerischen Abiturprüfung breiten Raum ein: mit 40 von 160 BE im Grundkurs macht sie sogar ein Viertel der Note aus. Das ist sicherlich Grund genug, sich eingehender mit ihr zu beschäftigen, zumal viele Schüler sie nur als lästiges Anhängsel betrachten. Die alte Frage, ob eine Übersetzung sinngemäß oder wörtlich sein soll, lässt sich sicher dahin beantworten, dass sie so wörtlich wie nötig, aber so frei wie möglich sein soll.

An dieser Stelle soll auf einige englische Konstruktionen eingegangen werden, die im Deutschen keine Entsprechung haben und daher vielen Schülern Schwierigkeiten bereiten bzw. Fehlerquellen darstellen.

Solche Konstruktionen sind zum Beispiel:

I. Partizipialkonstruktionen

Häufig wird die Konstruktion in Schülerarbeiten beibehalten, was zuweilen zu Unklarheiten oder sogar falschen Übersetzungen führt. Die wichtigsten Möglichkeiten, englische Partizipialkonstruktionen ins Deutsche zu übertragen, sind:
- Übersetzung mit Relativsatz,
- Übersetzung mit einem (temporalen oder kausalen) Nebensatz,
- Übersetzung durch einen oder zwei Hauptsätze mit „und“ (Parataxe).

1. Engl. Partizipialkonstruktion → dt. Relativsatz

   “A lack of mentors and role models, the working parent … all reflect the changing social and economic pressures affecting youth today.”
   „Ein Mangel an Ratgebern und Vorbildern, berufstätige Eltern … dies alles spiegelt die sich verändernden sozialen und wirtschaftlichen Zwänge wider, die sich auf die heutige Jugend auswirken.“

2. Engl. Partizipialkonstruktion → dt. (temporaler, kausaler oder modaler) Nebensatz

   a) “Flung out of their native lands by war or persecution, … immigrants are crossing Europe's borders in unprecedented numbers.“ (gk 2002 II)
   „Da man sie durch Krieg oder Verfolgung … aus ihren Heimatländern wirft, überqueren Einwanderer die Grenzen Europas in noch nie dagewesener Zahl.“

   b) “… newcomers are still coming, close to four million in the last decade, not counting an unknown … number of illegal entrants.”
   „… immer neue Einwanderer kommen, nahezu vier Millionen im letzten Jahrzehnt, wobei man die unbekannte … Zahl von illegalen Einwanderern nicht mitrechnet.“

3. Engl. Partizipialkonstruktion → dt. Hauptsatz mit „und“ (Parataxe)

a) “… the traditional exchange of housework for economic support is becoming outmoded, shifting the foundations on which many marriages are based.”
„… der traditionelle Tausch von Hausarbeit gegen wirtschaftlichen Unterhalt ist allmählich überholt und verändert die Grundlagen, auf denen viele Ehen beruhen.“

b) “… America’s encounter with their land was … often violent, consuming much of the nation’s energies.”
„… die Begegnung der Amerikaner mit ihrem Land war … oft gewaltsam und sie zehrte stark an den Kräften des Volkes.“

c) “… crackdowns merely send refugees underground, forcing them to take ever deadlier risks to get in.” (gk 2002 II)
„… hartes Durchgreifen treibt die Flüchtlinge lediglich in den Untergrund und zwingt sie, immer lebensgefährlichere Risiken einzugehen, um ins Land zu gelangen.“

II. Gerundkonstruktionen

Das Gerund ist – vereinfacht gesagt – ein Substantiv, das von einem Verb abgeleitet ist. Es wird gebildet aus dem Verb + *ing*. Es kann im Satz als Subjekt (z. B. *Swimming is fun*) als Objekt (*I enjoy swimming*) oder als adverbiale Bestimmung (Präposition + Gerund) verwendet werden. Als Übersetzungsmöglichkeiten bieten sich – je nach Gebrauch – die Substantivierung des Verbs oder Infinitivkonstruktionen an.

Sätze, bei denen das Gerund als adverbiale Bestimmung verwendet wird, lassen sich entweder mit einer Infinitivkonstruktion oder mit einem adverbialen Nebensatz (mit „als“; „nachdem“; „indem“; „dadurch, dass …“) ins Deutsche übertragen.

1. Engl. Gerund → dt. Substantivierung

Easing entry requirements makes good economic sense …” (gk 2002 II)
„Vom wirtschaftlichen Standpunkt aus ist eine Lockerung der Einwanderungsbestimmungen durchaus sinnvoll, …“

2. Engl. Gerund → dt. Infinitivkonstruktion

a) “… exercising control over who knows what about you has come to be seen as an essential feature …” (gk 2002 I)
„… Kontrolle auszuüben über das, was jemand über einen weiß, wird zunehmend als ein grundlegender Wesenszug … angesehen.“

b) “… America is the only country where people are cajoled into buying food products because they are ‘sinfully delicious’.”
„… Amerika ist das einzige Land, in dem die Leute beschwatzt werden, Nahrungsmittel zu kaufen, weil sie ‚sündhaft köstlich‘ sind.“

3. Engl. (Präposition +) Gerund → dt. Nebensatz

a) “Vowing to act tough on illegal immigrants … plays well with the masses.” (gk 2002 II)
„Wenn man hoch und heilig versichert, hart gegen illegale Einwanderer … vorgehen zu wollen, kommt dies bei den Massen gut an.“

b) “… it isn’t surprising that some of them give vent to their own fantasies by responding physically to the fictitious battle being played …”
„… es ist nicht verwunderlich, dass einige von ihnen ihren eigenen Phantasien freien Lauf lassen, indem sie auf die vorgetäuschte Schlacht … körperlich reagieren.“

III. Passivkonstruktionen

Das Passiv gehört zweifellos zu den gestärkten Kategorien in der englischen Sprache und wird sehr viel häufiger verwendet als im Deutschen. Daher kann man es oft nicht einfach durch ein deutsches Passiv wiedergeben, insbesondere wenn das Englische ein persönliches Passiv verwendet. (= *He* will be told later; *She* was being helped; etc.)
Als Alternative bietet sich an:

1. Engl. Passiv → dt. unpersönl. Ausdruck (= „man“)
   a) “The emotional and educational impact on these children is just now beginning to be addressed …”
   „Man beginnt eben erst damit, sich der Auswirkungen auf die Gefühlswelt und die Erziehung dieser Kinder anzunehmen …“
   b) “Such factors are still assumed to play their part in producing crime.”
   „Man nimmt immer noch an, dass diese Faktoren ihren Teil zur Entstehung von Kriminalität beitragen.“

2. Engl. Passiv → dt. Aktiv
   “Among headteachers the argument is often put that uniform reduces competitiveness between fashion-conscious people …” (gk 2001 II)
   „Schulleiter bringen oft das Argument vor, dass Uniformen den Konkurrenzgeist zwischen modebewussten Schülern abbauen …“

IV. Veränderung der Wortart

Manchmal ist es erforderlich, bei der Übertragung des Textes die Wortart zu verändern, entweder aus stilistischen Gründen oder weil das Deutsche keine direkten Entsprechungen kennt. Die häufigsten Beispiele hierfür sind:

1. Engl. Nomen → dt. Verb oder Adjektiv
   Hierher gehören Ausdrücke wie “to make a complete mess of sth” (etwas total durcheinander bringen); “to have difficulty in doing sth.” (sich schwer tun mit etwas), “some sort of material” (ein bestimmtes Material) oder “in effect” (tatsächlich).
   a) “Most people have long accepted the need to provide some information about themselves …” (gk 2002 I)
   „Die meisten Leute haben sich längst damit abgefunden, dass sie ein bisschen Information über sich preisgeben müssen …“
   b) “Easing entry requirements makes good economic sense …“ (gk 2002 II)
   „Vom wirtschaftlichen Standpunkt aus ist eine Lockerung der Einwanderungsbestimmungen durchaus sinnvoll …“
   c) “… it is possible to discern among the young an insensitivity to nuances of language.”
   „… man kann bei Jugendlichen feststellen, dass sie unempfindlich sind für feine Unterschiede in der Sprache.“

2. Engl. Verb → dt. Adverb
   Das Englische bezeichnet die Art und Weise eines Geschehens häufig durch verbale Fügungen, denen im Deutschen Adverbien entsprechen, z. B.: “to be likely to do sth.” (wahrscheinlich etw. tun), “to happen to do sth.” (zufällig etw. tun), “to keep doing sth.” (weitermachen) und “to be sure to do sth.” (sicherlich etw. tun).

a) "Successive generations are likely to be more thoroughly assimilated …"
„Nachfolgende Generationen sind wahrscheinlich besser angepasst …"

b) "… the region not only did not falter economically, but continued right on with an industrial expansion …"
„… die Gegend wurde nicht nur nicht wirtschaftlich schwächer, sondern erlebte auch weiterhin einen industriellen Aufschwung …"

c) "… exercising control over who knows what about you has … come to be seen as an essential feature of a civilised society." (gk 2002 I)
„… Kontrolle auszuüben über das, was jemand über einen weiß, wird … zunehmend als ein grundlegender Wesenszug einer zivilisierten Gesellschaft angesehen."

V. Fremdwörter

Ein heftig umstrittenes Thema bei Übersetzungen ist, inwieweit man Fremdwörter stehen lassen darf, bzw. wann man sie durch ein deutsches Wort ersetzen muss. Völlige Einigkeit wird man hier nicht erzielen, aber als Faustregel gilt, dass allgemein gebräuchliche Fremdwörter und Fachbegriffe (wie z. B. Computer, Horizont, Alternative, Demokratie, usw.) verwendet werden dürfen, dass man das Fremdwort jedoch immer dann, wenn es ein gutes deutsches Wort dafür gibt, ersetzen sollte (*career* = Berufsweg, Laufbahn; *creatures* = Geschöpfe; *consumption* = Verbrauch).
Gelegentlich kann es auch notwendig sein, ein Fremdwort durch ein anderes zu ersetzen, wenn das ursprüngliche z. B. als zu stark oder zu schwach erscheint.

Beispiele:

1. Ersatz der Fremdwörter notwendig

a) "… the emotional and educational impact …"
„… die Auswirkungen auf die Gefühlswelt und die Erziehung …"

b) "According to experts on adolescent development, children now spend significantly less time in the company of adults than they did a few decades ago."
„Nach Aussagen von Fachleuten für die Entwicklung von Jugendlichen verbringen Kinder jetzt bedeutend weniger Zeit in der Gesellschaft von Erwachsenen als dies vor einigen Jahrzehnten der Fall war."

2. Fremdwörter werden beibehalten

a) "New information technology offers huge benefits …" (gk 2002 I)
„Die neue Informationstechnologie bietet riesige Vorteile …"

b) "Such factors are still assumed to play their part in producing crime."
„Man nimmt immer noch an, dass diese Faktoren ihren Teil zur Entstehung von Kriminalität beitragen."

c) "No issue generates more emotion … Vowing to be tough on illegal immigrants … (gk 2002 II)
„Kein Problem weckt mehr Emotionen … Wenn man hoch und heilig verspricht, hart gegen illegale Einwanderer vorzugehen …"

3. Ersatz eines Fremdwortes durch ein anderes

"Britain pulled back from total abolition." (gk 2001 II)
„Großbritannien zog sich von der kompletten Abschaffung wieder zurück."

Tips for the Exam

- Good preparation makes for a clear conscience, less excitement and fewer mistakes!

- **Select** the task according to the following criteria:
  Interest in the topic
  Comprehension of the text and the assignments
  Difficulty of the translation (40 BE!)
  Attractiveness of a composition topic (40 BE!)

- Make a **timetable** for the three parts and check during the exam whether you abide by it. It is better to drop a task for the time being than to get stuck with it. Return to it after you have finished the rest. Reserve some time at the end to go over your work again carefully.

- Be sure to understand exactly what the **questions** require you to answer. Sometimes there are double or triple aspects in one question. Highlight the passages in the text with different markers for the different questions before you answer them in your own words. You may quote – but not excessively.

- Please don't forget a question! This always happens to some students. It really is advisable to answer the questions in the given order.

- Before you write your **composition**, read the topical question carefully, and outline your ideas and arguments on a separate piece of paper. Make sure you consider a proper introduction and conclusion.

- **Use the whole time** that is at your disposal. Before you hand in your exam, make sure to **check** the following points:

Questions:	Do my answers really and completely correspond to the questions?
Composition:	Does the content cover the topic?
Translation:	Have I overlooked any words? Are the tenses translated correctly?
Whole text:	Tenses? Prepositions? Expressions?
If you have time:	Look up words you are not confident with in your dictionary.

Colloquiumsprüfung

I. Allgemeines zum Prüfungsablauf und zu den angeführten Beispielen

1. Das Colloquium dauert in Bayern 30 Minuten und besteht aus zwei Teilen:
   - ein 10-minütiges Referat zum ausgewählten Schwerpunkt, ggfs. unter Einbeziehung einer Textvorlage[1], und ein 5-minütiges Gespräch darüber mit weiterführenden Fragen zum Themenkreis, dem das Referat zugeordnet ist,
   - eine 15-minütige Prüfung zu Lerninhalten aus zwei der übrigen Ausbildungsabschnitte, wobei die vom Kursleiter im Laufe der vier Semester benannte Begleitlektüre mitberücksichtigt wird.
2. Die Textvorlagen sind als **Beispiele** aus der Praxis (nicht etwa als Muster) zu verstehen, da Textwahl und Fragestellung wesentlich vom behandelten Themenkreis und dem Niveau des Grundkurses abhängen.

II. Referat zum Schwerpunktthema und weiterführende Fragen (Dauer: etwa 15 Minuten)

1. Vor der Prüfung bekommt der Kandidat das Thema des Kurzreferats und ggf. einen Text schriftlich vorgelegt; es steht eine Bearbeitungszeit von 30 Minuten zur Verfügung. Ein zugelassenes einsprachiges Wörterbuch darf benutzt werden; evtl. schriftliche Notizen dürfen in der Prüfung herangezogen werden.
   Bedenken Sie jedoch, dass eine „Lesung" ohne Blickkontakt mit dem Prüfungsausschuss wenig überzeugend wirkt und zu Punkteabzug führt, wenn die Kriterien des freien Vortrags nicht mehr erfüllt sind.
2. Um dem Prüfling den Einstieg in das Referat zu erleichtern, kann (wie in unseren Beispielen) ein kurzer Text (evtl. ein Hörtext auf Band, eine Karikatur) vorgelegt werden, an den sich die Aufgabenstellung anschließt.
   Das Thema soll vom Prüfling sachgerecht und folgerichtig, in möglichst einwandfreiem Englisch abgehandelt werden. Deshalb kommt der Gliederung des Referats besondere Bedeutung zu. Es ist sinnvoll, die Hauptgliederungspunkte schriftlich festzuhalten und auf ihre Stimmigkeit innerhalb der Gesamtdarstellung zu überprüfen.
   Verlieren Sie dabei den zeitlichen Rahmen (10 Minuten) nicht aus dem Auge. Überlegen Sie sich, welche Punkte durch Beispiele illustriert bzw. bei Zeitmangel gestrafft werden können.
3. Ratschläge aus der Prüfungspraxis:
   Die Referatzeit sollte voll ausgeschöpft werden, da andernfalls die Zusatzfragen entsprechend früher einsetzen und damit der Prüfling weniger Gelegenheit hat, sein Wissen im Zusammenhang darzustellen. Außerdem deutet ein zu kurzes Referat auf nicht sonderlich fundierte Kenntnisse im Schwerpunktbereich oder auf wenig differenziertes Erfassen des Themas hin.

1 Für das Kurzreferat ist die Vorlage eines Textes nicht erforderlich; es kann auch ein freies Thema aus dem Schwerpunktbereich gestellt werden. In der Praxis wird jedoch oft ein Text vorgelegt.

4. Bei den anschließenden Fragen zu Problemen, die im Referat angeschnitten wurden bzw. zum Schwerpunktthema insgesamt, sollte der Prüfling mit angemessener Ausführlichkeit antworten. Es reduziert sich dadurch die Zahl der Zusatzfragen und damit auch die Gefahr, den Faden zu verlieren.
   Es ist für den Ausschuss leichter, sich ein positives Bild von der Sprechkompetenz des Prüflings zu machen, wenn dieser nicht ständig durch Zusatzfragen zum Weitersprechen ermutigt werden muss.

   Sollten Sie einmal eine Frage nicht beantworten können, geben Sie das gleich zu erkennen. Das wirkt sich weniger nachteilig aus als mühevolle Hilfestellung durch den Prüfer. Gerade in der Fremdsprache hängt die Geläufigkeit des Ausdrucks ganz wesentlich von der Klarheit der Gedanken ab.

III. Bewertung

1. Die Leistungen der beiden Prüfungsteile werden mit je zwei Punktzahlen bewertet. Die erste Punktzahl wird für die Gesprächsfähigkeit, die zweite für die fachlichen Kenntnisse und Fähigkeiten erteilt. Die vier Punktzahlen werden zur Vierfachwertung der Abiturprüfung addiert:

Beurteilungsbereiche:	1. Gesprächsfähigkeit	2. fachliche Kenntnisse und Fähigkeiten
Prüfungsteile:		
1 Kurzreferat (ca. 10 Minuten) und Gespräch über das Referat (ca. 5 Minuten)	maximal 15 Punkte	maximal 15 Punkte
2 Gespräch über Problemstellungen aus zwei weiteren Semestern bzw. Themenkreisen unter Einbeziehung der Begleitlektüre	maximal 15 Punkte	maximal 15 Punkte

   Die **Punktsumme** der Colloquiumsprüfung (Vierfachwertung) ergibt sich aus der Addition der vier Punktwerte.

   Hinsichtlich der **Gesprächsfähigkeit** wird z. B. beurteilt, ob der Prüfling seine Überlegungen in freier Rede zusammenhängend vorträgt, seine Ausführungen logisch gliedert, seinen eigenen Standpunkt begründen und auf Fragen, Einwände und Anregungen des Prüfers eingehen kann.

   Hinsichtlich der **fachlichen Kenntnisse** wird z. B. beurteilt, inwieweit der Prüfling fähig ist, das Thema zu erfassen, ob er die relevante Fachsprache beherrscht, fachspezifische Verfahrensweisen anwenden, Fakten einordnen sowie Sachverhalte und Probleme zutreffend beurteilen kann.

Colloquiumsprüfung im Fach Englisch
Referatsthema ohne Beigabe von Materialien: Lord of the Flies

Lord of the Flies

Task:

Lord of the Flies is more than an adventure story. Show how the boys try to establish their own society and what it leads to.
Try to determine in the course of your talk if the author presents an optimistic or pessimistic view of human nature.

Helps to prepare your talk

This is how you could practise your presentation about the given topic:
- First organise your thoughts along the subdivisions of the task: establish a *structure* with key words and fill in the appropriate *examples* from the book
- After that you might compare your personal outline with the suggestions below
- Correct or enlarge it according to your needs, then *practise free speech* on the basis of it and see how long you take.
- Add or remove points or examples if necessary.
- You might give it a second try with a friend listening and pointing out your language mistakes afterwards. This could help you to detect your own *typical mistakes* in oral production.

Note:
- In your talk you should use the Present Tense as it is commonly used when talking about texts.
- Don't forget to include evidence from what you remember of the novel.
- Concentrate on the task without too many digressions into other interesting aspects (You may, however, mention them in passing to impress the examiner with your profound knowledge!).

Suggestions for your structure

You may begin with a **brief summary of the plot**, *then proceed by dealing with the questions of the task.*

Establishment of their own society

Getting organised:	Calling the others (conch), meeting, introductions, election of Ralph as "chief", they agree on rules and discipline
Immediate tasks and co-operation:	Exploring the island, building a fire as a signal for rescuers, hunting for food, putting up shelters
Division:	2 tribes (forms of society): democratic civilized tribe versus dictatorial savage tribe (hunters)
Rise of the savage tribe:	Painted faces; increasing nakedness; violence against Piggy; the killing ritual; fear of the beast; hunters create totem (Lord of the Flies)
Decline of the civilized tribe:	Assembly rules are disrupted; Ralph loses almost all followers
Triumph of savagery:	Feast and killing of Simon; attack on Ralph's camp; robbery of the spectacles; killing of Piggy; hunters set fire to the island and chase Ralph
Rescue:	Ironically by an adult war party (fun and games?)

Optimistic view? Ralph and Piggy as role models for a reasonable society. The children are rescued in the end, grown-ups take control. It becomes clear that Jack has been wrong.

Pessimistic view? Innocent children, without outside influence, develop into merciless savages; a tropical paradise turns into hell; the world of adults seems no better. Author's message: typical of human nature.

Opinion: It is also my opinion that man is essentially good, needs good leaders and educators; the world develops towards democracy and reason

Or: I share the author's pessimism: man is ruining his planet with his inborn aggression, reason is weaker than the forces of evil

Additional questions you may be asked after your presentation

1. What elements of adventure stories do you see in the book?
2. What is the significance of the pig's head?
3. What makes the figure of Simon so special?
4. What do you think of the film version you know?

Colloquiumsprüfung im Fach Englisch
Referatthema mit Textgrundlage: Home-schooling

Home-schooling

Just how bad are American schools? And how deeply do conservative Americans distrust their government? One answer to both these questions is provided by the growth of home-schooling. As many as 2m American students – one in 25 – may now be being taught at home. (…)

Home-schooling is a fairly recent phenomenon. When Ronald Reagan came to power in 1981, it was illegal for parents to teach their own children in most states. Today it is a legal right in all 50 states. Twenty-eight states require home-schooled children to undergo some kind of official evaluation, either by standardised tests or by submitting a portfolio of work. Thirteen states simply require parents to inform officials that they are going to teach their children at home. In Texas, a parent doesn't have to tell anyone anything.

The main reason why legal restrictions on home-schooling have been swept away across so much of America is the power of the Christian right. (…) The religious conservatives turned to home-schooling in the 1970's in response to what they saw as the school system's lurch to the secular left – and they still provide most of the movement's political muscle on Capitol Hill. (…)

So there is certainly an ideological edge to many home-schoolers. But do not be misled. First, this is a bottom-up[1] movement with parents of whatever political stripe[2] making individual decisions to withdraw their children (rather than following orders from higher up). Second, (…) home-schoolers simply believe that they can offer their children better education at home. One-to-one tuition, goes the argument, enables children to go at their own pace. And children can be taught "proper" subjects based on the Judeo-Christian tradition of learning, rather than politically correct flimflam[3].

From: The Economist, February 28th, 2004

1 *bottom-up, adj.:* deciding sth. on practical details before thinking about general principles
2 *stripe:* persuasion
3 *flim-flam:* information or ideas that are not true or seem very stupid

Task:
Give a summary of the article in your own words as far as is appropriate. Show in how far the ideas behind home-schooling are typically American.

Helps to prepare your talk
If you have chosen the American or English systems of education as the main topic of your oral exam (Colloquium) you should, of course, be familiar with the most characteristic aspects of either of the two. You can get a lot of information from the internet or by consulting one of the many books on *Landeskunde,* which always contain special sections on the English or American school systems. Besides, you will probably be familiar with at least the most important elements through stories, books, and films *(Harry Potter; Dead Poets Society);* these works of fiction provide you with more substantial information than newspapers or television, where interest in school is mainly aroused only in cases of spectacular high school massacres.

Brief outline

In the first part of your talk, you are asked to give a summary of the text. Since it is very clearly structured, it is fairly easy to relate its contents.

The writer arouses the reader's attention by beginning with two very provocative questions: one on the quality of American schools, the other on the political implications of home-schooling. To prove his point, we are given the information that 4 % of American students are taught at home.

The next part of the text deals with the legalisation of home-schooling in the US within the last 25 years and the varying mechanisms of controlling it in different states, which is followed by an outline of the reasons for the growth of this movement.

In the last paragraph, the writer gives some reasons why parents might prefer home-schooling to sending their children to free public education.

In the second part, you are asked to relate home-schooling to typically American values and ideas. Here are some points that could be part of your answer:

- In many areas of the US, free public education has a very bad reputation (as opposed to Germany, where private education is often sneered at) because, in fact, its academic standard can be very poor
- Private, individual initiative takes precedence over state or government measures and institutions
- A deep-rooted distrust of any central or state government, especially among conservative Americans
- An equally deep-seated resentment among Christian fundamentalists of a state controlled learning curriculum (e. g. Darwin – evolution of species)

Questions you might be asked in the discussion about the talk

1. What are the advantages and disadvantages of home-schooling? (The writer quotes the argument that children can "go at their own pace", (ll. 20/21)
2. Show some of the differences between the American and the German school systems!
3. Compare the different attitudes towards private and public education in Germany and the USA!
4. What is your personal opinion on home-schooling?
5. Is education a private or a public affair?

Colloquiumsprüfung im Fach Englisch
Referatgrundlage Cartoon: US Immigration

US Immigration

© Copyright 2006 Mike Lane – All Rights Reserved. www.politicalcartoons.com

Task:

Describe and analyse the cartoon.
Outline how immigration has changed in American history with special reference to Hispanics.

Helps to prepare your talk

The United States as a "nation of immigrants" has been a favourite subject-matter for many years in your English textbooks: the first settlements in the 16th century, the Pilgrim Fathers and Plimoth Plantation, the beginning of mass immigration from many European countries (e. g. Ireland, central Europe) in the 19th century, the change in immigration after World War II with people now coming mainly from Asian and Central and South American countries …

In preparing the theme for your oral exam at home, you should consult the internet and you will find a lot of information on the development of the American population in books on *Landeskunde;* it will also be very useful to read American newspapers: there will always be articles on the topic, since this a very important issue in American domestic politics. So you can come up with at least a few important dates or figures, which will always be very useful in your talk, as well as in the ensuing discussion.

Brief Outline

Describing the cartoon is fairly easy because it contains only a few elements:

- The small crouched figure of a workman obviously of Hispanic origin, who is weighed down by a huge sombrero
- The figure of a grinning white American man dressed in a black suit who is dancing on the brim of the sombrero, balancing his dance with a briefcase in his left hand
- The captions:
  The headline *Hat Dance* referring to the folk dance which is associated with Mexico and the Hispanic population of the south-western United States
- The briefcase inscribed *US Business Lobby,* which clearly identifies the dancer as an American businessman
- The words *Cheap Immigrant Labor* which run along the brim of the workman's sombrero
- Take into account the expressions on the faces and the posture of the two figures: the depressed, almost squashed Mexican worker who carries the weight of an obviously jovial, sly American, whose face and thin legs express some uncertainty as if he knew he was doing something illegal.

What does the gesture of the businessman's right hand convey? What does the flower between his teeth stand for? Answering these two questions can lead to your analysis of the cartoon, which will be based on the ambiguous attitude of many white Americans, who on the one hand take advantage of the cheap labour of many, mainly illegal, immigrant workers from south of the US American border, whereas the American government tries to stop illegal immigration. Public opinion on this topic is very divided, too, which leads to inconsistent attitudes and even hypocrisy. The businessman shows this ambiguity in the rather uncertain way he daintily dances on the hat, which looks rather like balancing on insecure ground. So the popular Mexican Hat Dance becomes quite a dreary, dubious and drab performance.
The second part of your task asks you to give a brief outline of the history of immigration in North America with special focus on the more recent developments after World War II and the shift from European immigration to people coming from Spanish-speaking countries of South and especially Central America. Here you can use the information you learned at home: a few important figures and dates might still be present in your memory and you should note down these key references on your worksheet (e. g. the Immigration and Nationality Act of 1952 which introduced among others, quotas for people coming from Asia and other regions of the world; the Immigration Reform Act of 1986 which granted amnesty to more than 2,000,000 illegal immigrants; the very recent failure of introducing new legislation during the Bush administration (e. g. the Comprehensive Immigration Reform Act of 2007 would – among others – have provided legal status for the approximately 12 million illegal immigrants); a percentage of almost 20 % of the American population projected for Hispanics in 2025 …

Questions you might be asked in the discussion about the talk

1. Melting Pot – Salad Bowl – Pizza … how do these concepts of immigration differ from each other?
2. How is (Hispanic) immigration reflected in American films or literature?
3. How and where is immigration reflected in American everyday culture?
4. Changes in immigration legislation after 9/11
5. Which are the main differences between the American and the German attitude towards immigration?

Grundkurs Englisch 2000
Textaufgabe I

Do Parents Know Their Kids?

Jocks[1], preps[2], punks, Goths[3], geeks[4]. They may sit at separate tables in the cafeteria, but they all belong to the same generation. There are now 31 million kids in the 12-to-19 age group, and demographers predict that there will be 35 million teens by 2010. […] In many ways, these teens are uniquely privileged. They've grown up in a period of sustained prosperity and haven't had to worry about the draft[5] (as their fathers did) or global conflicts (as their grandparents did). Cable and the Internet have given them access to an almost infinite amount of information. Most expect to go to college, and girls, in particular, have unprecedented opportunities; they can dream of careers in everything from professional sports to politics, with plenty of female role models to follow.

But this positive image of American adolescence in 1999 is a little like yearbook photos that depict every kid as happy and blemish-free. After the Littleton, Colo., tragedy[6], it's clear there's another dimension to this picture, and it's far more troubled. In survey after survey, many kids […] say they feel increasingly alone and alienated, unable to connect with their parents, teachers and sometimes even classmates. They're desparate for guidance, and when they don't get what they need at home or in school, they cling to cliques or immerse themselves in a universe out of their parents' reach, a world defined by computer games, TV and movies, where brutality is so common it has become mundane. […]

Many teens say they feel overwhelmed by pressure and responsibilities. They are juggling part-time jobs and hours of homework every night; sometimes they're so exhausted that they're nearly asleep in early-morning classes. Half have lived through their parents' divorce. Sixty-three percent are in households where both parents work outside the home, and many look after younger siblings in the afternoon. Still others are home by themselves after school. That unwelcome solitude can extend well into the evening; mealtime for this generation too often begins with a forlorn touch of the microwave.

In fact, of all the issues that trouble adolescents, loneliness ranks at the top of the list. […] Teenagers may claim they want privacy, but they also crave and need attention – and they're not getting it. […]

Loneliness creates an emotional vacuum that is filled by an intense peer culture, a critical buffer against kids' fear of isolation. Some of this bonding is normal and appropriate; in fact, studies have shown that the human need for acceptance is almost a biological drive, like hunger. It's especially intense in early adolescence, from about 12 to 14, a time of "hyper self-consciousness," says David Elkind, a professor of child development at Tufts University. "They become very self-centered and spend a lot of time thinking about what others think of them," Elkind says. "And when they think about what others are thinking, they make the error of thinking that everyone is thinking about them." Dressing alike is a refuge, a way of hiding in the group. When they're 3 and scared, they cling to a security blanket[7]; at 16, they want body piercings or Abercrombie[8] shirts.

If parents and other adults abdicate power, teenagers come up with their own rules. Bullying has become so extreme and so common that many teens just accept it as part of high school life in the '90s. Emory University psychologist Marshall Duke, an expert on children's friendships, recently asked 110 students in one of his classes if any of them had ever been threatened in high school. To his surprise, "they all raised their hand." […]

Even the best, most caring parents can't protect their teenagers from all problems, but involved parents can make an enormous difference. Kids do listen. […] Seize any opportunity to talk – in the car, over the breakfast table, watching TV. Parents have to work harder to get their points across. Ellen Galinsky, president of the Families and Work Institute, has studied teenagers' views of parents. "One 16-year-old told us, 'I am proud of the fact that my mother deals with me even though I try to push her away. She's still there.'" So pay attention now. The kids can't wait.

From an article by Barbara Kantorowitz and Pat Wingert in:
Newsweek, 10 May 1999, pp. 48–52

1 jocks (AmE infml): athletes, especially ones with few other interests
2 preps (AmE infml): here: rich young people, noticeable for their expensive clothes
3 Goths: young people who like Gothic music (dark metal music about death and evil) and cultivate a certain style: body piercing, black clothes and lipstick, white make-up
4 geeks (AmE infml): boring people, dressed unfashionably
5 draft (AmE): obligatory military service; in the 60s /70s, this meant being sent to fight in the Vietnam war
6 the Littleton, Colo., tragedy massacre at a Colorado high school, where on April 20, 1999, two boys killed twelve fellow pupils and a teacher, injured many more, then killed themselves
7 security blanket: soft blanket or toy that little children like to hold to comfort themselves
8 Abercrombie: an expensive, trendy brand of clothes

Worksheet:

maximum number of points attainable

I. Questions on the text

Read all the questions first, then answer them in the given order. Use your own words as far as is appropriate.

1. In what way are today's teenagers a "uniquely privileged" (l. 4) generation? — 10
2. Outline the various problems young people are confronted with. — 20
3. How do adolescents react to their sense of isolation? What psychological explanations are given in the text? — 20
4. What does the text say about the extent and the causes of bullying at American high schools? — 10
5. What is the writer's message to parents? — 10
6. Show that the writer uses a variety of means to make his text interesting and convincing. — 10

II. Composition

Choose *one* of the following topics. Write about 120 to 150 words. — 40

1. The "infinite amount of information" provided by cable TV and the Internet – a blessing or a curse?
2. Raising and teaching teens – not an easy job these days?

III. Translation

Translate the following text into German: — 40

Total: 160

What is most bizarre about America's spate of school shootings is not that they have occurred, but America's reaction to them: plenty of public handwringing about moral decay and media violence. Inevitably, there have been further calls to beef up security at schools.

But these are all side issues, which have nothing to do with what really distinguishes America from other countries. Young people everywhere, like many of their elders, have violent fantasies. If America is in moral decline, then so is most of the rest of the world, which just as avidly consumes violent films and rock videos. Mentally disturbed people anywhere can sometimes pose a threat to others. And all schools, not just those in America, remain vulnerable to someone looking for innocent victims. But, of all rich countries, only America makes it possible for teenage misfits, the insane or anyone else determined to cause mayhem to get their hands so easily on such a terrifying array of weapons.

From: *The Economist,* 24 April 1999

Lösungvorschlag

I. Questions on the text

1. Today's adolescents have been able to enjoy an uninterrupted period of wealth and peace. At the same time the media and the World Wide Web offer them more information than ever before. Boys in the U.S. do not need to do military service any more and educational and professional career options are wide open, especially for girls, who can follow the examples of many successful women.

2. Many teenagers suffer from a sense of alienation and solitude. They find it difficult to communicate with their elders, and sometimes even with their peers. They look for orientation in their cliques and escape into a world of their own, where they are not reached by their parents, and which is mainly ruled by violent computer games, films and TV programmes. Many of them are stressed by jobs and responsibilities in their homes, which interfere with their school assignments. Every other youngster has experienced their parents' divorce, even more have to look after themselves, as both parents work, and some have to take care of younger brothers and sisters in the afternoon. On the one hand they ask for privacy, on the other they are very much in need of attention which they fail to get.

3. To overcome their sense of isolation teenagers try hard to integrate into peer groups and adopt lifestyles and behaviour patterns of the current youth culture. For example, they wear expensive clothes that are supposed to be 'in' and are worn by everybody else, and follow the fashion of body piercings. Hiding in a group gives them security. This is explained by people's overall, almost biological desire to be accepted, particularly in early adolescence, when young people develop a strong sense of self-awareness. They are obsessed with people's opinion of themselves and feel constantly observed by others.

4. Bullying at American high schools seems to have become so widespread and extreme that many teenagers regard it as normal. The text gives the example of a class in which all students admit to have suffered from it.
   As to the causes of this practice the author explains that the adults' influence on children has weakened, which creates a vacuum of guidance and behaviour patterns. The children fill it with rules of their own, which they seek to enforce on others.

5. Even if parents cannot prevent their children from having problems, they should at least try to exercise an influence on them. Rather optimistically the writer believes that children will listen to their advice. He quotes one kid who admits that he appreciates his mother's attempts to get through to him. Thus the author recommends that parents should always try hard to reach their children and never give up.

6. Already the title poses an interesting question, at least for adults. The first line of the article, with its colourful enumeration of juvenile subculture groups will further hold the readers' attention, as well as the examples later on (Abercrombie shirts, piercings).

   The author also tries to make his text interesting by employing a number of colourful images like the simile: *"adolescence ... is ... like yearbook photos"* (l. 10), and metaphors, for example in lines 19/20: *"juggling part-time jobs"* and *"dressing alike is a refuge"* (l. 36/37). He tries to convince the reader by giving facts, figures, and percentages, and by mentioning surveys. Furthermore, his references to and quotations from authorities and kids underline that he has thoroughly investigated the issue.

II. Composition

1. The "infinite amount of information" provided by cable TV and the Internet – a blessing or a curse?

   Note: It is practically impossible to concentrate a composition of this kind into 120-150 words. There is hardly a teacher who would not tolerate a wider margin.

   A recent survey in Britain showed that about 80 % of the teenagers have their own TV sets, and PCs have established a growing presence in people's homes. It is true that the dozens of simultaneous channels you can watch on cable TV do occasionally offer invaluable information, and the billions of bytes roaming the Internet transport much of the world's knowledge. Educational programmes on TV have never been better and there is hardly a modern student who does not consult the Web to research a topic he needs for school.
   So much about the "blessing", but is there really a "curse"? Apart from the dangers of indiscriminate viewing for children and the false picture they may get of reality, apart from the potential influence of violent computer games – information as such cannot be negative. The only complication is localizing islands of usefulness in a sea of facts. But there are always parents and instructors to channel the children's viewing, and search engines to guide you through the Internet. The choice, as always, is yours.

2. Raising and teaching teens – not an easy job these days?

   Being a teenager myself I find it hard to place myself in the position of my parents and teachers, and evaluate the difficulties they may have had with me. From what they never fail to tell me about the idyllic conditions in their own youth, their excellent relationship with their own parents, and their own academic standards I guess that I don't compare favourably. All I can say in my defence is that times are changing. We have a lot more possibilities and freedom and don't want to fall back behind other kids' privileges. It is therefore difficult for parents to enforce the conditions they remember. There is so much to do outside our homes and school. Why shouldn't we meet our friends as much as possible and spend our pocket money as we see fit? So raising and teaching us is probably not easy, but who knows if we may not have the same or even more problems with our own kids one day?

III. Translation

Was an der Flut von Schießereien an Schulen in Amerika am eigenartigsten[1] ist, ist nicht die Tatsache[2], dass sie sich ereignet haben, sondern wie Amerika darauf reagiert[3]: jede Menge öffentliches Händeringen über moralischen Verfall und Gewalt in den Medien. Wie nicht anders zu erwarten war, gab es weitere Aufrufe, die Sicherheitsvorkehrungen an Schulen zu verstärken.
Aber dies sind alles Randprobleme, die nichts damit zu tun haben, was Amerika von anderen Ländern wirklich unterscheidet. Überall haben junge Leute – wie auch viele ältere Menschen – Gewaltfantasien. Wenn Amerika in moralischem Verfall begriffen ist, dann auch der Großteil der restlichen Welt, der ebenso begierig[4] gewaltstrotzende Filme und Rockvideos konsumiert. Überall können Geistesgestörte manchmal für andere eine Bedrohung darstellen. Und alle Schulen, nicht bloß amerikanische, bleiben verwundbar durch jemanden, der nach unschuldigen Opfern Ausschau hält. Aber von allen reichen Ländern ermöglicht es einzig Amerika jugendlichen Außenseitern, Verrückten oder allen Anderen, die entschlossen sind, ein Chaos anzurichten so leicht Zugriff zu erhalten auf ein solch Schrecken erregendes Waffenarsenal.

Anmerkungen:

1 *am bizarrsten* wird natürlich auch anerkannt
2 Stilistisch bedingte Einfügung
3 Auch möglich: *reagiert hat*
4 Ein Beispiel, wie man durch eine kleine Erweiterung des Grundbegriffes (gierig) die Bedeutung genauer treffen kann

Grundkurs Englisch 2000
Textaufgabe II

On Sundays the Pecks went to church, of course, and on Wednesday evenings Laura had her Ladies' Circle. On holidays there were the formal visitors: Justin's business associates and their wives, along with their starched, ruffled[1] children. But you couldn't say that the Pecks had *friends,* exactly. They kept to themselves. They were suspicious of outsiders.

Daniel was a tall, cool, reflective boy, and from the beginning he planned to study law. Therefore Caleb would take over the importing business. In preparation for this Caleb attended the Salter Academy[2], walking there daily with his friend Paul and a few of the neighborhood boys. He worked very conscientiously, although sometimes his mother suspected that his heart wasn't in it. Coming home from school he could be waylaid by any passing stranger, he fell willingly into conversation with all sorts of riffraff. He had no discrimination. And he still followed organ grinders. With his pocket money he bought tawdry musical instruments, everything from pennywhistles to a cheap violin sold him by a sailor; he could make music out of anything. He played these instruments not only in his room but outdoors as well, if he wasn't caught and stopped. More than once he was mistakenly showered with coins from someone's window. When Laura heard about it she would grow dark in the face and order him to remember his name. She shut him in the parlor, where he continued to spill out his reckless, made-up tunes on the massive piano draped in fringed silk. Unfortunately the Creole gardener, Lafleur Boudrault, had taught him ragtime. A disreputable, colored kind of music. Justin, home in his study doing the accounts, would raise his head to listen for a minute and frown, but then he shrugged it off.

In 1903, Caleb graduated from the Salter Academy. The day after his graduation Justin took him down to his office to show him around. Caleb would be spending his days in an office above a warehouse, behind a roll-top desk, dealing with ledgers and receipts and bills of lading[3]. Still, it was a fine opportunity for a young man with ambition, Caleb. Caleb?

Caleb turned from the single, sooty window, through which he had been gazing though it was impossible to see the harbor from there. He said that he would prefer to be a musician.

At first Justin couldn't take it in. He was politely interested. Musician? Whatever for?

Then the situation hit him in the face and he gasped and caved in. He felt for the chair behind him and sat down, preparing bitter, harmful words that would convey all his horror and disgust and contempt. But music was so – no young man would ever seriously – music was for women! For parlors! He felt nauseated by the sight of this boy's intense brown eyes. He could hardly wait to chew him up and spit him out and stamp on what was left.

Instead, all that came from his mouth were strange vowel sounds over which he had no control.

He had to be carried away in his office chair by two men from the warehouse. They laid him in his buggy and folded both arms across his chest, as if he were already dead, and then Caleb drove him home. When Laura came to the door she found Caleb on the topmost step with his father curled in his arms like a baby. But Justin's eyes were two hard, glittering pebbles, and she could feel his rage. "What *happened?*" she asked, and Caleb told her, straight out, while struggling upstairs with his burden to Justin's high carved bed. Laura's face grew as dark as coffee but she said not a word. She had the kitchen maid fetch the doctor from down the street, and she listened stonily to the doctor's diagnosis: apoplexy, brought on by a shock of some sort. He did not hold out much hope for recovery. If Justin lived, he said, one side would likely be paralyzed, although it was too soon to say for certain.

Then Laura went downstairs to the parlor where Caleb stood waiting. "You have killed your half of your father," she said.

On Monday, Caleb started work behind the roll-top desk.

From *Searching for Caleb* by Anne Tyler, copyright © 1975 by Anne Tyler Modarressi. Used by permission of Alfred A. Knopf, a division of Random House, Inc.

[1] ruffled: wearing ruffles (dt. Rüschchen)
[2] Salter Academy: a local private boys' school
[3] bill of lading: a list of goods delivered by a ship or other means of transport

Worksheet

maximum number of points attainable

I. Questions on the text

Read all the questions first, then answer them in the given order. Use your own words as far as is appropriate.

1. What impression does the reader gain of the Pecks' social background and family life? Give evidence from the text. — 20
2. What do we learn about Caleb in the second paragraph? Explain in particular the role music plays in his life. — 20
3. Why does Justin show his son around the office? Describe and explain Caleb's behaviour in this situation. — 10
4. How does Justin react when he hears about his son's plans for the future? — 10
5. What role does Caleb's mother play in his decision to start work in the office? — 10
6. Give two examples of metaphorical language and explain their function. — 10

II. Composition

Choose *one* of the following topics. Write about 120 to 150 words. — 40

1. Money, power, prestige, intellectual challenge – to which of these or other aims would you give priority in your future career?
2. Which should come first – personal fulfilment or responsibility towards one's family?

III. Translation

Translate the following text into German: — 40

160

Pressures to join the family business, or to do something our parents can relate to or consider "respectable" are a huge problem for many young people starting their careers today.

Although there's nothing new about this phenomenon, it has become more pronounced. The world of work has changed considerably in the past 30 years: there are more graduates than ever before, and new opportunities exist in fields which our parents' generation could never have dreamed of.

Family pressures can manifest themselves in a number of different ways –from a guilt-including expression of disappointment to a real threat of excommunication. Some parents will bully their children into doing what they wish, while others may try to bribe them with offers of cash (or withhold it).

Neil Crawford, a psychotherapist and an expert in family businesses, says: "Young people in this situation are often faced with a dilemma: do they please their parents and be grateful or should they go their own way?"

From an article by Hilary Freeman in: *The Guardian,* 23 October 1999

Lösungvorschlag

I. Questions on the text

1. *The relevant information can be found in the first two paragraphs*

   The Pecks, who own an importing business, seem to be respectable, well-to-do upper middle-class people, who can afford to employ a kitchen maid and a gardener. They associate with business friends, but they hardly entertain any friendly relations with them: the business partners, their wives and their children are "formal visitors" (line 2) and the Pecks keep "to themselves." (line 4) They seem to be reputable members of society, who can afford to send Daniel to university and Caleb to a private school, which is characteristic of the higher classes. Accordingly they tell their son "to remember his name" (line 16) and not to mix with "riffraff". (l. 10)
   They seem to lead an orderly family life, go to church every Sunday (l. 1), Mrs. Peck attends a ladies' circle every Wednesday evening (l. 1/2) and they receive visitors on holidays. But apart from that there seems to be very little communication: Justin retreats to his study when he is at home, Laura shuts Caleb in the parlour, and both fail to realise their boy's true interests.

2. Caleb is a very diligent student at a local boys' school, he works well although he is not enthusiastic about his studies. Much to his parents' dismay he is not appropriately aware of his family background, and easily associates with all sorts of people his parents do not approve of.
   His parents cannot understand that he runs after organ grinders, which only shows his love for music. He spends his pocket money to buy all kinds of simple musical instruments and plays them in his free time. His parents are very much against this and try to prevent it, but music is the only thing that counts in his life.

3. *Don't forget that it is not enough to describe Caleb's behaviour, the author also wants you to <u>explain</u> it.*

   When Caleb has finished school, his father shows him around the office in the importing firm to acquaint him with his future workplace. Whereas Mr Peck seems to be proud of offering him an opportunity to rise in the business world, Caleb appears somehow absent-minded. He looks out of the window, not concentrating on what his father points out to him, and finally tells Justin straight out that he would rather be a musician.
   It is obvious that Caleb doesn't care for his father's business and has made up his mind long ago. So he doesn't concentrate on the warehouse, which, for all he knows, will never be his world.

4. At first his father doesn't quite realise all the implications of his son's answer and casually inquires, "Whatever for?" On second thoughts, however, he realises what he has heard and that it would destroy all the dreams and the hopes he has placed in him. In a state of shock he has to sit down, and tries to compose himself to give him a piece of his mind and to show Caleb all his contempt. However, he cannot do that because he has a stroke and loses all control over his body.

5. *Note that the text does not explain Laura's role in Caleb's decision to start a career in an office. It is, however, not difficult to find out since it is implied in what she says in the end.*

   When she has heard the doctor's diagnosis Mrs Peck simply says to Caleb, "You have killed your half of your father." Instead of telling him that he has had a stroke – which would have been appropriate in the situation – she puts pressure on her son and arouses feelings of guilt in him. Caleb obviously can't stand this pressure and finally gives in, probably to make amends for his behaviour.

6. *You will certainly have noticed that the text abounds in metaphors: the author speaks of "starched, ruffled children" (l. 3), he says that Caleb "was ... showered with coins"(l. 15) and that he continued" to spill out ... tunes" (l. 17). "Justin's eyes were two hard, glittering pebbles" (l. 42/43) is another case in point. We have decided to take the following two examples:*

   a) *"Then the situation hit him in the face..." (line 31)*
   After his initial failure to understand his son's announcement, Justin suddenly realises the full implications of what Caleb has said and is deeply shocked by the whole situation. Instead of simply stating that Justin was shocked or upset by what it meant, the author uses this metaphor, which is much more vivid, graphic and thus makes it much easier for the reader visualise Mr. Peck's state of mind.

   b) *"He could hardly wait to chew him up and spit him out and stamp on what was left." (lines 35/36)*
   Justin doesn't have words for what his son has just told him: that he would throw away a respectable job, an opportunity, and instead take an – in Justin's view – inferior, disreputable occupation that would ruin his family name. As there are no words to express Justin's anger and contempt for Caleb the author uses this metaphor to show the father's aggressions and his wish to destroy him.

II. Composition

1. Money, power, prestige, intellectual challenge – to which of these or other aims would you give priority in your future career?

   Don't we all dream of having endless resources of money, of being able to fulfil all our wishes without ever having to worry that our bank accounts get into the red? Or of holding a powerful position in which we can change circumstances according to our ideas? In reality, however, most of us have to realise that the dream is only for the happy few. And it is perhaps for the best that most of our dreams do not come true. For "money is not everything", as the proverb says, and power tends to corrupt people, as the recent political scandals have shown.
   Of course, I sometimes envy the rich and the powerful, but there are other things that make a job rewarding to me. If it is intellectually demanding and requires taking competent decisions, if I have to cooperate with a team which is governed by mutual respect, I would be very happy.
   It goes without saying, of course, that I also expect a decent salary and that my work carries some prestige, but they are not foremost in my expectations.

2. Which should come first – personal fulfilment or responsibility towards one's family?

   Note that personal fulfilment and responsibility towards one's family are not necessarily opposed to each other, since a lot of people do find personal fulfilment in the care for their families. What is meant here is probably the attitude of workaholics, both male and female, who live entirely for their work and neglect their families, especially their children.

Everyone of us knows such cases: both parents are successful in their professional lives, they have achieved everything they wanted but their children drop out of school, or even worse, they turn to petty crime. Parents can't understand this, since they provided their children with everything money could buy. In their search for the reasons husband and wife then begin to blame each other and their marriage may well end up in divorce.
What these people fail to see is that there is more to a happy family than the financial means for a carefree life. Children do not only need money but their parents' time, affection and, above all, their love. It is, of course, very hard to cope with the requirements of a full-time job, a married life, the household chores and the education of the children. The couple should really consider postponing their self-realisation until the children can look after themselves.

III. Translation

Der moralische Druck[1], in das Familienunternehmen einzusteigen oder etwas zu tun, das unsere Eltern als „anständig" bezeichnen oder akzeptieren[2] können, stellt für viele junge Leute, die jetzt ins Berufsleben eintreten, ein riesiges Problem dar.
Obwohl dieses Phänomen[3] keineswegs neu ist, so ist es doch[4] deutlicher zu Tage getreten. Die Arbeitswelt hat sich in den letzten 30 Jahren erheblich verändert: Es gibt mehr Hochschulabsolventen als jemals zuvor, und es gibt neue Möglichkeiten in Berufsfeldern, von denen die Generation unserer Eltern nicht einmal träumen konnte.
Der Druck, den die Familie ausübt, kann sich auf unterschiedlichste Art und Weise zeigen – von einem Ausdruck der Enttäuschung, der Schuldgefühle hervorruft, bis zur wirklichen Drohung mit dem Ausschluss aus dem Familienkreis[5]. Manche Eltern schüchtern ihre Kinder so lange[6] ein, bis sie tun, was sie wollen, während andere womöglich[7] versuchen, sie dadurch gefügig zu machen[8], dass sie ihnen Geld anbieten[9] (oder vorenthalten).
Neil Crawford, ein Psychotherapeut und Fachmann, was Familienunternehmen betrifft, sagt: „Junge Leute in dieser Situation stecken oft in einer Zwickmühle: Sollen sie es ihren Eltern Recht machen und dankbar sein oder sollen sie ihren eigenen Weg gehen?"

Anmerkungen:

1 Der Singular ist im Deutschen gebräuchlicher
2 wörtl.: für ...halten, ansehen
3 Um das Fremdwort zu vermeiden, wäre „Vorgang" möglich
4 Einfügung aus stilistischen Gründen
5 Zusatz zur Verdeutlichung
6 „will" steht hier nicht als Futur, sondern zum Ausdruck einer gewohnheitsmäßigen Handlung, die im Deutschen mit „pflegen zu", „oft", „häufig", usw. wiedergegeben wird.
7 „may" bezeichnet hier die Möglichkeit
8 wörtlich: zu bestechen
9 im Deutschen ist die Verbalkonstruktion zu bevorzugen

Grundkurs Englisch 2001
Textaufgabe I

A Princely Pioneer

Once upon a time there was a prince who unwisely confided to the media that while tending his beloved garden, he often talked to his plants. He also warned his future subjects about losing touch with their natural surroundings and their rich cultural heritage. But the people scoffed and said it was the fuddy-duddy Prince who was out of touch. And as for talking to his plants – well, they shook their heads and remembered the madness of the Prince's forebear, King George III, who famously struck up a conversation with a tree that he had mistaken for the King of Prussia.

These days Britain's Prince of Wales is still considered a tad eccentric: after all, who in his right mind would have lost the love of the fairytale Princess Diana? But increasingly, Charles is winning applause for his not-so-crazy campaign to combat what he calls "the wanton destruction that has taken place … in the name of progress." For 30 years the Prince has been in the forefront of efforts to promote kinder, gentler farming methods; protect Britain's countryside from urban sprawl; improve city landscapes; and safeguard the nation's architectural heritage. And whereas his was once a lonely if plummy voice crying in the wilderness, the Prince has seen many of his once maverick opinions become mainstream.

Charles is not the first royal concerned about nature. Mad King George dabbled in botany when he wasn't losing his mind or the American colonies, and Charles' father, the Duke of Edinburgh, has long supported wildlife causes. But it is Charles who has become the crusader, with a vision of Britain that may border on the romantic but is in synch with Britons alarmed by what is happening to their green and pleasant land. He has the energy and dedication to get things done. "My problem," he has said, "is that I become carried away by enthusiasm to try and improve things, and also feel very strongly that the only way to progress is by setting examples and then hoping others will eventually follow."

An example people are following is organic farming, which Charles has adopted wholeheartedly on his own farmlands in the Duchy of Cornwall and surrounding his country home at Highgrove in western England. Charles once noted that when he decided to go organic, which means forswearing artificial fertilizers and pesticides, the experts were very polite, "but what they were saying about this latest demonstration of insanity once they were out of earshot can only be surmised." Today the experts have been confounded[1]. The duchy's Home Farm near Highgrove is 100 % organic and highly profitable and serves as a model for farmers around the country at a time when farm incomes are falling and organic produce is in high demand, fetching premium prices in shops and supermarkets.

Charles is throwing himself into another pioneering project: a radical way to meet Britain's need for new housing. Appalled by suburban developments made up of identical boxlike dwellings that eat into the countryside, the Prince is creating a model township called Poundbury on duchy land adjoining the town of Dorchester, south of Highgrove. The houses – 220 so far, with an additional 2,280 planned – are not identical but come in different sizes and styles that pay homage to traditional English architecture and materials. Some are privately owned, others government subsidized. All are highly energy efficient. The town layout prefers people over cars: front doors give onto streets that are safer for children because the roads are too winding to allow cars to speed. A 1998 British government report cited Poundbury as an example for future developments because its efficient use of space permits a higher population density, thus fighting sprawl. As a skeptical journalist noted after touring Poundbury, "the Prince of Wales has got it right."

From an article by Christopher Redman in: *TIME*, 26 April 2000

[1] to confound s.b.: *here:* to prove s.b. wrong

Worksheet:

maximum number of points attainable

I. Questions on the text

Read all the questions first, then answer them in the given order. Use your own words as far as is appropriate.

1. How did the British public view Prince Charles in the past and what were the reasons for this view? 10
2. To what extent has the Prince's image changed? (Refer to lines 8–16) 10
3. How has Charles influenced British farming? 10
4. Describe the characteristic features of Poundbury. Why has Charles launched this project and how has it been received? 20
5. What is the writer's personal attitude towards the Prince and his activities? Examine in detail how this attitude is conveyed. 20
6. What use of a literary genre does the writer make in the first paragraph and to what effect? 10

II. Composition

Choose *one* of the following topics. Write about 120 to 150 words. 40

1. "Saving the planet starts at home." Discuss.
2. Cities are sometimes called "urban jungles". Is this characterization justified?

III. Translation

Translate the following text into German: 40

160

The British public has taken against genetically modified crops in a big way. Activists uproot them and supermarkets attempt not to furnish their customers with them. This week the Prince of Wales [...] came out against them for the umpteenth time, a piece of non-news that still managed to provoke headlines throughout the country.

Europeans have in general been more skeptical about genetically modified crops than Americans, who have so far swallowed the idea, and the food, with relatively few qualms. And among the Europeans the British have been particularly adamant in their refusal to have anything to do with such things. The recent history of British agricultural politics – the killing of millions of cows for fear that their increasing madness was spreading into the population – has left the public distrustful of "unnatural" tinkering with the food chain. The prince says that he wants us to reject all genetic modification and instead "work with nature for the benefit of humankind."

From *Getting Nostalgic about Nature* by Oliver Morton in: *Newsweek,* 14 June 1999, p. 80

Lösungsvorschlag

I. Questions on the text

1. The British public has so far tended to regard Prince Charles as a bit old-fashioned and eccentric, even mad. People talked about him rather contemptuously because he talked to his plants and split with his wonderful wife. They pointed out that he might have inherited his madness from his ancestor, King George III., who had talked to a tree which he believed to be the King of Prussia.

2. The Prince's image has changed to a large extent. He may still be regarded as a bit eccentric because he divorced the universally admired Princess Diana, but he is increasingly respected for his critical views on what is done in the name of progress. Especially his views on farming methods, the destruction of the countryside, modern architecture and city landscapes, which were once considered to be strange, have now been universally acclaimed.

3. Charles has shown British farmers that organic farming, i. e. farming without artificial fertilisers and pesticides, is not only possible but can be highly profitable. First introduced against the experts' advice on his own farmlands in Cornwall, his organic farming now serves as a model for farmers in the whole country.

4. Poundbury is a model for urban development, which the Prince of Wales created because he was horrified by the characterless suburbs eating into the countryside. The key features of his project are houses of different sizes and styles that respect British architectural traditions as well as a blend of private ownership and social housing. Moreover, all the buildings are highly energy efficient, and the winding streets are safer because they prevent cars from speeding. The project has been highly successful, which can be seen from the approval it obtained from different sources, including the government.

5. *As this is a predominantly expository text which is supposed to give the reader objective information, you have to look for implicit indications of the writer's attitude. These are for example the structure of the text, stylistic devices, the choice of words or the quotations. If you take these into account, you will soon notice that the author sympathises with the Prince of Wales.*

   The writer of this text is definitely sympathetic towards Charles. The first indication of his attitude is the structure of the article. The author first mentions the critical voices before he proves them wrong and quotes the supporters of the Prince. These – direct and indirect – quotations are inserted in order to prove that Charles is right. The experts are said to be confounded (ll. 30 f), a government report sees the Poundbury project as "an example" (l. 44) and the very last opinion is uttered by a journalist, who thinks that Charles "has got it right." (l. 46) Moreover, the author's choice of words conveys a very positive image of the Prince. Thus we hear that Charles is conducting a "not-so-crazy campaign" (l. 10), that he has "a vision of Britain" (l. 20) as well as "the energy and dedication to get things done" (ll. 21 f).

6. *You will easily notice that the present text begins like a fairy tale (Once upon a time …). That is certainly surprising in a TIME article.*

   The article begins like a fairy tale. Not only is the opening line "Once upon a time" (l. 1) typical of such a story, but there are also other ingredients, like an old-fashioned, slightly eccentric prince and his subjects.

Since TIME articles do not normally begin in such a way, such an introduction certainly arouses the reader's curiosity. Moreover, it makes you expect a prince who is rather ignorant of the world.
When you read on, however, you will soon discover that Charles is not as unworldly as the first paragraph suggests, and so the beginning forms a stark contrast to the rest of the text. The use of this genre certainly emphasises the prince's "not-so-crazy" ideas.

II. Composition

1. **"Saving the planet starts at home."**

   Note that this year's exams were written when US President Bush's energy plan was discussed in America, which places importance on increasing the supply of energy rather than reducing its consumption.
   The Bush administration has just announced that it will solve the present energy crisis by boosting production: exploiting the Arctic, building 38,000 new miles of pipeline and 1,900 new – mainly nuclear – power plants in the next 20 years. Those measures were presented as the solution to our problems.
   Environmentalists are shocked. For decades most experts have agreed that Americans lived too well, used too much energy and were responsible for most of the world's emissions of carbon dioxide. If people didn't mend their ways, scientists warned, they would be in danger of destroying their living conditions on this planet. "Saving the planet starts at home," they said, "everyone of us has to drive smaller cars, use fewer household appliances, and turn down the central heating", to name only a few things. For me that is still the point, for it will take at least 10 to 15 years for Bush's plan to take effect. And in the meantime all we can do is to try and save the planet in our homes.

2. **Cities are sometimes called "urban jungles". Is this characterization justified?**

   This is a subject where a look into your dictionary may help you. A ***jungle*** *in this sense is defined as "an unfriendly or dangerous place or situation, especially one where it is very difficult to be successful or to trust anyone" (OALD) or as "a place that is very untidy and where a lot of things have been placed close together." (DCE)*

   A lot of writers, especially in America, have described the cities as jungles. Upton Sinclair and Theodore Dreiser depicted them as unhealthy places, where human beings are mistreated and die as a consequence of the unspeakable conditions of working class and slum life. All this was certainly true in the nineteenth and early twentieth centuries, and some of it may be still be true in the inner cities of present day America. But to portray today's cities as jungles would be unfair or at least one-sided. Sure, there is still traffic congestion and pollution, substandard housing and crime, but most big cities today have taken great efforts to revitalise their centres. The movement of new urbanism, which started in the 1980's, has been very successful in creating compact, pedestrian-friendly, liveable communities where people like to meet and live on neighbourly terms with each other. Of course the task has not yet been completed, but at least we are on the right track.

III. Translation

Die britische Öffentlichkeit hat deutlich Partei gegen genmanipulierte Getreidearten ergriffen. Aktivisten reißen sie aus der Erde, und Supermärkte versuchen, sie ihren Kunden nicht anzubieten. Erst[1] in dieser Woche hat sich der Prinz von Wales zum x-ten Male dagegen ausgesprochen, was zwar[2] nichts Neues war[3], aber trotzdem[2] für Schlagzeilen überall im Land sorgte[4].

Im Allgemeinen standen die Europäer genetisch veränderten Getreidesorten skeptischer gegenüber als die Amerikaner, die bis jetzt sowohl die Idee als auch die Lebensmittel ohne nennenswerte Bedenken geschluckt haben[5]. Und unter den Europäern sind die Briten mit ihrer Weigerung, etwas mit solchen Dingen zu tun haben zu wollen, besonders unnachgiebig gewesen. Die jüngste Geschichte der britischen Landwirtschaftspolitik – das Töten von Millionen von Kühen aus Angst davor, dass ihr zunehmender Wahnsinn auf die Bevölkerung übergreift – hat die Öffentlichkeit gegenüber „unnatürlichem" Herumbasteln[6] an der Nahrungskette misstrauisch gemacht. Der Prinz möchte[7], dass wir jegliche genetische Veränderung ablehnen und statt dessen „mit der Natur zusammen zum Wohle der Menschheit arbeiten sollen."

Anmerkungen

1 Zusatz zur Verdeutlichung
2 Zusätze zur Verstärkung
3 *a piece of non-news* (= eine Nichtnachricht) kann man nicht wörtlich ins Deutsche übertragen
4 *managed to provoke* wurde zu „sorgen für" zusammengezogen
5 Das Wortspiel mit „etwas schlucken" für akzeptieren sollte man im Deutschen so belassen
6 „Herumpfuschen", „Herumdoktern" wären stärker
7 „Der Prinz sagt, dass er will, dass wir … ablehnen" wurde zu „… möchte, dass wir … sollen." zusammengefasst

Grundkurs Englisch 2001
Textaufgabe II

During the night after his first day Marcus woke up every half-hour or so. He could tell from the luminous hands of his dinosaur clock: 10.41, 11.19, 11.55, 12.35, 12.55, 1.31 … He couldn't believe he was going to have to go back there the next morning, and the morning after that, and the morning after that, and … more or less every morning for the rest of his life, just about.

He just wasn't right for schools. Not secondary schools, anyway. That was it. And how could you explain that to anyone? It was OK not to be right for some things (he already knew he wasn't right for parties, because he was too shy, or for baggy trousers, because his legs were too short), but not being right for school was a big problem. Everyone went to school. There was no way round it. Some kids, he knew, got taught by their parents at home, but his mum couldn't do that because she went out to work. Unless he paid her to teach him – but she'd told him not long ago that she got three hundred and fifty pounds a week from her job. Three hundred and fifty pounds a week! Where he was going to get that kind of money from? Not from a paper round, he knew that much. The only other kind of person he could think of who didn't go to school was the Macaulay Culkin[1] kind. They'd had something about him on Saturday-morning TV once, and they said he got taught in a caravan sort of thing by a private tutor. That would be OK, he supposed. Better than OK, because Macaulay Culkin probably got three hundred and fifty pounds a week, maybe even more, which meant that if he were Macaulay Culkin he could pay his mum to teach him. But if being Macaulay Culkin meant being good at drama, then forget it: he was crap at drama, because he hated standing up in front of people. Which was why he hated school. Which was why he wanted to be Macaulay Culkin. Which was why he was never going to be Macaulay Culkin in a thousand years, let alone in the next few days. He was going to have to go to school tomorrow.

He was quiet at breakfast. 'You'll get used to it,' his mum said as he was eating his cereal, probably because he was looking miserable. He just nodded, and smiled at her; it was an OK thing to say. There had been times when he knew, somewhere in him, that he would get used to it, whatever it was, because he had learnt that some hard things become softer after a very little while. The day after his dad left, his mum had taken him to Glastonbury with her friend Corinne and they'd had a brilliant time in a tent. But this was only going to get worse. That first terrible, horrible, frightening day was going to be as good as it got.

He got to school early, went to the form room, sat down at his desk. He was safe enough there. The kids who had given him a hard time yesterday were probably not the sort to arrive at school first thing; they'd be off somewhere smoking and taking drugs and raping people, he thought darkly. There were a couple of girls in the room, but they ignored him, unless the snort of laughter he heard while he was getting his reading book out had anything to do with him.

What was there to laugh at? Not much, really, unless you were the kind of person who was on permanent lookout for something to laugh at. Unfortunately, that was exactly the kind of person most kids were, in his experience. They patrolled up and down school corridors like sharks, except that what they were on the lookout for wasn't flesh but the wrong trousers, or the wrong haircut, or the wrong shoes, any or all of which sent them wild with excitement. As he was usually wearing the wrong shoes or the wrong trousers, and his haircut was wrong all the time, every day of the week, he didn't have to do very much to send them all demented.

From: Nick Hornby, *About a Boy.* London: Victor Gollancz 1998

[1] Macaulay Culkin: famous American child actor

Worksheet:

maximum number of points attainable

I. Questions on the text

Read all the questions first, then answer them in the given order. Use your own words as far as is appropriate.

1. Describe the situation Marcus finds himself in during the night. 10
2. What role does Macaulay Culkin play in Marcus' thoughts? 20
3. What does the reader learn about the boy's family background and about his relationship to his mother? 10
4. How does Marcus see his fellow pupils? What thoughts and feelings do they evoke in him? 10
5. How is Marcus characterized in the text, explicitly and implicitly? 20
6. What narrative perspective is used in this passage and what is the effect on the reader? 10

II. Composition

Choose *one* of the following topics. Write about 120 to 150 words. 40

1. "Schools should concentrate more on developing social skills than on teaching pupils facts and facts only." Discuss.
2. Leaving school as soon as possible may be tempting for quite a few pupils. Weigh the pros and cons.

III. Translation

Translate the following text into German: 40

160

Whatever happened to school uniform? In the 1960s and 70s it seemed to be on its way out. But then something happened. Britain pulled back from total abolition. Today that group of scruffy adolescents at the school gates will – more likely than not – be wearing variants on the same basic blue, black or green dress code[1].

Much of the rest of the world would probably see Britain's school uniforms as an anachronism – so why have many schools voted to retain them? "They appeal to parents," says Malory Wober of the University of Michigan. "Uniform represents order and the majority of British parents still want that from schools." Among headteachers the argument is often put that uniform reduces competitiveness between fashion-conscious people and obscures the differences between rich and poor children.

British teenagers like the challenge of a uniform. One head said: "When I think of the efforts they go to to subvert the rules I think it's almost an essential part of growing up."

From *The strange fashion for uniforms* by David Mosford in:
The Times Educational Supplement, 14 January 2000

[1] dress code: set of rules about what clothes you must wear in a school, business etc.

Lösungsvorschlag

I. Questions on the text

1. Marcus spends a troubled night. He wakes up frequently because he worries about his first day in the new school, which didn't go well, and about the fact that he will definitely have to go back there in the morning. In his opinion he is not "right for schools" (l. 6), but he realises that this attitude will not convince anyone, and nothing can be done about it.

2. He remembers Macaulay Culkin because this hero of the film "Alone at Home" doesn't have to go to school but can afford to be taught by a private tutor. He envies him for this but knows that he cannot compare himself to him: Culkin makes a lot of money because he, unlike Marcus, is self-confident and enjoys appearing in public. So, on the one hand, the child actor serves as a role model for him, but on the other, he is convinced that he could never be like him.

3. Marcus is the only child of a broken marriage. He now lives with his mother, who goes to work and struggles to keep up a reasonable standard of living. It seems they cannot afford much: they go camping and he wears unfashionable clothes and shoes, and his mother probably cuts his hair. They apparently get along well. He accepts his mum's life and opinions and appreciates her attempts to soften the effects of the divorce on him.

4. The boy mentions some kids who made him miserable on his first day at school. In his imagination, he blows them up into being secret drug-takers and rapists. The girls in the classroom take no notice of him, but he suspects, in his pessimistic mood, that they laugh about him behind his back, as most children, "in his experience" (l. 40) always try to detect flaws in other kids' appearance in order to make fun of them. He realises that he fulfils all the conditions for making a perfect victim.

5. *Remember that <u>explicit</u> or direct characterisation is achieved through statements and comments by the narrator himself or other characters. <u>Implicit</u> or indirect characterisation is possible through conclusions the reader may draw on the basis of a character's behaviour, opinions, choice of words or way of talking.*

   Marcus tells the reader explicitly that he is a shy person and lacks the confidence to stand "up in front of people" (l. 21). By reading between the lines and by what he says about other people we come to understand that he is also vulnerable (his sleeplessness after his first school day, his dismay at his parents' separation). He accepts his shortcomings, which are partly due to his mother's financial situation. Also he is reasonable enough to realise he will have to continue at school, and to acknowledge the soundness of his mother's reaction ("You'll get used to it", l. 25 – "it was an OK thing to say", ll. 26 f). Even though he remembers that the shock of his father's abandoning the family wore off after some time, he cannot come to terms with his pessimism about further "terrible, horrible, frightening" (l. 31) days to come.

6. *The narrative perspective is the point of view from which the story is told – from the outside through an <u>omniscient</u> narrator, or from the inside, when a <u>first-person narrator</u> or a <u>third-person narrator</u> is used. The latter may pretend to know everything (and be omniscient again) or proceed from his own limited perspective. The author can also present several third-person narrators. It is also possible, especially in modern fiction, that third-person narrators use the <u>stream-of-consciousness</u> technique, where we enter a character's conscious and even subconscious mind, or, which is the case in*

this passage, an interior monologue in reported thought, where a person's thoughts and feelings are reported in an organised way, in the past tense

Here the author uses a third-person point of view and the technique of reported thought. In three scenes (Marcus in bed, at the breakfast table, at school) all past and present facts relevant to the boy's situation are presented. He lets the reader participate in his thoughts and takes him into his confidence, so that he will see everything through the protagonist's eyes, share his feelings and take his side. The effects achieved are thus comparable to those of a first-person narrative, with an additional touch of objectivity through the presentation by a third-person narrator.

II. Composition

1. Schools should concentrate on social skills

It is often helpful to look up the key words of a topic in your dictionary (Here: social skills (ability to meet people easily and deal well with them), DCE, or socialization, DCE/OALD)

To develop a child's ability to meet people easily and deal with them is clearly a major educational aim. Families already supply behaviour guidelines, but as they are only small units, they cannot entirely prepare young people for their integration into larger social groups. It is therefore necessary that schools prepare children for their future social roles. It would, however, be excessive to demand that they should concentrate more on social skills, at the cost of reducing the traditional syllabus. Interaction in the classroom already provides the children with enough possibilities to find out which attitudes will be acceptable among their peers. This gives them a far better insight into the demands of social integration than a new school subject could do. It goes without saying that teachers should keep their eyes open for conflicts or anti-social views and try to exert their influence to make the students aware of values and behaviour patterns which would enable them to become acceptable members of society.

2. Leaving school as soon as possible

There will be moments in the life of any pupil when you become frustrated with school and think of dropping out. What a temptation to leave it all behind: bad marks, trouble with teachers and parents, no end of studies, lack of interest in most subjects! It seems more appealing to step out into real life, to earn your own money, to become independent and to follow your real inclinations. While your mates do their homework and prepare for exams you can take your date to the disco!
On the other hand, as a dropout you have only limited career options and will find it extremely hard to reverse your earlier decision. If you later realize that your true professional goal would have required further study, it may be too late. You will hardly find the opportunity or energy to make a fresh start and become a doctor or a lawyer after all. So it is better to fight a passing frustration and carry on at school as long as you can.

III. Translation

Was ist bloß[1] aus der Schuluniform geworden? In den sechziger und siebziger Jahren schien sie schon im Rückzug begriffen zu sein. Aber dann ist etwas passiert. Großbritannien zog sich von ihrer kompletten[2] Abschaffung wieder[1] zurück. Heute wird jene Gruppe schlampig gekleideter Jugendlicher an den Schultoren höchstwahrscheinlich wieder verschiedene[1] Varianten der im wesentlichen gleichen blauen, schwarzen oder grünen vorgeschriebenen Kleidung tragen.

Ein großer Teil der übrigen Welt würde wahrscheinlich die britischen Schuluniformen als unzeitgemäß betrachten – warum haben sich dann viele Schulen für ihre Beibehaltung[3] entschieden? „Sie kommen gut bei Eltern an," sagt Malory Wober von der Universität von Michigan. „Die Uniform steht für Ordnung, und die Mehrheit britischer Eltern wünscht sich das immer noch von den Schulen." Von Schulleitern wird oft das Argument vorgebracht, dass Uniformen den Konkurrenzgeist zwischen modebewussten Schülern abbauen und die Unterschiede zwischen reichen und armen Kindern verschwimmen lässt.

Britische Jugendliche lieben die Herausforderung einer Uniform. Ein Schulleiter sagte: „Wenn ich an die Anstrengungen denke, die sie unternehmen, um die Regeln zu unterlaufen, so glaube ich, dass dies fast ein wesentlicher Teil des Entwicklungsprozesses ist."

Anmerkungen:

1 Stilistisch bedingte Einfügungen
2 Als Zeichen des guten Willens: ein Fremdwort durch ein anderes ersetzen
3 Eine immer wieder brauchbare Technik: Verbalkonstruktionen nominal übersetzen

Grundkurs Englisch 2002
Textaufgabe I

What the Internet cannot do

"It is impossible that old prejudices and hostilities should longer exist, while such an instrument has been created for the exchange of thought between all the nations of the earth." Thus Victorian enthusiasts, acclaiming the arrival in 1858 of the first transatlantic telegraph cable. People say that sort of thing about new technologies, even today. The wildest optimism has greeted the Internet. A whole industry of cybergurus[1] has enthralled audiences (and made a fine living) with exuberant claims that the Internet will prevent wars, reduce pollution, and combat various forms of inequality. However, although the Internet is still young enough to inspire idealism, it has also been around long enough to test whether the prophets can be right.

Grandest of all the claims are those about the Internet's potential as a force for peace. One guru, Nicholas Negroponte, has declared that, thanks to the Internet, the children of the future "are not going to know what nationalism is". His colleague, Michael Dertouzos, has written that digital communications will bring "computer-aided peace" which "may help stave off future flare-ups of ethnic hatred and national break-ups". The idea is that improved communications will reduce misunderstandings and avert conflict.

This is not new, alas, any more than were the claims for the peace-making possibilities of other new technologies. In the early years of the 20th century, aeroplanes were expected to end wars, by promoting international communication and (less credibly) by making armies obsolete, since they would be vulnerable to attack from the air. After the first world war had dispelled such notions[2], it was the turn of radio. "Nation shall speak peace unto nation," ran the fine motto of Britain's BBC World Service. Sadly, Rwanda's[3] Radio Mille Collines[4] disproved the idea that radio was an intrinsically pacific force once and for all.

The mistake people make is to assume that wars are caused simply by the failure of different peoples to understand each other adequately. Indeed, even if that were true, the Internet can also be used to advocate conflict. Hate speech and intolerance flourish in its murkier corners, where governments find it hard to intervene. Although the Internet undeniably fosters communication, it will not put an end to war.

What about the belief that the Internet will reduce inequality? According to a recent study, American households with annual incomes above $75,000 are more than 20 times as likely to have Internet access as the poorest households. Bill Clinton, struck by the "digital divide" between rich and poor, argues that universal Internet access would help to reduce income inequality.

But, as the cost of using the Internet continues to fall, the true reason for the digital divide will become apparent. The poor are not shunning the Internet because they cannot afford it: the problem is that they lack the skills to exploit it effectively. So it is difficult to see how connecting the poor to the Internet will improve their finances. It would make more sense to aim for universal literacy than universal Internet access.

Yet, even inequality may, in some cases, be reduced thanks to the Internet. A computer programmer in Bangalore or Siberia can use the Internet to work for a software company in Seattle without leaving home, and can expect to be paid a wage that is closer to that of his virtual colleagues at the other end of the cable. The effect is to reduce income inequality between people doing similar jobs in different countries, but to increase the inequality between information workers in poor countries and their poorest compatriots.

The Internet changes many things. It has had a dramatic impact on the world of business. Firms can now link their systems directly to those of their suppliers and partners, can do business online around the clock, and can learn more than ever about their customers. For individuals, e-mail has emerged as the most important new form of personal communication since the invention of the telephone.

The extent to which the Internet will transform other fields of human endeavour, however, is less certain. Even when everyone on the planet has been connected to the Internet, there will still be wars, and pollution, and inequality. As new gizmos[5] come and go, human nature seems to remain stubbornly unchanged; despite the claims of the techno-prophets, humanity cannot simply invent away its failings.

From: *The Economist,* 19 August 2000

1 cybergurus: *(derog.)* computer experts

2 to dispel a notion: to prove it wrong

3 Rwanda: African country, notorious for its ethnic conflict between the Hutu and the Tutsi tribes

4 Radio Mille Collines: a Hutu radio station that was accused of encouraging the massacre of large parts of Rwanda's Tutsi population

5 gizmo: *(infml)* a small piece of equipment, often one that does something in a new and clever way

Worksheet:

maximum number of points attainable

I. Questions on the text

Read all the questions first, then answer them in the given order. Use your own words as far as is appropriate.

1. Why does the writer mention "the first transatlantic telegraph cable" (ll. 3/4)? Examine other historical references that reveal a similar intention. — 20
2. What claims do Negroponte and Dertouzos make for the Internet and how does the writer view them? — 10
3. What, according to Bill Clinton, should be done about the "digital divide" (l. 32) in the US and what does the writer think of this proposal? — 10
4. Prove that the headline does not cover all the aspects dealt with in the text. — 20
5. What conclusion about the potential of the Internet for human progress does the writer reach in the final paragraph? — 10
6. How does the writer's use of language reflect his attitude? — 10

II. Composition

Choose *one* of the following topics. Write about 120 to 150 words. — 40

1. Surfing the Internet is a conscious decision to waste time. Discuss
2. Do you think books will ever become obsolete?

III. Translation

Translate the following text into German: — 40

160

New information technology offers huge benefits, but it comes at a price: less and less privacy. Most people have long accepted the need to provide some information about themselves in order to vote, pursue a business or even borrow a library book. But exercising control over who knows what about you has also come to be seen as an essential feature of a civilised society. Without the "right to be left alone", to shut out on occasion the prying eyes of both government and society, other political and civil liberties seem fragile. Today most people in rich societies assume that, provided they obey the law, they have a right to enjoy privacy whenever it suits them.

They are wrong. Despite a raft of laws, treaties and constitutional provisions, privacy has been eroded for decades. The power to gather and disseminate data electronically is growing so fast that it raises the unsettling question: in 20 years' time, will there be any privacy left to protect?

From: *The Economist,* 1st May 1999

Lösungsvorschlag

I. Questions on the text

1. *Note that the first transatlantic cable (lines 3/4) was a new technology in its day. Similar inventions the author refers to are aeroplanes (l. 17) and the radio (l. 20).*

   The author mentions the first transatlantic telegraph cable because – like most technological advances – it was received with great expectations when it was first installed. Enthusiasts in those days thought that the increasing exchange of ideas between different nations would abolish old prejudices and hostilities. This example serves the writer as proof of his thesis that the optimism that usually accompanies the introduction of new technological inventions is always almost exaggerated or even unfounded. In order to corroborate his thesis he also points out that in the 20th century the arrival of aeroplanes and of the radio were expected to promote international communication and understanding, or even render the military obsolete.

2. *The quotations you need for the first part of the question are to be found in the second paragraph. In order to determine the author's view, however, you have to look at the third, and mainly at the fourth paragraph.*

   Both experts see the Internet as a force for peace. Nicholas Negroponte expects it to abolish all kinds of nationalism, and Michael Dertouzos even claims that it will help to prevent future eruptions of racial hatred and nationalism, thus reducing misunderstandings and averting conflicts. The author thinks that these expectations are no more true than the predictions made about former new technologies. Even if it were true, he says, that wars are caused by the failure of mutual understanding, the Internet can also be abused to stir up hatred instead of calming it down.

3. *The "digital divide" means that there is a difference between rich and poor people with regard to their access to Internet technology.*

   Former US president Bill Clinton suggested that everybody should have the same chances to have Internet access. In his view such a step would contribute to more equality of income. The argument is that the poor have a low income because they cannot afford to use modern technology. The author, however, thinks it is the other way round: the poor avoid using the Internet because they lack the skills to do so. In his view teaching them basic skills like reading and writing would help them more.

4. *Every writer tries to word a headline in a way that attracts the greatest number of readers. In our time articles that praise the Internet as a cure for all kinds of problems are abundant and will go largely unnoticed. A differing view, however, is certain to be read by a lot of people who have doubts about the new technology. If you read the text carefully you will also find passages that show the reader what the Internet can accomplish.*

   It is the writer's main purpose to warn the reader not to expect too much of the new medium Internet. Thus the headline seems to cover the subject matter adequately.
   On the other hand, there are also passages in which the reader is told what the Internet can do. In the last but one paragraph the author points out that it brings about a lot of changes. Business life is in fact revolutionised by linking the computers of different firms, which can now buy and sell around the clock, and the invention of e-mail has dramatically changed personal communication. Even before, the author has also pointed out that the Internet has contributed to raising the wages of computer programmers, even in poor countries (ll. 41/42). On the negative side, we are also told that the Internet can be and is used to stir up hatred and intolerance (l. 26). These examples show that the headline covers only one aspect of the text.

5. *Read the question carefully: you are to determine the writer's conclusion about human progress, which includes technology and human nature.*

   The writer says clearly that the Internet will change a lot of things, although it is not yet certain to what extent it will do that. The one thing that is certain, however, is that it cannot change human nature. Even if everyone in the world is connected, that will not be the end of "wars, and pollution, and inequality" (l. 52). These negative aspects seem to be deeply rooted in human nature.

6. *Two devices are obvious: the writer's choice of words ("cybergurus"), and his use of contrasting conjunctions such as however, but and yet.*

   When the writer of the present text talks about eminent computer scientists, he refers to them in a rather derogatory way as "cybergurus" (l. 5) or simply "gurus" (l. 11), further down as "techno-prophets" (ll. 53/54), who cannot "invent away" (l. 54, an expression that the author has coined himself). Moreover, he shows that he is far from sharing their enthusiasm by calling their inventions "gizmos" (i. e. devices whose names one does not remember) that "come and go" (l. 52).
   Another device that reflects his attitude is the antithetical structure: he quotes the enthusiasts of technology, only to state his own opinion in a remark that is introduced by conjunctions expressing contrast, such as "but" (l. 34), "however" (l. 7) or "yet" (l. 39). Thus he signals to his readers that he disagrees with the optimistic estimations of the "gurus".

II. Composition

1. Surfing the Internet is a conscious decision to waste time. Discuss.

   Note that the expression "surfing the Internet" was coined to point out that it was similar to "channel surfing", i. e. changing channels on a TV set at random. A lot of people, however, use the phrase also to describe targeted research on the Internet.

   Everyone of us has heard about computer addicts, sitting in front of their monitors for hours on end. They casually click on links, thus browsing aimlessly through the World Wide Web. If you ask them afterwards what they did, they will have a very hard time explaining their activity. That is the type of person who wastes her or his time on the net, although I doubt that they take a conscious decision to do it. Like all addicts, they can't help it.
   On the other hand, if you "surf the Internet" doing serious, purposeful research for a subject you can hardly call it "a waste of time". Of course, while trying to find relevant scientific, or literary, material, we may also become distracted by a lot of fascinating information. But that is just like browsing the shelves of a bookshop, and nobody would call that a waste of time.

2. Do you think books will ever become obsolete ?

   To some of us it may still sound like science fiction but the 100 % bookless school is already a reality – in California. The children there work with modern computer programs instead of old-fashioned books, and their principal claims that test scores have gone up since they went digital. So, it seems we can do without books.
   We should not forget, however, that a lot of people would deplore the replacement of books by computers and television. They fear that it would be a great loss for our culture, and that our children will be – at best – semiliterate if the texts they read only appear on a computer monitor.
   I think that the fears and hopes are rather exaggerated. Just look at the facts – online booksellers have been immensely successful since the arrival of the Internet. Sales figures for books are in fact higher than ever before. It seems that more and more people enjoy the pleasure of being alone with a book. Perhaps rather than killing books, the Internet encourages people to buy and read them.

III. Translation

Die neue Informationstechnologie bietet riesige Vorteile, aber sie hat auch ihren Preis: immer weniger Privatsphäre. Die meisten Leute haben sich längst damit abgefunden, dass sie ein bisschen Information über sich preisgeben müssen[1], um wählen zu können, ein Geschäft zu betreiben oder auch nur, um ein Buch aus der Bücherei auszuleihen. Aber die Kontrolle darüber zu behalten, wer was über einen weiß, wird auch zunehmend[2] als ein grundlegender Wesenszug einer zivilisierten Gesellschaft angesehen. Ohne das „Recht, in Ruhe gelassen zu werden", gelegentlich die neugierigen Blicke sowohl der Regierung als auch der Gesellschaft auszuschließen, erscheinen auch[3] die anderen bürgerlichen und politischen Freiheiten zerbrechlich. Heute gehen die meisten Leute in den wohlhabenden Gesellschaften davon aus, dass sie, wenn sie gesetzestreu sind, auch das Recht haben, ihre Privatsphäre zu genießen, wann immer es ihnen gefällt.

Sie irren sich. Trotz einer Unmenge von Gesetzen, Verträgen und Verfassungsbestimmungen wird die Privatsphäre schon[4] seit Jahrzehnten ausgehöhlt. Die Macht, auf elektronischem Wege Daten zu sammeln und zu verbreiten, wächst so schnell, dass sie die beunruhigende Frage aufwirft: Wird in 20 Jahren überhaupt[5] noch eine Privatsphäre da sein, die man schützen kann?

Anmerkungen

1 *the need to* gibt man am besten verbal wieder

2 *to come to be* wird im Deutschen mit dem Adverb „zunehmend" wiedergegeben

3 Zusatz zur Verdeutlichung

4 *wird … schon* zur Wiedergabe des Present Perfect

5 Zusatz zur Verdeutlichung

Grundkurs Englisch 2002
Textaufgabe II

The Dinner

It was June, the first really decent day of the summer. Nicole was eating her dinner with her legs sticking out the kitchen door, grabbing the bit of sun before it was hijacked by next door's wall. All four of the daughters had sunglasses parked on top of their heads. Laurence, the son, had sunglasses as well, like the ones Edgar Davids, the Dutch footballer, wore. On Edgar Davids they looked impressive, terrifying, even sexy. On Laurence they looked desperate – he looked like a day-old chick that had just been pushed out of the nest. Larry's heart went out to him.

And that was why he wasn't turned in to the girls' chat that evening. He was trying to come up with a nice way to tell poor Laurence to bring the glasses back to the shop. So he'd heard none of the usual prying and slagging, the good-natured torture and confession that he loved so much.

He was wondering if Laurence still had the receipt for the goggles when he heard Vanessa asking, "What's he do for his money?"

"He's an accountant," said Stephanie.

Larry sat up: no daughter of his was going to get stuck with a bloody accountant.

"At least, he would be," said Stephanie, "if they let him work."

"What's that mean?" said Larry.

They all looked at him. The aggression and fear in his voice had shocked even him.

"They won't let him work," said Stephanie.

"Who won't?"

"I don't know," she said. "The government."

"Why not?"

"Because they haven't granted him asylum yet."

"He's a refugee?"

"Yeah. I suppose so."

"Where's he from?"

"Nigeria."

Larry waited for the gasps, but there were none, not even from Mona[1]. He wished now he'd been listening earlier. This mightn't have been a boyfriend she was talking about at all, it could have been someone she'd never even met.

But Vanessa put him right.

"You should see him, Da[2]. He's gorgeous."

And all the other girls nodded and agreed.

"Dead serious-looking[3]."

"A ride[4]."

He stood up.

"He is not gorgeous!" he shouted.

Nicole laughed, but stopped quickly.

"He's not gorgeous or anything else! Not in this house!"

He realized that he was standing up, but he didn't want to sit down again. He couldn't.

Mona spoke. "What's wrong?"

He looked at six faces looking up at him, waiting for the punch line, praying for it.

Frightened faxes, confused, and angry.

There was nothing he could say. Nothing safe, nothing reassuring or even clear. He didn't know why he was standing there.

"Is it because he's black?" said Mona.

Larry didn't let himself nod. He never thought he'd be a man who'd nod: yes, I object to another man's color. Shame was rubbing now against his anger.

"Phil Lynott was black, love," Mona reminded him.

Phil Lynott had been singing "Whiskey in the Jar" when Larry and Mona had stopped dancing and kissed for the first time.

And now he could talk.

"Phil Lynott was Irish!" he said. "He was from Crumlin[5]. He was fuckin' civilized!"

And now Stephanie was right in front of him, tears streaming from her, and he couldn't hear a word she was screaming at him. And he wished, he wished to Christ they could start all over again, that he could sit down and listen and stop it before all this had to happen.

It was Mona who rescued him. "We'll have to meet him," she said. This was just after she'd hit the table with the frying pan.

"No," said Larry.

"Yes, Larry," she said, and he knew she was right. If he kept saying no they'd all leave, all the girls. It was what he would have expected of them. "Stand up for your rights." That was what he'd roared after them every morning, on their way out to school. "Get up, stand up. Don't give up the fight."

The house was empty now. Mona had imposed a ragged[6] peace. Larry and Stephanie had hugged each other, yards of brittle space between them. The girls had taken her down to the local. They'd be talking about him now, he knew. Racist. Bastard. Racist. Pig.

"It could be worse, love," said Mona.

Larry looked at her. "He could have been an estate agent," she said.

From: Roddy Doyle, *The Dinner*, in: *Guess who's Coming for the Dinner*, 2001

1 Mona: Larry's wife

2 Da: Dad

3 dead serious-looking *(teenage-slang):* stunning

4 a ride: *here:* fantastic

5 Crumlin: a part of Dublin

6 ragged: *here:* unstable, not likely to last

Worksheet:

maximum number of points attainable

I. Questions on the text

Read all the questions first, then answer them in the given order. Use your own words as far as is appropriate.

1. What do the first two paragraphs tell us about the relationship between Larry and his children? — 10
2. Outline the step-by-step escalation of the conflict between Larry and his daughters. — 20
3. Trace the development of Larry's inner conflict. — 20
4. What different feelings does Larry evoke in the reader? — 10
5. Describe the role Mona plays in this scene, her position in the family and her character. — 20

II. Composition

Choose *one* of the following topics. Write about 120 to 150 words. — 40

1. What can be done at school to promote racial and cultural tolerance?
2. "Stand up for your rights" – a maxim for your life?

III. Translation

Translate the following text into German: — 40

160

Immigration is the subject Europe's politicians would rather not talk about. No issue generates more emotion, and few others seem as difficult to solve. Vowing to act tough on illegal immigrants and false asylum seekers plays well with the masses; but crackdowns merely send refugees underground, forcing them to take ever-deadlier risks to get in. Easing entry requirements makes good economic sense, since Europe needs 75 million new workers over the next 50 years to replenish its aging population.

The Continent's long-standing "zero immigration" policy seems premised on[1] the hope that the problem will go away: if you build a "Fortress Europe", they won't come. But they're still coming. Flung out of their native lands by war or persecution or poverty – or simply the promise of a better life – immigrants are crossing Europe's borders in unprecedented numbers. Europe may still resist the idea that it is a continent of immigrants. But in order to thrive, it has no choice but to become one.

From *Sea of Promise* by Ranesh Ratnesar in: *TIME*, 19 February 2001, p. 16f.

1 premised on: based on

Lösungsvorschlag

I. Questions on the text

1. Without doubt, Larry enjoys the company of his children. It is mentioned that he loves to listen to their teenage conversations and bantering at the dinner table. He does not insist on formal behaviour and does not mind Nicole eating with her legs "out the kitchen door" (l. 2). However, he objects to his son's choice of sunglasses. He feels sorry for him, because in his opinion they do not suit him and he tries to think of a "nice way" (l. 9) to persuade him to take them back to the shop.

2. *Note: Questions 2 and 3 both deal with Larry's argument with his daughters. Make sure to differentiate between the external aspects and his own inner conflict.*

   Larry starts to interfere when he overhears Stephanie mentioning her involvement with an accountant, a profession he obviously objects to, and he proceeds with a kind of cross examination. When she admits that he is black, he freezes in disbelief. The girls' enthusiastic praise of his good looks makes him stand up and shout out his protest: "Not in this house!" (l. 39). This openly racist attitude shocks his daughters. Larry puts himself further in the wrong when he weakly claims only to disapprove of the man's nationality rather than his skin colour. This brings Stephanie to tears and to shout at him in anger. His wife's resolute protest ends the argument for the time being and establishes a temporary truce.

3. Larry's fatherly preoccupation with his son's sunglasses is interrupted when he realises that Stephanie might be having a relationship with a "bloody accountant" (l. 15). He is even more disturbed when he learns that the man is not allowed to work. He is aware that his voice betrays "aggression and fear" (l. 18), which makes him uneasy for the first time. To his disappointment, the other family members do not share his shock at the young man being an African. His brief hope that they are not talking about a potential boyfriend of Stephanie's is shattered. His dismay turns into anger and he categorically forbids admitting the man to his house. When the issue of colour is brought up, he wavers and begins to feel ashamed. He realises that he has gone too far and wishes to undo everything. After a last weak protest, he is relieved that his wife settles the matter. He knows that otherwise his girls would have left, following his own educational rule of standing up for one's rights.

4. In the beginning, Larry is portrayed as a loving father. But the reader begins to be disappointed in him when he first objects to a man being an accountant, and even more when he utters his racist views. Likewise, his choice of words ("bloody accountant", "fuckin' civilized") contribute to the reader's reservations. However, his admission of shock and shame at his own behaviour, and that he was wrong compensate for his rudeness, and the reader will get the impression that Larry reacted out of parental protectiveness and will forgive him.

5. *Note: Be sure to cover the three aspects of role, position and character*

   Mona is first mentioned when she ignores Larry's shock at the man's African origin. She has participated in their children's conversation from the beginning and cannot find anything wrong in it. To save the situation, she reminds her husband that a black singer, with his song, had contributed to their own romance. When he stubbornly continues to defend his views, she "rescued him" (l. 58) from his impossible position, bangs the frying pan on the table and decides that they are indeed going to meet the African. Then she accomplishes reconciliation between her husband and their children.

Mona's behaviour shows that she is a determined woman who enjoys the respect of her family. She seems to be sensitive to her husband's dilemma and helps him to repair his relationship with his children. As a liberal thinker, Mona is on her children's side in the conflict, but she does not abuse Larry for his views and comforts him in the end.

II. Composition

1. What can be done at school to promote racial and cultural tolerance?

Here it will help to consult your dictionary about the definition of tolerance. This can provide you with an idea for your introduction.

The dictionary says that tolerance is the willingness to allow people to do, say, or believe what they want without criticising them. In the case of racial tolerance, one might add that everyone should be accepted no matter what skin colour they were born with. This ethical principle is widely shared and explicitly mentioned in the Bavarian Law of Education, which stresses the important aim to promote the understanding between peoples. Accordingly, teachers are called upon to interfere if individual students should, with their opinions or behaviour, express narrow-minded, negative stereotypes of racial or cultural minorities, or defend exaggerated nationalistic views. Such opinions must be discussed in class whenever they arise. In many subjects like history, languages, or geography, other cultures are examined and compared with our own. Here comparisons should never be drawn in a way that our culture is shown to be better than others, but just as a different one. These differences between cultures must be presented as something both acceptable and even valuable.

2. "Stand up for your rights!" – a maxim for your life?

Most of you will remember the incident we are using in our introduction: On December 1, 1955, a black woman named Rosa Parks deliberately took her seat in the "white" section of a bus in Montgomery, Alabama, and was arrested. Martin Luther King then organized a bus boycott, which triggered off the Civil Rights Movement in America.

Rosa Parks, by sitting down on a Montgomery bus, stood up for an ignored but constitutional right, fully aware that she would get into trouble.
Admirable as this may be the question remains whether standing up for your rights is a rule that should be invoked in all circumstances. In our daily lives, we constantly come up against situations where we must decide whether to put our foot down or ignore what we consider unjust. If we oppose our parents when they forbid us to see a certain boy or girl, if we protest against a teacher's unfair treatment, we might get into trouble, but we could also gain respect and succeed. In any case, we will have won a moral victory, which makes us a better person and develops our character. On the other hand, it might be wise to first weigh up the causes and consequences. If we feel that fundamental rights are being violated we should run the risk, but fighting for trifles is not worth the effort and only makes us appear quarrelsome.

II. Translation

Einwanderung ist das Thema über das Europas Politiker lieber nicht sprechen würden. Kein Problem weckt mehr Emotionen[1] und wenig andere scheinen so schwer lösbar zu sein. Wenn man hoch und heilig versichert[2], hart gegen illegale Einwanderer und Scheinasylanten vorgehen zu wollen, kommt dies bei den Massen gut an – aber hartes Durchgreifen treibt die Flüchtlinge lediglich in den Untergrund und zwingt sie, immer lebensgefährlichere Risiken einzugehen, um ins Land zu kommen. Vom wirtschaftlichen Standpunkt aus ist eine Lockerung der Einwanderungsbestimmungen durchaus[3] sinnvoll, weil Europa in den nächsten 50 Jahren 75 Millionen neue Arbeitskräfte[4] benötigt, um seine alternde Bevölkerung zu ergänzen.

Die seit langem bestehende Politik des Kontinents, keine Einwanderung zuzulassen[5] scheint auf der Hoffnung begründet zu sein, dass das Problem verschwinden wird: Wenn man eine „Festung Europa" errichtet, werden sie nicht kommen. Aber sie kommen immer noch. Da sie durch Krieg oder Verfolgung oder Armut oder einfach nur[3] wegen der Hoffnung auf ein besseres Leben aus ihren Heimatländern geworfen werden, überschreiten Einwanderer die Grenzen Europas in noch nie da gewesener Zahl[6]. Mag Europa sich auch[3] weiterhin gegen die Vorstellung sperren, dass es ein Einwanderungskontinent ist – um aber weiter[3] im Wohlstand zu leben hat es keine andere [3] Wahl als einer zu werden.

Anmerkungen

1 Im Deutschen nur Plural möglich. Alternative Übersetzung: bringt mehr Gefühle ins Spiel

2 Wörtlich: *geloben*

3 Stilistisch bedingte Einfügungen

4 *Arbeiter* geht hier nicht, da sicher auch höher qualifiziertes Personal gebraucht wird

5 *Null-Einwanderung* wäre zu unidiomatisch. Vielleicht auch: *totale Einwanderungssperre*

6 Im Deutschen ist der Singular vorzuziehen

Grundkurs Englisch 2003
Textaufgabe I

Kings of Spray

Judging from the crowd, it could have been any trendy gallery opening in New York or London. Rail-thin fashionistas[1] clutched Gucci[2] bags as they wobbled around on stiletto heels. Slender young men adjusted horn-rimmed glasses before cooing over a painting's "sense of color" and "emotion". The only people who seemed out of place were the artists themselves – a small clutch of bleary-eyed wanderers with hooded sweat shirts and matted hair – who go by the "tags" Mak 1, Mantis and Eeb. They work not in oils or pastels but in spray paint, producing graffiti art that has made them the talk of Cape Town. And they've always done their best work under cover of night, when nobody else is looking.

Now Cape Town's art establishment can't take its eyes off them. Impressed by the enormous murals brightening large swaths of the city – many supporting causes like antiretroviral drugs[3] for AIDS patients or quitting smoking – gallery owners have begun inviting the graffiti artists to exhibit their work on canvases. The shows have become so popular that some of the artists can now make a living solely off their graffiti. Advertisers, corporations, political candidates – even private art collectors – are commissioning their work. Two of the country's top graffiti artists, Mak 1 and Falko, have been hired to decorate buildings for the 2004 Summer Olympics in Athens. At home they lecture at universities and recently organized a "graffiti tour" of the township where they painted their first murals.

So it came as a surprise two months ago when city officials announced a crackdown on graffiti. "We were shocked," says Mantis. "One minute we're the kings of Cape Town, and the next minute everyone wants to see us disappear." Indeed, officials hoping to lure tourists and investors suddenly decided that graffiti – which had gone largely unpoliced – was unsightly.

Contemporary graffiti art started in the 1980s in Cape Town's mixed-race, or "colored", communities. Inspired by television images of New York buildings and subway trains covered with graffiti, a few young artists created their own tags, spray-painting their signatures on walls.

Today graffiti has spread to the affluent southern suburbs and is becoming popular elsewhere in the country as well. Two of Cape Town's most admired artists – Mantis and Tyler Murphy – are white. "The graffiti scene is the only place in cape Town where everyone is judged strictly on skill. We don't care what you look like because so many of us are rootless ourselves, trying to create a culture that's not like the one we grew up with," says Murphy.

Even graffiti art's staunchest opponents are reluctant to criticize their murals, which not only are stunning but also incorporate such elusive values as racial harmony and opportunity for the disenfranchised[4]. Officials are careful to distinguish the murals from tags, the ugly signature scrawls that mar the city landscape. While they're hoping to eradicate tagging, they don't want to ban murals outright. "We simply want to regulate them, the way you would regulate putting up a billboard," says Executive Councilor for Safety and Health Ian Neilson. City councilor Jean-Pierre Smith, who hired graffiti artist Sky 189 to paint a mural for his campaign, is worried about the impact on the artists' livelihood. "We're just seeking to clean up the city, not to criminalize their profession," he says.

Some believe officials have fixated on graffiti because Cape Town's bigger problems – poverty, homelessness, crime – are so intractable. Six months ago art editor Roger Lucey commissioned three graffiti artists to paint a piece on the front wall of his suburban home, prompting his outraged neighbors to file a complaint with the city council. "My neighbors say I'm bringing crime into the area, but it's just a bloody piece of art work," he says. "They're so afraid of young people's real problems that they fix on small things like this." Like that of all art, it seems, graffiti's appeal lies squarely in the eye of the beholder.

From: *Newsweek,* April 29, 2002

1 fashionistas: people who follow all the latest fashions

2 Gucci: Italian fashion designer

3 anti-retroviral drugs: drugs for people who are infected with HIV

4 disenfranchised: *here:* disadvantaged

Worksheet:

maximum number of points attainable

I. Questions on the text

Read all the questions first, then answer them in the given order. Use your own words as far as is appropriate.

1. Describe and characterize the people attending the gallery opening referred to in the first paragraph. — 10
2. In what way has the popularity of graffiti art affected the lives of some artists? — 10
3. How has the city officials' attitude towards graffiti changed? Explain how they justify their new policy. — 20
4. Trace the origin and the spread of graffiti art in South Africa. What does Murphy consider so special about the graffiti scene? — 10
5. Describe Roger Lucey's experience and compare it to what is expressed in the title and in the first paragraph. — 10
6. What does the text reveal about the writer's personal attitude towards graffiti? Give evidence from the text. — 20

II. Composition

Choose *one* of the following topics. Write about 150 to 200 words. — 40

1. "Let's stop subsidizing the arts – the taxpayers' money should be used for more important things." Discuss.
2. Like graffiti, the video clip has become a standard element of contemporary youth culture. Do you consider it art or "trash"?

3. Comment on the cartoon.

From: *New Yorker & Artist's Album* (1970)

III. Translation

Translate the following text into German: 40/160

The mode of representation that prevails in murals painted in the 1980s and early 1990s shows black people as victims. Murals of this type tend to have an accusatory tone, their objective focused on the public representation of the injustices suffered by the black community at the hands of the white Apartheid regime. In these murals the depiction of blacks and whites almost always follows simple patterns: black people are represented as powerless receptors[1] of someone else's treatment, while whites assume the role of oppressors. A mural painted in 1982 by students of the Fort Hare University campus, for example, depicts scenes of violence commemorating the 1976 Soweto Riots. Blacks are shown as innocent victims of white oppression and martyrs; the responsibility for their suffering is so unmistakable and so universally understood to be on the part of the whites that there is no need to even represent the perpetrators.

From: "Negotiating Identity: Urban Community Art in South Africa", in: *Art a Journal of the African World* (2001)

1 receptor: noun derived from the verb "to receive"

Lösungsvorschlag

I. Questions on the text

1. *When you read the first paragraph carefully, you will find out that there are two different kinds of people: the fashion-conscious audience and the graffiti artists themselves.*

   The fashion-conscious visitors to the gallery are wearing stiletto heels and horn-rimmed glasses and are carrying Gucci bags as well as other trendy accessories. Throwing in supposedly clever remarks about the paintings they are trying to prove their expertise in art. In contrast to them the graffiti artists themselves seem to be "out of place" in their sloppy and scruffy outfits – people you do not expect at a gallery opening.

2. *To answer this question, read the second paragraph carefully.*

   Gallery owners invited graffiti artists to present their pictures on canvas. These exhibitions have become so popular that they have brought the sprayers sufficient means to live on. They produce their art at the request of various people (advertisers, corporations, politicians and collectors), some of them teach at universities or organize graffiti tours through their townships. Two top artists have even been engaged to decorate buildings for the 2004 Olympic Games.

3. *Keep in mind: Graffiti artists distinguish between pieces, i. e. the paintings on the walls, called murals in this text, and tags, the ornamental signatures of graffiti artists.*

   The traditional attitude of the city authorities had not only been to tolerate but even to praise graffiti artists, hoping to attract tourists and investors. Two months ago, however, they decided to take action against them. All of a sudden, their art was considered to be ugly. But officials are careful to point out that they are not against all graffiti – in fact murals are still accepted as an artistic expression of the underclass as long as they observe certain rules, whereas the tags – i. e. the sprayers' ugly signature scrawls – are felt to spoil the appearance of the city.

4. South Africa's graffiti art started in the 1980s in the "coloured" areas of Cape Town where young people tried to emulate the example of New York. Today, however, it has spread to the prosperous suburbs of the city and become popular all over the country. As white artist Tyler Murphy points out the graffiti scene is different from other circles of society in that it doesn't judge you on the colour of your skin but only on your artistic skill.

5. *Art editor Roger Lucey's experience is described in the last paragraph. It reveals the prejudices people still have against graffiti artists.*

   When Roger Lucey had graffiti artists paint a picture on the front wall of his house, his neighbours complained to the city authorities. They were not offended by the mural itself but accused Lucey of bringing crime to their area. This shows that a lot of people are still prejudiced against graffiti artists. This experience stands in sharp contrast to the headline and the beginning of the text, which suggest that South Africa's society greatly admires graffiti painters, or at least has given them a kind of cult status.

6. *The present text seems to be written from an objective point of view, showing understanding for the city officials as well as the artists. However, in certain passages the author's positive attitude to graffiti is revealed. Very often adjectives reveal a writer's attitude.*
(l. 11: murals brightening … the city;
ll. 35/36: … murals, which are not only stunning but also incorporate … values;
l. 50: … like that of all art, …)
We have underlined some typical expressions that you may use when answering such a question.

Although the present article is an expository text, i. e. it wants to inform the reader, the writer does not refrain from showing his attitude towards graffiti. Adjectives like "brightening" (l. 11) or "stunning" (l. 36) reveal his positive view of the murals. And in the very last sentence he even classifies graffiti as "art" (l. 50). Moreover, he points out the positive messages that the murals convey (ll. 36/37). And when referring to the opponents of graffiti he adopts quite a critical attitude. He mentions for example some people's suspicion that the officials have only focused on graffiti because they are incapable of solving the town's bigger problems such as "poverty, homelessness and crime". (l. 45)

II. Composition

1. **"Let's stop subsidizing the arts – the taxpayer's money should be used for more important things." Discuss.**

Pros
- *We badly need money to create jobs, for schools, kindergartens, etc.*
- *Subsidizing the arts only serves a minority – the majority of citizens are indifferent to art or even disapprove of it.*
- *Art lovers can pay the full price for their hobby – just as the crowds at sports events or pop festivals.*

Cons
- *The arts are not of minor importance – they educate people and help create well-rounded personalities*
- *Art galleries, symphony orchestras and theatres make a city attractive*
- *If the state does not support the arts, private sponsors will step in and try and influence the artists.*

Quite a few people think that due to the limited budget of the state, we ought not to squander our limited resources on subsidising the arts. Given a choice between spending money on arts and improving institutions like kindergartens, schools and universities the choice should be clear as to what really benefits the citizens. Subsidising the arts means forcing most taxpayers to spend their money on something they do not care about or even detest. Why not make the theatre-goer and music lover pay the full price for their extravagant hobbies, just as the crowds at spectator sports?
The answer is quite simple: because it would be the end of the fine arts. Our cities would not have any theatres or symphony orchestras if the tickets cost more than one hundred dollars per person. Most towns would certainly be rather dull places without any cultural institutions. They would become less attractive to visitors as well as to the local population. The arts have always educated people, inspired and uplifted them. And we must not forget that they have also captured the minds of young people and encouraged them to emulate the great masters. Let's face it: we cannot celebrate our great cultural heritage and hope that we get it for free.

2. **Like graffiti, the video clip has become a standard element of contemporary youth culture. Do you consider it art or "trash"?**

Most adults associate the term video clip with MTV and its showering young people with blaring pop music. They would hardly see it as a new art form and most would even agree that it is just trash. If we consider that the aim of most of these films is to promote the sale of CDs they seem to have a point. Just look at some of those videos: the so-called star is filmed singing on a stage, in a car or even just sitting on a chair. Such films are really without artistic merit and seem to confirm the prejudice. But then we mustn't forget that the medium is still young and capable of development. As soon as the clips had been established as a staple element of youth culture, gifted directors began to create wonderful videos using all sorts of tricks and gimmicks, many of of them even trying to convey a message to the young people. Some of their films have come to be regarded as video classics. With video clips it is the same as with all other artistic genres: they are not art or trash per se but it depends on what you make of them.

3. **Comment on the cartoon.**

When asked to analyse a cartoon, you should first describe the scene, the persons and the action portrayed in the picture. Then you should try and explain the message (what /who does the cartoonist want to criticise, which current problem does he refer to, who does he side with/against, etc.). Finally you may say whether you agree with the cartoonist or if you disagree.
The following composition was written by a student of the Gabelsberger-Gymnasium Mainburg in the 2003 Abitur exam. We would like to thank him for giving us the permission to reprint his (slightly abridged) essay:

The cartoon obviously shows a gallery opening. In the background, the wall is covered with paintings in impressive old frames. People are staring at the pictures, while in the foreground a crowd of visitors has gathered around the artist. The artist himself is in the centre of the cartoon, wearing a beret (status symbol of artists) and holding a glass of wine in his right hand. This would not be strange if the artist wasn't a monkey.
A closer look at the paintings reveals that they are full of coarse and childish drawings; clearly a reference to modern art. The cartoon has no caption, the picture speaks for itself. So what is behind all this? There are different ways to interpret the cartoon. Maybe it is a conservative view of modern art, a criticism of paintings that look like a mess, something even a monkey could do. But I think there is more to it. It is also a criticism of people who lack an opinion of their own concerning art. Those people are impressed by anything in a golden frame. To them art is something fashionable, a status symbol, and they interpret a message into anything.
To sum up, it is an interesting, multi-layered cartoon, which offers itself to different ways of interpretation and – although it appeared in 1970 – still holds good today.

III. Translation

Die Darstellungsweise, die auf Wandgemälden vorherrscht, die in den 1980er und frühen 1990er Jahren entstanden sind[1], zeigt Schwarze als Opfer. Wandgemälde dieser Art haben häufig[2] einen anklagenden Ton, wobei ihr Ziel auf die öffentliche Darstellung der Ungerechtigkeiten gerichtet ist, die die schwarze Gesellschaft von Seiten des weißen Apartheidregimes hinnehmen musste[3]. Auf diesen Wandgemälden folgt die Darstellung von Schwarzen und Weißen fast immer einfachen Mustern: Schwarze werden als machtlose Wesen dargestellt, die die Behandlung durch andere ertragen[4], während die Weißen die Rolle des Unterdrückers einnehmen. Ein Wandbild, das 1982 von Studenten auf dem Gelände der Fort Hare Universität gemalt wurde, zeigt zum Beispiel Gewaltszenen, die an die Unruhen von Soweto im Jahre 1976 erinnern.

Die Schwarzen werden als unschuldige Opfer weißer Unterdrückung und als Märtyrer gezeigt; die Verantwortung für ihr Leiden – wie[5] wirklich jeder[6] unmissverständlich erkennt – liegt bei den Weißen, sodass man die Übeltäter nicht einmal darstellen muss.

Anmerkungen

1 wörtl.: gemalt wurden

2 „to tend to" – wörtl.: *neigen zu;* sollte durch ein Adverb (z. B. *oft, häufig*) wiedergegeben werden

3 wörtl.: *erduldete*

4 „powerless receptors of … treatement" wurde erweitert zu „machtlose Wesen, die Behandlung ... ertragen"

5 Eine Möglichkeit, passive Verben des Sagens und Denkens ins Deutsche zu übertragen: ein eingeschobener Hauptsatz mit „so" oder ein Nebensatz mit „wie"

6 „jeder erkennt" zur Wiedergabe von „is ... universally understood" – engl. Passiv wurde in deutsches Aktiv umgewandelt

The Bean Trees

One block down and across the street, old Bobby Bingo sold vegetables out of his dilapidated truck. Lou Ann had been tempted by his tomatoes, which looked better than the hard pink ones at the grocery; those didn't seem like tomatoes at all, but some sickly city fruit maybe grown inside a warehouse. She had finally collected the nerve to ask how much they cost and was surprised that they were less than grocery tomatoes. On her way home she made up her mind to buy some more.

"Hi, tomato lady," Bingo said. "I remember you."

She flushed. "Are they still forty-five a pound?"

"No, fifty-five. End of the season."

"That's okay," she said. "It's still a good price." She looked at every one in the box and picked out six, handling them to the old man one at a time with her free hand. With her other hand she adjusted the baby on her hip taking extra care, as she had been instructed, to support his wobbly head. "Your tomatoes are the first good ones I've had since back home." She felt her heart do something strange when she said "back home".

Bobby Bingo had skin like a baked potato. A complete vegetable man, Lou Ann thought, though she couldn't help liking him.

He squinted at her. "You're not from here? I didn't think so." He shook out a wad of odd-sized plastic bags, chose one with red letters on it, and bagged the tomatoes. "Seventy-five," he said, weighing them up and down in his hand before he put them on the scales. "And an apple for Johnny," he said, picking out a red apple and shaking it at the baby.

"His name's Dwayne Ray, and he thanks you very much I'm sure but he don't have any teeth yet." Lou Ann laughed. She was embarrassed, but it felt so good to laugh that she was afraid next she would cry.

"That's good," Bingo said. "Soon as they get teeth, they start to bite. You know my boy?"

Lou Ann shook her head.

"Sure you do. He's on TV every night, he sells cars. He's a real big guy in cars."

"Sorry," she said. "I don't have a TV. My husband took it to his new apartment." She couldn't believe, after deceiving her own mother and grandmother for two entire weeks, that she was admitting to a complete stranger on the street that her marriage had failed.

He shook his head. "Don't worry about it. Makes me sick every time he comes on. Don't even call himself by his own name – 'Bill Bing' he says. 'Come on down to Bill Bing Cadillac[1],' he says. 'Bill Bing has just the thing.' I always wanted him to be a real big guy, you know. Well, look at him now. He don't even eat vegetables. If he was here right now he would tell you he don't know who I am. 'Get rid of that old truck,' he says to me. 'What you need to sell garbage for? I could buy you a house in Beverly Hills[2] right now,' he says to me. 'What?' I tell him. 'You crazy? Beverly Hills? Probably they don't even eat vegetables in Beverly Hills, just Alaska King Crab and bread sticks!' I tell him. 'You want to make me happy, you give me a new Cadillac and I can sell my vegetables out of the trunk.'" Bingo shook his head. "You want grapes? Good grapes this week."

"No, just the tomatoes." She handed him three quarters.

"Here, take the grapes. Johnny can eat the grapes. Seedless." He put them in the bag with the tomatoes. "Let me tell you something, tomato lady. Whatever you want the most, it's going to be the worst thing for you."

From: Barbara Kingsolver, *The Bean Trees,* 1988

1 Cadillac: one of the most expensive and prestigious cars made in the US

2 Beverly Hills: a residential area of Greater Los Angeles, famous as the home of many film stars

Worksheet:

maximum number of points attainable

I. Questions on the text

Read all the questions first, then answer them in the given order. Use your own words as far as is appropriate.

1. Describe Lou Ann's personal situation; take into account her thoughts and feelings. — 20
2. Analyse the relationship between Bobby Bingo and his son as it is seen by the father. — 20
3. Show how a personal relationship develops between Lou Ann and Bobby Bingo; examine the role of fruit and vegetables in this process. — 20
4. What mode of presentation and narrative perspective are used in the text? What is the effect on the reader? — 10
5. Examine the stylistic level of this passage and determine its function. — 10

II. Composition

Choose *one* of the following topics. Write about 150 to 200 words. — 40

1. "Children begin by loving their parents. After a time they judge them. Rarely, if ever, do they forgive them." (O. Wilde) Do you agree?
2. Genetically engineered vegetables – blessing or curse?
3. Germans have often been smiled at for worrying about the quality of their food. Write a letter to the editor of a British or American magazine to justify these fears.

III. Translation

Translate the following text into German: 40/160

The Bean Trees[1] is an engaging novel for high school[1] students. The story begins with Taylor Green's determination not to become pregnant in high school[1] and thus face a premature marriage that would likely result in her being stuck in Pittman County, Kentucky, the rest of her life. The story is uplifting, never depressing or sad, yet the subject matter is substantial and varied, ranging from the long-term effects of child abuse to the plight of Guatemalan political refugees.

The characters are admirable and engaging, and almost all are women. Yet, though this is basically a woman's novel, it is not a story without men; both Taylor and Lou Ann exhibit interest in the opposite sex. Furthermore, Taylor is tough enough to elicit admiration from even the most macho males in the class. And Taylor's independent, adventuresome spirit appeals to their yearning to go into the world.

From: Karen and Philip Kelly, "Barbara Kingsolver's *The Bean Trees:* A New Classroom Classic", *English Journal* (1997)

1 nicht übersetzen

Lösungsvorschlag

I. Questions on the text *(We use the American spelling)*

1. Lou Ann is a young woman who had a baby not long ago – little Dwayne Ray still has a "wobbly head" (l. 13) and no teeth. Her husband left her and the baby two weeks ago, a fact she has not even admitted to her mother and grandmother so far. It surprises her that she reveals her situation to a stranger. Lou Ann may be the daughter of a single mother herself, as no father is mentioned. Her financial situation must be precarious – she hardly dares to ask about the price of the tomatoes. It seems that she has come from the country and still has no love for city life: the tomatoes are "sickly city fruit" (l. 3 f.) and when she thinks of "back home" she feels a sudden homesickness welling up in her (l. 14). The sadness of her situation weighs heavily on her, she hardly laughs anymore, and when she actually does it "felt so good" (l. 23) she is afraid it might make her cry.

2. Bobby Bingo's son is so much on the old man's mind that Lou Ann's baby boy immediately reminds him of Bill and gives him the opening to complain about him to a total stranger. He tells her that he had high hopes for his son and wanted him to become "a real big guy" (l. 34 f.). On the surface his expectations have come true: Bill is now a wealthy Cadillac dealer and appears in his own TV commercial every night. Yet Bobby is disillusioned with his son ("makes me sick" l. 32) who has apparently cut himself off from his roots: his family name was not elegant enough for him so he changed it to Bing, and he seems to be embarrassed by his father's simple way of life, to an extent that he would pretend not to know him if he met him in the street. The vegetables his father sells so lovingly are just "garbage" (l. 37) for Bill. Old Bingo is not willing to change over to his son's world, to give up his old truck and live in a new house in Beverley Hills – their philosophies are irreconcilable. In the end Bobby bitterly remarks that what you want very much will turn out wrong.

3. Their relationship begins when the old man recognizes the young woman who had been his customer before. He addresses her as "tomato lady", which makes her blush (l. 8). Lou Ann takes an instant liking to this "complete vegetable man" (l. 15). Her acceptance of the price and her praise of the tomatoes are certainly well received, and Bingo offers a free apple to her toothless baby, which makes her laugh and warm to him further. The child reminds Bingo of his own son, and the two strangers begin to exchange confidential and embarrassing facts about their lives. Lou Ann, to her own surprise, begins by telling him about her husband having abandoned her, and Bingo responds by criticising his son's attitude and disregard of his father's way of life. As for the role of vegetables, one can say that Lou Ann's appreciation of the old man's tomatoes made him open up to her, the involuntary humour in his expecting Baby Dwayne to eat the apple relaxes her, and the "vegetable man's" gift of the seedless grapes is a further token of his sympathy for the "tomato lady".

4. ***Mode of presentation:*** *a way in which events are related to the reader or listener in a narrative text. If a story is told in* ***condensed form*** *as a series of events,and the narrator describes the situation and tells the reader directly what he wants him to know we speak of* ***panoramic presentation;*** *if the action and incidents are shown in detail by the characters' words, feelings and thoughts we speak of* ***scenic presentation.*** *Usually writers use a mixture of both modes. For "perspective" see Tips for Questions on the Text (p. VIII).*

   In this text the author combines scenic presentation with the device of a third-person narrator. He confines the point-of-view to what Lou Ann sees, feels and thinks: they looked better, she was surprised, she made up her mind (all in the first paragraph). What we get to know about Bobby Bingo is revealed exclusively by what he himself says. All information is passed on through dialogue, thoughts and actions. The author never comments, which is typical of the scenic mode of presentation. So the reader becomes a participant in the narrative process. He is called upon to make his own discoveries, evaluate the events himself, and draw his own conclusions.

5. *An author's style basically defines itself by his choice of words, the complexity or simplicity of his sentence structure and his use of stylistic devices (see: Figures of Speech, p. I). Make sure to comment on the function of the author's style as well describing its effect.*

   Throughout the text the writer uses simple and everyday expressions. Neither in the dialogues nor in the descriptions are difficult or latinised words to be found. The verbal exchanges are always colloquial and contain grammatically incorrect forms ("he don't have any teeth", l. 22 f.) and incomplete sentences ("You crazy?", l. 38). The sentences are generally short in the conversations, only slightly longer in some other passages, with simple subordinate clauses. No stylistic devices are used.
   The author's style reflects and underlines the status and the credibility of the characters: they are simple people – the country girl and the old man who sells vegetables from his pickup truck. Their problems are plain and concrete and couldn't have been expressed in an elaborate style.

II. Composition

1. **"Children begin by loving their parents. After a time they judge them. Rarely, if ever, do they forgive them." (O. Wilde) Do you agree?**

   Oscar Wilde is famous for his witty aphorisms. The quotation in question, however, sounds wise and is worth thinking about.
   The love small children feel for their parents is obvious. Mum and Dad are the people they trust unconditionally. Parents are idolized, small injustices will not be noticed or easily forgiven. Children are absolutely convinced that their parents love them and return their love with fervour.
   As they grow older their increasing knowledge of the world makes them more and more aware of the fact that even their parents are not beyond criticism and they often find fault with them. Children in their puberty begin to revolt and feel hindered by their parents' rules. They criticise their strictness, their lack of generosity and understanding. This judgment is quite natural and helps to establish the children's own set of values.

The last part of the quotation, however, is far too pessimistic. In cases of severe mistreatment, when children were routinely beaten or damaged for life, it may be possible and even justified that no absolution is ever granted. But I don't agree that this happens "rarely". We all grow up and change our perspectives. Most of us will be parents ourselves and will understand why our own fathers and mothers reacted in certain ways. And, besides, forgiveness is a very human and Christian virtue.

2. **Genetically engineered vegetables – blessing or curse?**

This is the classic argumentative essay type where you had best start out with a short list of pros and cons on your draft:

Pro	*Cons*
• *disease and plague resistant*	• *health hazard, side effects?*
• *higher yield*	• *difficulty of control?*
• *cheaper production*	• *customer information?*
• *possibility of increased nutritional value*	• *religious and ethical objections*

Man has always tried to outsmart nature and to improve food production. The cubic tomato is the transporter's dream and the environmentalist's nightmare. Both supporters and opponents of genetic manipulation use reasonable arguments.

Many concerned critics hold that interference with the evolutionary process is dangerous, unethical and possibly irreversible. What if artificial crops replace the traditional ones before we realize their side-effects? The cubic tomato may be easy to handle, but what if we lose the good old tasty one? Nobody can guarantee that experimental vegetables can be so safely confined within their areas of growth that their seeds don't spread and contaminate the rest.

Proponents of genetic engineering, however, praise its advantages. They claim that production costs can be cut considerably by developing plague and disease resistant as well as more productive crops. This would also reduce health hazards for consumers by minimizing the application of fungicides, herbicides and chemical fertilizers and better satisfy the needs of growing populations, especially in the Third World.

In conclusion: the dangers of gene manipulation should not be dismissed. But whereas these have not been proved so far, the advantages of gene manipulation are already visible. The only possible course of action would be to tolerate engineering but subject it to strict supervision. Let us give the cubic tomato a chance, as long as people can choose from other alternatives.

3. **Write a letter to the editor of a magazine justifying German worries about the quality of food.**

Letters can be of two types: personal and formal. All letters should consist of five parts: address and date, recipient's name and address (especially in formal letters), salutation, main body and closing. The following example is a formal letter, with respective salutation and closing formulas, a polite tone and absence of colloquial language. It also contains a reference (Re) to the article in question which is necessary in business letters. The salutation, if you don't know the recipient's gender, is "Dear Sir or Madam". In this case one closes the letter with "Yours faithfully". When you address the person by name you write "Yours sincerely".

Fritz Grüner
Weinbergerstr. 29
81241 München

The Editor
Newsweek Inc.
251 West 57th Street
New York, NY 10019

May 8, 2003

Re: Your article "Germans worry too much about food" of April 21, 2003

Dear Sir,

In the last issue of your prestigious magazine I came across an article in which the attitude of Germans insisting on quality food is treated too lightly for my taste. Your columnist seems to imply that people should not worry too much about what they eat. This does not offend me or my countrymen in any way but I would still like to make a case for organic food.

The world moves forward fast, but have we already forgotten how tasty food once was, before chicken batteries and greenhouse products replaced free roaming poultry and garden vegetables? Is it altogether dismissible to fear that artificially fertilized plants and the indiscriminate application of herbicides represent a health hazard? Many scientists have blamed the rise of allergies on these procedures. Is it cowardly to avoid mass produced beef in the times of BSE? I find it hard to believe that only Germans should be worried and that other countries should go for junk food with enthusiasm. While we cannot turn back the wheel of progress and abolish industrialized agriculture altogether most Germans insist on at least being given a choice, even if it costs more. Organic sauerkraut with sausages from happy pigs is a treat that, unfortunately, isn't appreciated much elsewhere.

Yours sincerely,

F. Grüner

III. Translation

The Bean Trees ist ein spannender[1] Roman für High School Schüler. Die Erzählung beginnt mit Taylor Greens Entschluss, während ihrer High School Zeit nicht schwanger zu werden, um sich nicht dem Risiko[4] einer Frühehe auszusetzen[2], die wahrscheinlich dazu führen würde, dass sie für den Rest ihres Lebens in Pittman County, Kentucky, hängen bleiben würde[3]. Die Geschichte stimmt einen positiv und ist nie deprimierend oder traurig, und doch ist die Thematik gehaltvoll und abwechslungsreich. Sie reicht von den langfristigen Auswirkungen des Kindsmissbrauchs bis zum Elend der politischen Flüchtlinge aus Guatemala.

Die handelnden Personen sind bewundernswert und sympathisch, und fast alle sind Frauen. Und doch ist es, auch wenn dies hauptsächlich ein Frauenroman ist, keine Geschichte ohne Männer – sowohl Taylor als auch Lou Ann zeigen sich am anderen Geschlecht durchaus[4] interessiert. Zudem besitzt Taylor genug Härte, um sogar bei den ausgeprägtesten Machos[5] ihres Jahrgangs[6] Anerkennung hervorzurufen. Und außerdem[4] spricht Taylors Unabhängigkeitsstreben und Abenteuerlust ihre Sehnsucht an, in die Welt hinaus zu gehen.

Anmerkungen:

1 „engaging" hat einige Bedeutungsvarianten: *einnehmend, gewinnend, fesselnd.* Es kommt im Text zweimal vor (hier: *spannend – sympathisch*)

2 „to face" – wörtlich: *gegenüber stehen, sich aussetzen, rechnen müssen mit*

3 Das gerund „being stuck" als adverbiale Bestimmung wird mit einem Nebensatz übersetzt

4 stilistisch bedingte Einfügungen

5 „macho", vor allem als Adjektiv, ist kaum mit einem deutschen Ausdruck wiederzugeben

6 „class" im High School System umfasst den ganzen Jahrgang („the class of 2003") – *Klasse* wird natürlich auch akzeptiert

Grundkurs Englisch 2004
Textaufgabe I

Must the Backpackers Stay Home?

The horror of the Bali bombings[1] and the attacks in Kenya[2] confirm that tourists are now in the terrorists' cross hairs[3]. Soft targets, that euphemism of the month, seem to be softest when they're wearing shorts or sinking a few brews. Terrorism doesn't lend itself to easy gradations of tragedy. But for me, the deliberate attempt to kill tourists – and those who work with them – is among the most distressing developments of the past year. Taking aim at resorts in the developing world hurts those who can least afford it. In many poor countries, tourism is the fastest-growing sector of the economy and the one that offers the easiest pathway from poverty to a better and happier life. In Kenya, tourism employs about 500,000 people and has become one of the most important sources of foreign exchange. Those benefits are now at risk. As for Bali, the financial effects of the bombs are likely to be catastrophic. Employment on the island may fall more than 20 % next year. And since Bali was a flagship destination for all of Southeast Asia, the ripple effect from the bombings may be felt throughout the region.

But this isn't just a matter of dollars and cents. The freedom to travel safely and cheaply is one of the great blessings of our time – something that immeasurably expands the range of human experience. If we ever manage to build a world based on mutual respect and understanding between peoples, tourism will deserve much of the credit. That's particularly true for one class of traveler: backpackers – precisely the group targeted in the Bali attack. Few modern social developments are more significant and less appreciated than the rise of backpacker travel. The tens of thousands of young people who wander the globe are building what may be the only example of a truly global community. Nobody has an accurate way of guessing the size of the backpacker market, but the growth of the Lonely Planet[4] brand offers somewhat of a proxy[5]. The first Lonely Planet guidebook was stapled together on an Australian kitchen table in the early 1970s; 30 years later, the company publishes more than 600 titles.

Backpackers are not only more likely to respect local cultures than those tourists served by the mass market, but they are also, in their own way, valuable to host economies. Backpackers may spend less on vacation than their parents, but most of what they do spend stays local. Mark Hampton of the university of Surrey in Britain, who has studied tourism in Indonesia, estimates that 70 % of backpackers' vacation expenditures go to locally owned businesses – like small hotels and restaurants – compared with only about 30 % of the cash spent by "mass" tourists, who often stay in big hotels owned by foreign firms.

The bombs in Bali have placed the phenomenon of young people tasting the world at threat. I find that unbearably sad. More than 30 years ago, I discovered Europe by hitchhiking around it each summer, sleeping on beaches and in cheap hostels, breezing into Barcelona on the back of a motorbike, watching French kids in Nîmes cover a table with the ripe ingredients for a perfect ratatouille[6], selling my blood in a clinic off Omonia Square in Athens for $8 – enough for a few more days on the islands. I learned more from those trips than from years in school, and I'd begun to look forward to the day when my daughters would light out on their own adventures – to go see their relatives in Australia or hike in Tibet or do things in Bali that they wouldn't want to tell Dad about. But that was before our world was curdled. So add one more reason to hate what the terrorists have done: they've stolen our dreams.

From: *Time,* December 16, 2002

1 Bali bombings: terrorist attack on a Bali disco in October 2002, in which many young tourists were killed and injured

2 attacks in Kenya: terrorist attack on a Kenyan hotel in November 2002, in which Israeli tourists and local Kenyans were killed and injured

3 cross hairs: if you are in someone's cross hairs you are the target

4 Lonely Planet: guidebooks especially designed for backpackers

5 proxy: *here*: a parallel statistic

6 ratatouille: typical French dish consisting of mixed vegetables

Worksheet:

maximum number of points attainable

I. Questions on the text

Read all the questions first, then answer them in the given order. Use your own words as far as is appropriate.

1. Explain in detail why the writer considers the terrorist attacks in Bali and Kenya especially "distressing" (l. 5). Refer to the first paragraph. 20
2. "Terrorism doesn't lend itself to easy gradations of tragedy" (ll. 3/4). Explain the meaning of the sentence and its function in the context. 10
3. How does the writer evaluate travel and tourism in general? 10
4. Outline the particular role of backpackers. 20
5. The writer gives the reader details from his youth. What kinds of experiences does he mention and why does he refer to them? 20

II. Composition

Choose *one* of the following topics. Write about 150 to 200 words. 40

1. "Certainly, travel is more than the seeing of sights; it is a change that goes on, deep and permanent, in the ideas of living" (Miriam Beard). Discuss.
2. The more dangerous the better – high-risk adventure holiday activities are booming. How do you explain this trend?
3. You have just returned from a disastrous, but expensive holiday. Write a formal letter of complaint to the travel agency. Be diplomatic but firm.

III. Translation

Translate the following text into German: 40/160

Maps from the 13th century clearly showed the way to Paradis[1], an island east of India so inaccessible no one could prove it was a myth. The destinations medieval scholars inscribed across the Mappa Mundi[2] appear ridiculously unsophisticated to the modern traveller. Yet, more than ever, we continue to naively seek our ideal paradise lost.

Today, as the backpacker's bible, *Lonely Planet*[3], celebrates its 30th birthday, the quest for adventure has never been more widespread. Exotic destinations, out of reach to the average Seventies' family, are now easy to reach. Originally, the guide was a helmsman to the penniless and audacious youngster – an antithesis to the luxury of more conservative holidays. Yet, by opening up such remote destinations, *Lonely Planet*[3] led the way for the mass market. The authors[4] were lucky enough to be struck with inspiration at a time when the holiday market was altering dramatically.

From: *The Independent*, October 1, 2003

1 Paradis: nicht übersetzen
2 Mappa Mundi: lat.: Weltkarte; nicht übersetzen
3 Lonely Planet: nicht übersetzen
4 the authors: Mr and Mrs Wheeler, the founders of *Lonely Planet*

Lösungsvorschlag

I. Questions on the text

1. The writer sees the attacks as especially distressing because they were aimed at tourists, who are generally considered to be "soft targets", i. e. unprotected and unprepared for the bombings. Moreover they hit "those who can least afford it" (l. 6), the poor countries of the Third World. Not only is tourism the most important and fastest-growing economic sector in these areas, but it is also a means for the poor to improve their living standard because it brings foreign currency into the country and creates employment. If that is now at risk, it will not only be felt in the countries that were attacked but throughout the whole area. (ripple effect)

2. Note: *Before you set out to answer use your dictionary to look up*
   – *"lend itself to sth." – be suitable for being used in a particular way;*
   – *"gradation" – a small change or difference between points on a scale*
   (both definitions from DCE). So the sentence means that terrorism should not be used to determine differences of tragedy, i. e. what terrorist act is more tragic than another.

   The writer wants to say that any terrorist attack is tragic and that we should not try to assess which one is more and which one is less tragic. He makes this statement before he begins to write about his subject – the effect of terrorism on tourists – in order to avoid the reproach that he is too much concerned with tourism and values the victims of other terrorist attacks less, e. g. the businesspeople who died in the attacks on the World Trade Center.

3. The writer has a very positive attitude to travelling, he even calls it "one of the great blessings of our time" (l. 15). On the one hand he thinks that it gives tourists the opportunity to have invaluable experiences, on the other hand it contributes to the understanding of peoples and cultures to the extent that it will help us to "build a world based on mutual respect and understanding" (ll. 16/17).

4. What the author says about tourism in general is particularly true for backpacking, which is supposed to contribute especially to mutual respect and understanding between peoples. The masses of backpackers travelling around the world are creating "a truly global community" (l. 21), which is underlined by the fact that their numbers have been growing over the last 30 years. Moreover, the backpackers have a very positive effect on the economies of the countries they visit. Unlike ordinary tourists, who stay in big hotels that are under foreign ownership, the backpackers prefer to stay in small hotels and restaurants, which are owned by local people. Thus 70% of their money stays in the area they visit, in which it compares favourably to the 30% of traditional tourists.

5. Note: *Read the last paragraph carefully to answer the question. Begin by saying what the author did more than 30 years ago.*

   The author himself discovered Europe in pretty much the same way as backpackers do today. Living on a very low budget, he hitchhiked through it, slept either in very cheap hostels or on beaches, visited places more or less spontaneously ("breezing into …", l. 36) got into contact with the local people and experienced the local cuisine. When he ran out of money, he learned how to find the means for survival ("selling my blood", l. 38). On the whole, the writer thinks he learned more on these trips than in years at school. By referring to his own experiences the author manages to show what the terrorists have destroyed: his own children cannot have the same experiences which he could have as a young man because today's world is scared of terrorism. So he comes to the conclusion that the terrorists have "stolen our dreams" (l. 44)

II. Composition

1. **"Certainly, travel is more than the seeing of sights; it is a change that goes on, deep and permanent, in the ideas of living" (Miriam Beard). Discuss.**

   Ask most people what they expect of their holidays and they will answer that they have been so busy at their work all the year that they are just looking for a relaxing spot to lie on a beach and for a comfortable hotel that caters for all their wishes. Such travellers may just as well stay at home, for they do not experience anything new in their vacations. But as soon as they do a little sightseeing – an old church or a monument, or even a modern attraction – people will realize that travelling is more than just relaxing.

   Anyone who keeps his eyes open will notice that the buildings he sees in foreign countries differ from what he is used to at home. He will notice that people not only speak a different language but that they also have different customs, different lifestyles and that even manners vary from country to country. You will soon notice that travelling can be a truly mind-expanding and enriching experience. Once you have started to observe and perhaps imitate the ways and customs of the residents in the area you visit you will also begin to think about them and perhaps outgrow old prejudices. It will broaden your mind, and increase your knowledge of the world – and thus permanently change your ideas of living.

2. **The more dangerous the better – high risk adventure holiday activities are booming. How do you explain this trend?**

Most adults who travel want to find everything like at home – only better. Their usual food, beers, newspapers plus fine weather, beautiful beaches and a blue sea. For most young people such a holiday is boring, however. They seek adventure, want to do something out of the ordinary, try to go to the limit of their capacity. They would rather go bungee jumping, wild water rafting or abseiling. But it is not only young people who have such alternative ideas. According to a newspaper report a lot of German business executives have recently gone on such holidays. They are not only a change from the daily routine but also require personal courage, leadership qualities in extreme situations and mutual support, qualities these people also need in their positions.
It would be too simple, however, to leave the matter there. The latest trend in high-risk holidays are journeys to Afghanistan, Iraq or Chechenya, the war zones of this world. It seems to me that most people are not made for the regulated, uneventful and sedentary lives that we lead. So quite a few of us try to get the kick that we need by going on high-risk holidays.

3. **You have just returned from a disastrous, but expensive holiday. Write a formal letter of complaint to the travel agency. Be diplomatic but firm.**

Note: Here are some hints how to write a letter of complaint as well as some expressions you may use in your letter:
- *Include your name, address and phone number.*
- *If you have no name of a contact person, begin your letter with "Dear Sir or Madam," or "To whom it may concern,"*
- *Introduce the subject with "Re: …" (= lat. res/ dt. Betreff)*
- *Begin directly with the complaint: "I am writing to complain about …" or "On May 28th we booked a two-week holiday at your Leeds branch."*
- *State what went wrong: "Unfortunately the accomodation was far from luxurious …"*
- *Say how you would like to settle the matter, e.g.: "To resolve the problem, I would appreciate it if you could refund at least half the sum I paid …"*
- *State that you look forward to a reply. You may set a time limit and threaten further action.*
- *Close the letter with "Sincerely, Your name"*

Your letter may read like this:

Jim Myers
75, Scarborough Road
Leeds LS 16 5PT
Tel/Fax: (0)113-3894100

August 7, 2003

To
Worldtravel, Inc.
387, Ilkley Rd.
Leeds, LS 13 9PT

Re: My holidays in La Residencia, Marbella/Spain, from June 8, 2003

Dear Sir or Madam,

I am writing to you to complain about my summer holidays, which I booked at the Leeds branch of your travel agency earlier this year. The brochure from which I selected the apartment promised a quiet, modern style room in a luxury hotel overlooking a

crystal clear beach. It also said that the family rooms were equipped with a telephone, satellite TV, air conditioning and a kitchenette at the price of £349 per week.
When we arrived, however, we found that the hotel was a twenty-year-old rather shabby building, which was at least half a mile from the nearest beach. Not only did we have to walk the distance with our two little children but we also found the sea polluted with sewage from a nearby factory. Moreover, the air conditioning in the hotel was in disrepair so that the rooms were brutally hot and we could hardly sleep at night. As you can imagine, this was not the holiday we had imagined. We tried to get in touch with your local representative but he was not available. So we decided to fly back to Britain after three days. You will certainly understand that we want our money back. Would you please transfer the sum of £958 (price plus flight expenses) to our account until the end of the month. In case you have not refunded the required sum by August 31st, the case will from then on be dealt with by the lawyers of HELP, our consumer protection agency.

Sincerely,

Jim Myers

III. Translation

Landkarten aus dem 13. Jahrhundert zeigten klar den Weg nach *Paradis*, einer Insel, die östlich von Indien gelegen und so unerreichbar war, dass niemand beweisen konnte, dass es sich um ein Phantasiegebilde[1] handelte. Die Reiseziele, die die mittelalterlichen Gelehrten in die *Mappa Mundi* einzeichneten, erscheinen dem modernen Reisenden lächerlich naiv. Doch wir suchen heute[2] mehr denn je in kindlicher Weise[3] nach unserem idealen verlorenen Paradies.
Heutzutage, da die Bibel des Rucksacktouristen, der *Lonely Planet,* ihren dreißigsten Geburtstag feiert, ist die Suche nach Abenteuern so verbreitet wie nie zuvor. Exotische[4] Ziele, die für die Durchschnittsfamilie der siebziger Jahre unerreichbar waren, sind jetzt leicht zu erreichen. Ursprünglich war der Reiseführer derjenige, der den mittellosen und wagemutigen Jugendlichen als Lotse[5] diente – ein Gegensatz zu dem Luxus des traditionelleren Urlaubs. Doch indem er solche abgelegenen Urlaubsziele[6] erschloss, eröffnete *Lonely Planet* den Weg zum Massenmarkt. Die Autoren hatten das Glück, ihren plötzlichen Einfall[7] zu einem Zeitpunkt zu haben, als sich der Tourismusmarkt dramatisch veränderte.

Anmerkungen

1 als Alternative möglich: *Legende*
2 Zusatz zur Verdeutlichung
3 ‚*voller Naivität*' ist möglich; es wurde nicht gewählt, um die Wiederholung zu vermeiden
4 Möglich auch: *Ausgefallene Ziele* (um das Fremdwort zu vermeiden)
5 ‚helmsman' ist der Steuermann; Lotse wurde gewählt, weil das Bild im Deutschen gebräuchlicher ist
6 Urlaubs~ – Zusatz zur Verdeutlichung
7 möglich auch: *ihre Eingebung*

Grundkurs Englisch 2004
Textaufgabe II

From: Hanif Kureishi, *Love in a Blue Time*

Azhar's mother led him to the front of the lower deck, sat him down with his satchel, hurried back to retrieve her shopping, and took her place beside him. As the bus pulled away Azhar spotted Big Billy and his son Little Billy racing alongside, yelling and waving at the driver. Azhar closed his eyes and hoped it was moving too rapidly for them to get on. But they not only flung themselves onto the platform, they charged up the almost empty vehicle hooting and panting as if they were on a fairground ride. They settled directly across the aisle from where they could stare at Azhar and his mother.

The conductor came, holding the arm of his ticket machine. He knew the Billys, and had a laugh with them. He let them ride for nothing.

Mother's grey perfumed glove took some pennies from her purse. She handed them to Azhar who held them up as she had shown him.

'One and a half to the Three Kings[1],' he said.

'Please,' whispered Mother, making a sign of exasperation.

'Please,' he repeated.

The conductor passed over the tickets and went away.

'Hold onto them tightly,' said Mother. 'In case the inspector gets on.'

Big Billy said, 'Look, he's a big boy.'

'Big boy,' echoed Little Billy.

'So grown up he has to run to teacher,' said Big Billy.

'Cry baby!' trumpeted Little Billy.

Mother was looking straight ahead, through the window. Her voice was almost normal, but subdued. 'Pity we didn't have time to get to the library. Still, there's tomorrow. Are you still the best reader in the class? She nudged him. 'Are you?'

'S'pose so,' he mumbled.

Every evening after school Mother took him to the tiny library nearby where he exchanged the previous day's books. Tonight, though, there hadn't been time. She didn't want Father asking why they were late. She wouldn't want him to know they had been in to complain.

Big Billy had been called to the headmistress' stuffy room and been sharply informed – so she told Mother – that she took a 'dim view'. Mother was glad. She had objected to Little Billy bullying her boy. Azhar had had Little Billy sitting behind him in class. For weeks Little Billy had called him names and clipped him round the head with his ruler. Now some of the other boys, mates of Little Billy, had also started to pick on Azhar.

Big Billy lived a few doors away from them. Mother had known him and his family since she was a child. They had shared the same air-raid shelter during the war, Big Billy had been a Ted[2] and still wore a drape coal and his hair in a sculpted quaff. He had black bitten-down fingernails and a smear of grease across his forehead. He was known as Motorbike Bill because he repeatedly built and rebuilt his Triumph[3]. Sometimes numerous lumps of metal stood on rags around the skeleton of the bike, and in the late evening Big Bill revved up the machine while his record player balanced on the windowsill repeatedly blared out a 45[4] called 'Rave On'. Mother and the other neighbours were forced to shut their windows to exclude the noise and fumes.

Mother had begun to notice not only Azhar's dejection but also his exhausted and dishevelled appearance on hid return from school. He looked as if he'd been flung into a hedge and rolled in a puddle – which he had. Unburdening with difficulty, he confessed the abuse the boys gave him. Little Billy in particular.

Mother had taken Azhar's hand and instructed him to reply, 'Muck, muck, muck – you're common – common as muck!'

Big Billy was saying across the bus, 'Common! Why don't you say it out loud to me face, eh? But we ain't as common as a slut who marries a darkie.'

Mother's lips were moving but her throat must have been dry: no words came, until she managed to say, 'We're not Jews.'

'Nah,' said Big Billy. 'You no Yid, Yvonne. You us. But worse. Goin' with the Paki.'

From: Hanif Kureishi, "We're not Jews" in *Love in a Blue Time* (1997)

1 the Three Kings: the name of a bus stop

2 Ted (or Teddy boy): a member of a group of young men in Britain in the 1950s who liked rock and roll music and had their own style of clothes (narrow trousers, long jackets, pointed shoes)

3 Triumph: a make of motorcycle

4 a 45: a single record

Worksheet:

maximum number of points attainable

I. Questions on the text

Read all the questions first, then answer them in the given order. Use your own words as far as is appropriate.

1. What impression of Azhar's mother does the author convey to the reader in the first half of the text (ll. 1–30)?	20
2. Summarize what the reader learns about Big Billy.	20
3. Give a chronological synopsis of the conflicts and events culminating in the final confrontation of the two parents on the bus.	20
4. Show how the author uses language as an additional means of characterizing both parents. Refer to lines 54–59.	10
5. What will life at school be like for Azhar now? Look for indications in the text to support your prognosis.	10

II. Composition

Choose *one* of the following topics. Write about 150 to 200 words. 40

1. "If we were to wake up some morning and find that everyone was the same race, creed and color, we would find some other cause for prejudice by noon." (George Aiken). Discuss.
2. What can pupils, individually or as a group, do to combat bullying at school? Present your ideas in a speech for a meeting of pupils, parents and teachers.
3. Marriage isn't easy, as the divorce statistics prove. In today's global village, are racially mixed marriages more difficult than same-race ones?

III. Translation

Translate the following text into German: 40

160

Nationally, nonwhites make up 6 percent of the population, but in London the figure rises to between 30 percent and 60 percent depending on the locality. Yet there are those who believe a national culture is like the crown jewels, to be preserved and polished and protected from contamination. Prime Minister Tony Blair rightly calls these the "forces of conservatism". The irony is that similar forces of conservatism exist in the nonwhite populations of Britain. Many black and Asian Britons feel that they too would lose their roots if they became "too British". So they argue for separate schools and spaces, failing to understand that even if they lock up their young in insulated boxes, they will not stop change. The task is for all of us to create a modern British identity that has nothing to do with fusty old images of clotted cream[1] and Buckingham Palace.

From: *Newsweek*, September 18, 2000

1 clotted cream: dicker Schlagrahm (a speciality in Britain)

Lösungsvorschlag

I. Questions on the text

1. Azhar's mother is presented as a methodical person. She first accompanies her son to his seat on the bus before she fetches her shopping bags. The detail that she wears perfumed gloves reveals that she is an elegant woman. She also takes great care of her boy's education both in manners (she insists on his being polite and always saying please; l. 13) and in his performance at school. Every evening she takes Azhar to the library to provide him with new books to perfect his reading skills. It is important to her that Azhar is "the best reader in the class" (l. 23). When she learns of Azhar's problem at school she immediately calls on the headmistress to complain, but does not want her husband to know about this (l. 27) – he probably is not happy with her over-protectiveness.

2. Big Billy lives in their neighbourhood and has known Azhar's mother since their childhood. In the war they had sat out the bombing in the same air-raid shelter. As a youth he had been a Teddy boy and still hasn't quite given up to dress like one. He loves his motorbike and his constant meddling results in black fingernails and a greasy forehead. He shows total lack of consideration by disturbing his neighbours with his bike's roaring engine "in the late evening" (l. 39) and playing music at top volume. His boisterous entry onto the bus gives further evidence of his carelessness. On the other hand he knows how to make himself agreeable to people: he jokes with the bus conductor and rides for free. Big Bill encourages his son's bullying of Azhar ("… he has to run to teacher", l. 19). His behaviour towards Azhar's mother is more than rude – he calls her a "slut" to her face (l. 50). At the end of the text it becomes clear that he has primitive racial prejudices against "Yids" and "darkies".

3. *Note: The key word here is 'chronological': you have to present the events you find in the text in the order in which they occur in time.*

   Little Billy, who sits behind Azhar in the classroom, has picked on him for weeks, and other boys have followed his example. When they became more violent – they threw him into a hedge and rolled him in a puddle (l. 45) – Azhar finally had to explain to his mother what had been going on. She advised her boy to tell Little Billy he was "common as muck" (l. 48) and went to school the next day to complain. The head-mistress summoned Big Billy to her office and gave him to understand that she disapproved of the bullying. On their way home on the bus the Billies deliberately took their seats opposite Azhar and his mother and started to provoke them ("has to run to teacher", "cry baby"; l. 19 f). At first Azhar's mother tried to ignore them, but when Big Billy, apparently hurt by their calling them "common", addressed her directly with a vulgar and racist insult she weakly defended herself. Big Billy continued his abuse with a further remark about her having married a Pakistani.

4. The lines in question give evidence of Big Billy's attitude and character. His use of language proves that he is 'common' indeed. He speaks grammatically incorrect slang (to me face, we ain't) and in elliptic sentences (You no Yid; you us; but worse). His vocabulary is vulgar (slut) and racist (Yid, darkie, Paki).
   Azhar's mother, who has the same background as the Billies, has obviously tried to rise to a higher level. She does not reply in kind and is so taken aback by Big Bill's aggression that she can only manage a feeble answer; "We're not Jews" (l. 52). This is rather out of context, but it shows that she herself is not free of prejudice.

5. There are indications in the text that life will not be easier for Azhar in the future. The headmistress' criticism of Little Billy's behaviour goes no farther than expressing that she "took a dim view" (l. 30). This is definitely not enough to restrain Big Billy from encouraging his son to continue his bullying, given his character and reaction to the reprimand. His attitude and behaviour on the bus show that Azhar's mother's formal complaint has only increased his aversion to them.

II. Composition

1. **"If we were to wake up some morning and find that everyone was the same race, creed and color, we would find some other cause for prejudice by noon." (George Aiken). Discuss.**

   In 1776 the authors of the Declaration of Independence held that all men are created equal but it never entered their minds to include Native and African Americans. We have come a long way since then. Every kind of discrimination is now formally banned among all nations of the world. But does this mean we have reached the paradisiacal state where all people are brothers and sisters and respect their genetic differences? The quotation at hand strikes a pessimistic note about the human character. It states that people need prejudices and minorities they can regard as inferior to themselves.
   This may still be the case. A sad example in our country is the way some politicians are using the issue of Turkey's wish to enter the EU to gain support by mobilizing voters' lower instincts. It would support the validity of Aiken's observation but it does not follow that we should give way to this attitude. We cannot make the world a better place if we simply shrug our shoulders. Fortunately there have always been persons of integrity who continue to speak out against all kinds of open and hidden discrimination. They need our full support as citizens of the global village to rid the 21st century of all traces of prejudice. Hopefully, a remark like Aiken's will meet with incomprehension in the future.

2. **What can pupils, individually or as a group, do to combat bullying at school? Present your ideas in a speech for a meeting of pupils, parents and teachers.**

   Dear parents, teachers, fellow pupils,
   Thank you for inviting me to present my ideas concerning the problem of bullying in this institution.
   It goes without saying that this sad situation cannot continue. The sanctions proposed by our educators will undoubtedly send a clear signal that discrimination will not be tolerated here. It is, however, of the greatest importance that the problem must first of all be tackled in our classrooms and by the pupils themselves.
   Let me suggest three strategies that might help to eradicate bullying. First the school council should draft a joint resolution, based on contributions from the classes, which rejects any form of discrimination among pupils, to be pinned to the notice boards in the classrooms. Second, the form captains should make it their responsibility to intercede when pupils start to pick on individual children. And last but not least every individual student should make clear that he will not be siding with offenders but is prepared to speak out in favour of the victims and convince bullies that their attitude is undesirable.
   I hope that we can help the bully and the victim to sort out their problems without having to resort to the school authorities so that peace and mutual understanding will return to this school.
   Thank you for your attention.

3. **Marriage isn't easy, as the divorce statistics prove. In today's global village, are racially mixed marriages more difficult than same-race ones?**

'Love and marriage go together like a horse and carriage', as the old song goes, at least at the moment when bride and groom step to the altar. Maintaining this happy state is more than a growing number of couples can manage in the long run. If this is difficult enough for ordinary marriages – how much harder must it be for racially mixed ones?
Mixed marriages can be fascinating and rewarding and are normally contracted with a more than average share of love between the spouses. While in racially mixed societies like Brazil husbands and wives of different skin colours are not considered as exceptional, things are more complicated in countries with more racially uniform populations. Both partners will meet with raised eyebrows or open disapproval by less tolerant citizens and be constantly reminded of being different. This cannot but wear down the defences of the most loving and self-assured couples making them more vulnerable in marital crises. They might subconsciously blame their 'different' partner for making his or her life even more difficult. The additional discrimination that their children of mixed race will have to face will introduce further elements of stress into such families.
As long as the world has not become a truly global village racially mixed marriages are indeed more fragile.

III. Translation

Landesweit beträgt der Anteil der nicht-weißen Bevölkerung ungefähr 6 Prozent, aber in London steigt diese Zahl auf zwischen 30 und 60 Prozent, je nach der Gegend. Dennoch gibt es Leute, die glauben, dass eine nationale Kultur den Kronjuwelen gleicht, und etwas[1] ist, das erhalten und poliert und vor Verunreinigung geschützt werden muss. Premierminister Tony Blair nennt diese Leute zu Recht die „Kräfte des Konservatismus"[2]. Die Ironie dabei[3] ist, dass es ähnliche Kräfte des Konservatismus in den nicht-weißen Bevölkerungsgruppen[4] Großbritanniens gibt. Viele schwarze und asiatische Briten haben das Gefühl[5], dass auch sie ihre Wurzeln verlören, wenn sie „zu britisch" würden. Daher plädieren sie für getrennte Schulen und Lebensbereiche[6], und verstehen dabei[3] nicht, dass sie, selbst wenn sie ihre jungen Leute abkapseln[7], den Wandel nicht aufhalten werden. Es ist unser aller Aufgabe, eine moderne britische Identität zu schaffen, die nichts mehr[3] zu tun hat mit verstaubten alten Vorstellungen von ‚clotted cream', dem dicken Schlagrahm[8], und Buckingham Palace.

Anmerkungen:

1 Die Einfügung *etwas, das* erlaubt das Fortfahren mit dem Singular
2 Vager politischer Begriff. Auch möglich*: der Beharrung*
3 Stilistisch bedingte Einfügungen
4 Ermöglicht die Beibehaltung des Plurals, außerdem ein Beispiel für stilistische Verbesserungsmöglichkeiten durch Erweiterung des Grundworts
5 Auch: *meinen, denken. Gefühl haben* ist näher am englischen Wort, und ein Beispiel für eine oft nützliche Änderung der Wortart (hier: Verb – Substantiv)
6 Wieder eine Erweiterung des Grundworts
7 Die wörtliche Wiedergabe *in isolierte Schachteln sperren* ist weniger schön
8 *Dicker Schlagrahm* ist nur eine Umschreibung und nicht so genau wie *clotted cream*, daher die Verdeutschung als erklärenden Zusatz

Grundkurs Englisch 2005
Textaufgabe I

Pay up! Pay up! And play the game!

Class war is never far away in British education. It's sad but true that most of the best schools are fee-paying ones, which help their pupils win the excellent exam grades that lead on to a state-subsidised place at top universities.

The government wants to change that: it bullies top universities to take more state-school pupils, who are more likely to be from poor backgrounds. This week it issued tough new benchmarks for the numbers of state-school pupils that universities 'ought' to take. The result is pressure to admit as many state-school pupils as possible.

Distorting the system like this increases the chance that people will try to cheat it. Canny middle-class parents are now wondering if it's worth buying the best education they can afford for their children, for fear that they will be stigmatised when it comes to university entrance.

The game is to get the maximum quality of education for the minimum outlay, while ensuring that your child is not fingered as a class enemy when it comes to university entrance. How you manage this depends on money, religious belief and mobility.

If you have lots of cash, a bright child and don't want too much hassle, the best option is to send your offspring to an independent school from the start. It will be costly, but when your child is 16, you move him to the state sector for two years. The government's bean counters[1] will treat him as a state-school product. Applications to universities such as Cambridge, however, will list all his schools, showing what a well-trained chap he is. That should maximise his chances.

To play safe, you can also move house to somewhere grotty. Universities are paid extra for taking students from poor districts. You can always move back to a more salubrious area as soon as your child's application has been accepted.

If that's too expensive or disruptive, there are plenty of other options. The simplest is to move to the catchment area for a good state primary school. You can do the same thing later on, to get into a good (usually meaning solidly middle-class) state comprehensive. In London, house prices may be up to 20 % higher in the right catchment area – but you can regard that as an investment: sell the house once your child is safely enrolled, and you'll be unlikely to lose money on the deal. Or you can rent.

Many of the best state schools are church-run. Your chances of getting in are greatly strengthened if you can have a letter from your priest, saying that you attend Sunday worship regularly. Luckily for parents with wobbly faith (or a cynical lack of it) such schools are no longer allowed to interview.

The third option is to try for a place at a selective state school. This may mean moving to Kent or Buckinghamshire, two solidly Conservative counties that have preserved the 11 + exam[2], which selects children for high-performing schools. Your child will have her best shot at this exam at a private primary school. This needn't cost much: Merton Court, for example, a Kent school with stellar 11+ results, charges only £6,300 a year. Given what you save on school fees later, that's a bargain.

Another option is private tuition, used by one in four parents according to a recent survey. It can be expensive: £30 a session, say five times a week. But it has a big advantage: invisibility. Your child can arrive at university expertly tutored, but with impeccably plebeian credentials.

The government is constantly trying to change the rules to prevent such game-playing. One threat is to penalise university applicants on their parents' educational background as well as their own. Getting round that will be tricky: "Sophie, 17, seeks kind, preferably working-class, foster parents to see her through university admission and help her shed the disadvantages of her middle-class origins. No graduates need apply."

From: *The Economist,* 7 October 2004

1 bean counters: *here:* employees who care only about statistics
2 11+ exam: an exam that all children in Britain used to take at the age of eleven to decide which type of secondary school they should go to; it is still taken in a few areas

Worksheet:

maximum number of points attainable

I. Questions on the text

Read all the questions first, then answer them in the given order. Use your own words as far as is appropriate.

1. Explain why and how the government plans to influence university entrance procedures. Why are middle-class parents concerned? 20
2. Analyse the ways in which the area a family lives in can affect a child's educational prospects. 20
3. Apart from moving, how can middle-class parents ensure good education and easy university access for their children? Outline the different suggestions made in the text. 20
4. Examine how the ad (ll. 46–48) illustrates the writer's attitude towards his topic. Show how two other passages in the text produce a similar effect. 20

II. Composition

Choose *one* of the following topics. Write about 150 to 200 words. 40

1. "Teachers open the door. You enter by yourself." Discuss.
2. Money makes the world go round. Or does it?
3. Comment on the cartoon.

I'd put his name down for Eton if I could spell it!

From: www.cartoonstock.com

III. Translation

Translate the following text into German: 40/160

One of the fairest and most efficient ways to move up in society is through education. By providing a high quality university system, we ensure that talent is nurtured and rewarded. Unfortunately, not all pupils who could benefit from higher education get the opportunity. Some are not prepared academically, others lack the confidence to apply and a few are unable to demonstrate their intellectual capacity when traditional assessment methods are used.

Why worry about who gets into university? First, students at university learn not just from their teachers, but also from one another. Exposure to students from different backgrounds is an important contribution to a student's education. Second, students who attend university have better prospects in life than those who don't. They are more likely to get good jobs and make more money. Because of these advantages, it is vital that all members of society have a fair chance of reaping these benefits.

From: *How should students be selected in order to give anyone a fair chance?* by Steven Schwartz in: *The Guardian*, 23 September 2003

Lösungsvorschlag

I. Questions on the text

1. *The government's plans as well as the middle class reaction to them can be found in the first part of the text: lines 1–3 state why the government wants to change the system, lines 4–7 tell us what it wants to do and lines 8–11 say why middle-class parents are concerned. Read all the questions before you start with your answer: you are not supposed to analyse the ways in which parents try to outwit the system because that is referred to in questions 2 and 3.*

   In Britain pupils from fee-paying private schools have better chances to get a place at top universities than state-school pupils. Thus the system favours students from the middle and upper classes. The government wants to change this social injustice and tries to force the universities in question to accept more students from poorer backgrounds by introducing a quota for the number of pupils from state schools.
   Middle-class parents are concerned because they fear that buying a good education for their children will only put them at a disadvantage when they apply to top universities. So the parents try to outwit the system by making sure their children get a good education while at the same time appearing to be of a working-class background.

2. *In lines 21–39 the writer explains how parents can outsmart the system by moving to a different area. In your answer you just have to analyse how a family's place of residence may affect their children's chances of getting into a top university.*

   Since universities are given extra money if they take students from poor, dilapidated districts, the applications of children from those areas are more likely to be accepted. By moving there you can increase your child's chances of getting a place at a renowned university.
   But not all state schools are bad. In certain middle-class areas of the cities the state primary and comprehensive schools are so good that pupils can get a good education and will later be accepted at the top universities.
   Finally, there are even some high performing, selective state schools, especially in Conservative counties like Kent or Buckinghamshire, where they still have the traditional 11+ exam to select children for the secondary schools. Attending such a school also enhances the pupil's chances of getting a place at a top university.

3. *Apart from moving, the writer mentions three ways to outsmart the system of university admittance.*

   Parents who have enough money can send their children to a private school until they are 16 and enrol them at a state school for the two final years. Thus they can kill two birds with one stone: their children will get an excellent education but officially be counted as state-school graduates and be accepted by the universities.
   They can also try and get their children into a school run by the church. They are officially state schools and are often excellent. Although people's affinity to membership in the church may help get their children in, it is no longer a prerequisite.
   Finally, you may have your child take private lessons in addition to state-school tuition. That may be expensive, but as such lessons are not listed in official records it does not spoil the child's chances of university admission while at the same time it provides for an excellent education.

4. *Note that with this fictitious ad the writer pretends to give his readers advice on how to circumvent the government's regulations. It is, however, so exaggerated that the reader will not take it at face value.*

   The writer states that the government is constantly trying to change the rules in order to prevent people from outsmarting the system. Thus it might distribute university places according to the educational background of the applicant's parents. By suggesting that you advertise to find working-class foster parents the writer overshoots the mark and makes it clear to the reader that his ad is to be taken ironically.
   The text abounds in such irony. For example, he suggests to the reader to move to a dilapidated area in order to be admitted to a top university. "To play safe, you can also move house to somewhere grotty ... You can always move back to a more salubrious area as soon as your child's application has been accepted." (ll. 21–23). Nobody in his right mind would take such advice seriously and move to a slum – it can only be meant ironically.
   In the following paragraph his ironic attitude becomes even more obvious: "... there are plenty of other options. The simplest is to move to a catchment area for a good state primary school. You can do the same later on, to get into a good ... state comprehensive." (ll. 24–26). But as the reader will easily realise, moving frequently is not as simple as the author pretends.
   To sum up, the writer's attitude towards the government's efforts to give working-class students better chances is highly critical. He uses irony to point out that the government's efforts so far have been futile and only led to more cheating.

   Note that there are further examples of irony, e. g.: "Merton Court ... charges only £6,300 a year ... that's a bargain." (ll. 37–39) Hardly anyone will consider such a sum (~ 9,300 €) a bargain. Or take the writer's play on words when he states that people have to cheat to give their children "impeccably plebeian credentials"(l. 42f.)).

II. Composition

1. **"Teachers open the door. You enter by yourself." Discuss**

   This quotation is a Chinese proverb, meaning that teachers can awaken the pupils' curiosity and open their minds to a subject but that the pupil has to do the main work him- or herself, i.e. to learn. You can of course agree or disagree with the statement. We decided to deal with it in the light of today's educational debate.

   Teachers seem to have a very low standing in today's world. The public frequently blames them when children do not learn or do not learn enough. They are accused of failing to find a way of motivating their pupils. What all these criticisms have in common is that they presume the teacher has to make learning easy and fun for the students, who are hardly ever blamed for their lack of success.This proverb, however, sees education as the responsibility of both, teachers and students. The teachers can only try and get the pupils interested in a subject, i.e. they "open the door". The latter must then go on and strive in order to succeed, which means they must enter by themselves. By addressing the students directly ("you") the saying reminds them that they have to put in a lot of effort themselves.
   Of course not all teachers will find the right methods to arouse every students' interest. The saying really describes an ideal which people should strive to fulfil. Perhaps we should add two little words to the proverb: "Teachers should open the door. You must enter by yourself."

2. **Money makes the world go round. Or does it?**

There cannot be any doubt that money plays an important role in our lives. Money makes life more comfortable. If we possess enough of it we can buy whatever we want; we can afford to have the best doctors or lawyers, and it also gives those of us who have it a lot of power.

But does it really make the world go round? Is it really the driving force behind economic success, progress or political change? A lot of people would agree and point out that the triumph of the capitalist West over Communism in the 1990s was owed to the pursuit of profit. This view seems to be corroborated by the 1992 Clinton campaign motto "It's the economy, stupid", which helped him to win the elections.

However, this view leaves out that there are also other forces behind the developments in the world. What about people's values, beliefs, and religions as causes of change? Or simply human vanity? Many political leaders just have the ambition to wield power over their compatriots.

Finally we must not forget that money is only a tool in our hands. People can use it for their own advantage, but even then it is still the men and women behind it who make the world go round.

3. **Comment on the cartoon**

Note that Eton College is – besides Harrow School – one of the oldest and most prestigious public (i.e. private) schools in Britain. Despite all the reforms it has undergone, one of the safest ways to get your child in is still by registering him at birth. Most of its students are from upper-class families, who can afford to pay £ 7,460 (2005 figures) per term. The school is very popular with the Royal Family and has produced nineteen Prime Ministers.

The cartoon gives us a view into a family's living room, with the husband lying on the couch, drinking his beer and smoking a cigarette. He has obviously just read the paper and thrown it onto the floor. In the background we can see his wife with the baby on her arm. The room is barely furnished – apart from the couch there are a sofa table, a table lamp and a photo on the wall – probably the Queen. The caption tells us that the husband would like to register his baby for Eton College – one of the most distinguished and expensive public schools in Britain – but unfortunately he does not know how to spell it.

The traditional role allocation between husband and wife, the furnishings, the photo on the wall as well the fact that the man does not know how to spell Eton indicate that this is supposed to be a family of a poorer background.

There are different ways to interpret the cartoon. The most likely interpretation is a criticism of the importance the British government places on getting a top education for pupils from poor backgrounds, regardless of their abilities. Of course, Eton still has a selection procedure and an entrance examination, but if the government has its way and succeeds with its plan of introducing quotas for the admission of students from poor backgrounds to universities the day may not be far when the renowned public schools will also be targeted. But on the other hand the artist also wants to make fun of this lazy, uneducated man who fantasizes about sending his child to Eton but doesn't even have enough ambition to get off the couch to find out how to spell it.

III. Translation

Einer der gerechtesten und wirksamsten[1] Wege in der Gesellschaft aufzusteigen ist (über[2]) die Bildung. Indem wir ein Universitätssystem von hoher Qualität anbieten, stellen wir sicher, dass Begabungen gefördert und belohnt werden. Leider bekommen nicht alle Schüler, die von der höheren Bildung profitieren könnten, die Möglichkeit dazu. Einige sind von der Schule her[3] nicht ausreichend[4] vorbereitet, anderen fehlt das Selbstvertrauen[5], sich zu bewerben, und einige können ihre intellektuellen Fähigkeiten nicht zeigen, wenn herkömmliche Bewertungsmethoden angewendet werden.

Warum sollte man sich Gedanken darüber machen, wer Zugang zu den Universitäten erhält? Erstens lernen Studenten an der Universität nicht nur von ihren Lehrern, sondern auch voneinander. Das Zusammensein mit Studenten aus unterschiedlichen Verhältnissen ist ein wichtiger Teil[6] des Bildungsprozesses eines Studenten.

Zweitens haben Studenten, die eine Universität besuchen, bessere Aussichten im Leben als solche, die das nicht tun. Sie werden mit größerer Wahrscheinlichkeit[7] einen guten Arbeitsplatz[8] bekommen und mehr Geld verdienen. Aufgrund dieser Vorteile ist es unbedingt notwendig, dass alle Mitglieder der Gesellschaft eine faire Chance bekommen, diese Vorteile auch zu nutzen.

Anmerkungen

1 Natürlich kann man hier auch das Fremdwort „effizient“ verwenden.
2 Im Deutschen kann die Präposition (über) auch weggelassen werden.
3 „von der Schule her“ wurde gewählt, da die wörtliche Übersetzung (“in wissenschaftlicher/ akademischer Hinsicht“) im Deutschen zu hochtrabend klingt.
4 Zusatz zur Verdeutlichung
5 Alternative: der Mut
6 wörtl.: Beitrag (zur) …
7 wörtl.: Es ist wahrscheinlicher, dass sie einen Arbeitsplatz bekommen …
8 Im deutschen Singular statt engl. Plural.

Grundkurs Englisch 2005
Textaufgabe II

From: Gore Vidal, ***The City and the Pillar***, 1948

Breakfast was invariably unpleasant, possibly because it was the only meal the Willard family always had together.

Mr. Willard was already at the head of the table when Jim came into the dining room. Small, thin, gray, Mr. Willard tried to appear tall and commanding. It was the family's opinion that he would have had no trouble at all being elected governor, but for one reason or another he had been forced to allow lesser men to go to Richmond[1] while he remained a clerk at the courthouse, a bitter fate.

Mrs. Willard cooked breakfast in the adjoining kitchen, looking from time to time into the dining room to see if her children were down.

Jim, the firstborn son, was first to appear. Since this was a special day, he was cheerful.

"Morning, Father."

His father looked at him as though he could not quite place the face. Then he said "Good morning" and distantly stared to read the paper. He discouraged conversation between himself and his sons, especially Jim, who had made the error of being tall and handsome and not at all the sort of small, potentially gray son Mr. Willard ought to have had.

"You're down early," Mrs. Willard brought him his breakfast.

"Beautiful day, that's why."

"I don't think a quarter to eight is such an early hour," said his father from behind the *Richmond Times*. Mr. Willard had been brought up on a farm and one of the reasons for his life's success had been rising "at the crack of dawn."

"Good morning," Carrie same into the room.

"Morning, Carrie," Mr. Willard looked at his daughter with wintry approbation. Of his children, she alone gave him pleasure, she saw him great.

Finally, John entered. At fourteen, he was thin, nervous, potentially gray, except for black eyes.

"Hi." He sat down with a crash.

"Glad to have you with us," said his father, continuing the war.

"It's Saturday." John was a skilled domestic warrior, master of artillery. "Everybody sleeps late."

"Naturally," Mr. Willard looked at John and returned to his paper.

"Hey, Jim, they're playing baseball today over at the school. You going to play?" John struck his fist against his palm with a satisfactory sound.

"No, I'm going down to the cabin. For the whole weekend."

Mr. Willard struck again. "And who, if I'm not asking too much, are you going with?"

"Bob Ford. Mother said it was all right."

"Is that so? It is amazing to me why you want to sleep away from your own home which we have tried at such expense to make comfortable …" His father slowly unfurled the domestic banner, and charged. Jim refused to defend himself, beyond promising himself that one day he would throw a plate at this bitter old man he was forced to live with.

Meanwhile, he simply stared at his future weapon while his father explained to him how the family was a Unit and how be owed all of them a Debt and how difficult a time Mr. Willard had had making the Money to support them and though they were not rich, they were Respectable, and Jim's going around with the son of the town drunk did them no good.

During her husband's tirade Mrs. Willard joined them, a demurely pained expression on her face. When Mr. Willard had finished, she said, "Well, I think the Ford boy is nice and he does get good marks in school and his mother was a friend of ours no matter what we think of the father. So I don't see anything wrong with Jim seeing him."

"I don't mind," said Mr. Willard, "I just thought you would mind having your son exposed to that sort of a person. But if you don't, I have nothing more to say." Mr. Willard, having embarrassed his son and disagreed with his wife, ate fried eggs with unusual gusto.

Mrs. Willard murmured something soothing and Jim wished that his father were like Bob's father, drunk and indifferent.

From: Gore Vidal, *The City and the Pillar*, in:
Gore Vidal, *The City and the Pillar and Seven Early Stories*, Copyright © 1995 by Literary Creation Enterprises, Inc., Copyright © 1948, 1965 by E. P. Dutton & Co., Inc., Copyright © 1956 by Gore Vidal. Used by permission of Random House, Inc.

1 Richmond: capital of the US state of Virginia

Worksheet:

maximum number of points attainable

I. Questions on the text

Read all the questions first, then answer them in the given order. Use your own words as far as is appropriate.

1. Characterise Mr. Willard. Take into account his career, his attitude towards his family and the ideals and values he propagates in this excerpt. — 30
2. Analyse the relationship between Jim and his parents. — 20
3. Describe John's way of dealing with his father and explain how the author uses language to make the passage from line 27 to 32 entertaining. — 10
4. What does the reader learn about Bob Ford and his family? — 10
5. Explain the use of irony in the first paragraph (ll. 1/2) — 10

II. Composition

Choose *one* of the following topics. Write about 150 to 200 words. — 40

1. "Family isn't about whose blood you have. It's about who you care about." Discuss.
2. To what extent do parents have the right or the duty to participate in the decisions of their children who have reached the age of majority?
3. Comment on the cartoon.

Someday, Son, this will all be yours – unless I can come up with a better solution.

From: www.quantilex.com/art200101081.htm

III. Translation

Translate the following text into German: 40/160

Some parents carry a tremendous amount of guilt with them about the lack of time they spend with their children, so try to make up for it to them with quality events like going to a restaurant as a family. Parents such as these have a problem saying no to their children on virtually everything and any thoughts of disciplining are avoided at all costs. As for taking responsibility for their child's behaviour, that is impossible.

We tend to conceive of our children as some sort of reflection of ourselves. Children are now something we choose to have rather than mass produce to keep us going in our old age. So it's very important that they are perfect – something we can almost brag about.

There is also a tendency of some parents to be 'friends' with their children, and so they are afraid of setting consistent limits of behaviour. Children don't need more friends, especially old ones: what they need is parents.

From: *Big bullies* by Wendy Berliner in: *The Guardian*, 19 October 2004

Lösungsvorschlag

I. Questions on the text

1. Mr. Willard is described as a "small, thin, gray" (l. 4) and "bitter" (l. 39) domestic tyrant. Apparently he once had the ambition to become governor of Virginia but, to his disappointment, had to content himself with continuing as a clerk at the courthouse (l. 7). The author insinuates that he compensates for his shortcomings by trying to "appear tall and commanding" (l. 4) and by disciplining his family. During breakfast he sarcastically expresses his disapproval of his sons' late arrival and the company Jim keeps. With the exception of Carry, who seems to admire him, he hardly bothers about his children and doesn't look up from his paper when they appear. In the course of the conversation Mr. Willard voices his bitterness against his sons and hardly loses an opportunity to strike out at them with cutting remarks. He confronts them with his ideals and values: a family should be close, a "Unit" (l. 41), his children should be grateful for what he has done for them, especially for the financial sacrifices he made to sustain them and make them respectable (ll. 40–44). In this "tirade" (l. 45) the key-words – unit, debt, money and respectable – are ironically written in capital letters. When his wife shyly dares to utter an opinion he makes it clear that he disapproves of her, too.

2. Mr. Willard and his oldest son are a pair of opposites. Jim is "tall and handsome" (l. 14) and obviously his small, gray father finds this difficult to bear (l. 14 f.). He "discouraged conversation" (l. 13), especially with Jim, and uses every opportunity to put him in his place. He takes pleasure in 'striking' (l. 34), charging (l. 38) and embarrassing (l. 51) him and tries to make him feel guilty about breaking what is for him the family code of conduct. Jim remains polite and refuses to be baited into rebellion against the man fate has given him as a father – for now. One day, however, he will put his foot down and "throw a plate at this bitter old man" (l. 39). He would prefer to have a father like Mr. Ford who is an alcoholic but leaves his son alone. Mrs. Willard relates differently to her son and takes his side. She follows the argument of Jim and his father with a "pained expression" (l. 45) and defends his friendship with Bob but is lastly shown to be too weak to stand up against her husband.

3. John uses a more efficient strategy to defend himself against his father. He holds his own by cheerfully and colloquially greeting everybody, sits "down with a crash" (l. 26) and rather than finding excuses for his late arrival he reminds his father that everybody sleeps late on a Saturday – which takes the wind out of his sails.
   The entertainment value of this encounter lies in the author's choice of words. He depicts John as "potentially gray" (l. 24), which is funny in itself and alludes to Mr. Willard's resentment at not having children of that same description. Another amusing device is Mr. Vidal's use of military metaphors in a family context. Mr. Willard is "continuing the war" (l. 27), he "unfurled the domestic banner, and charged" (l. 37 f.). John is "a skilled domestic warrior, master of artillery" (l. 28), a veteran of many battles with his father and knows how to attack and weaken the enemy.

4. Bob, the son of the "town drunk" (l. 43) is Jim's friend, to his father's dismay. The boys intend to spend the weekend at "the cabin", probably with Mr. Ford (l. 33). Mrs. Willard characterizes Bob as being nice and a good student (l. 46 f.). Bob's mother is either dead or has left her family – Mrs. Willard emphasizes that she *was* their friend. So Bob lives with his father who does not bother much about him, he is "indifferent" (l. 54).

5. The irony used in the first sentence fits the dictionary definition as an unusual situation because the opposite of what is expected happens or is true (DCE). Most readers, hopefully, would not agree that breakfasts are "invariably unpleasant", particularly if they are the only meals the family shares – which is another unusual circumstance. The effect of this opening statement serves as a preparation for the following scene and makes the reader curious to learn more about such a strange family.

   Note: *The American Heritage Dictionary defines this case as a secondary meaning for irony: 'incongruity between what might be expected and what actually occurs'. In other words: ironic in this sense is synonymous with incongruous.*

II. Composition

1. **Family isn't about whose blood you have. It's about who you care about. Discuss.**

   Recently the German Minister of Justice proposed that parents should be prohibited from ordering laboratory tests to confirm their blood relationship with their children. The ensuing public debate has circled around the issue whether blood ties or the protection of already functioning families should be the determining factor.
   It is common knowledge that normally a family is constituted by the addition of genetically related offspring to a couple. The consequence is that parents will take pride in their sons and daughters as being reflections of themselves and assume full responsibility for their upbringing. Children, conversely, will feel protected in the confidence that mom and dad are the 'real' ones.
   On the other hand, the existence of unrelated families is a fact. S.O.S. Children's Villages, for instance, have succeeded in supplying true family backgrounds for orphans. Another case in point are the numerous families with adopted children, or parents who accept parenthood for children their partners have brought into the marriage. This works as smoothly as in families with genetic ties and proves that you are a family indeed when you care about each other.
   In my opinion the topical proposition cannot be regarded as a rule, but as a call for love in all families, no matter whether 'blood' is the ingredient or not.

2. **To what extent do parents have the right or the duty to participate in the decisions of their children who have reached the age of majority?**

   "As long as you live under my roof, you will do as I say" goes the parental argument that thwarts all children's attempts to give them one good reason for their denial of a sensible request. Such logic is difficult to tolerate for youths once they have finally come of age and can't accept that the freedom, which is legally theirs, is unjustly restricted.
   It is, however, hardly objectionable if parents "participate" in matters which will have an impact on their own finances or well-being. They can't be expected to give up their bedroom for their son's latest flame or sell their pension fund so that Junior can buy a Porsche. In such cases they certainly have the right to say no.
   The matter looks quite different when parents feel that big mistakes are about to be made like dropping out from school or college or marrying a table dancer. They won't be able to prevent such follies altogether but they do have the parental duty to convince their children that their plan would mean heading for disaster. If children refuse to take their advice they must be left to face the consequences. There are, however, areas that should be taboo to interventions. It would be degrading for a child who has reached the age of majority to be restricted in smaller issues like dressing or hairstyle, or where to go, and with whom, and until what time. They may, of course, try to participate in such decisions as friends would but must accept that their children have become grownups.

3. **Comment on the cartoon**

When asked to analyse a cartoon, you should first describe the scene, the persons, objects and the action portrayed in the picture. Then you should identify the title or/ and caption of the cartoon and relate it to the picture.
As a next step you should recognise and decipher the symbols and icons used in the cartoon, e. g. a dove stands for peace, chains for bondage, scales for justice, etc.
Then you should be able to relate the cartoon to the political or social situation to which it refers and you must try and explain the message (what/who does the cartoonist want to criticise, which current problem does he refer to, who does he side with/ against, etc.). Finally you may say, from your own experience and with your own arguments, whether you agree with the cartoonist or if you disagree.

The cartoon shows a son and a father standing in the latter's office, which offers a view of a production building through a large window. The caption – the father's words to his son – begins with the classical statement that all this, the father's lifework, will one day be his son's. After the dash comes an unexpected twist: "… unless I can come up with a better solution." Obviously the old man has misgivings whether his son will be up to the task of managing the firm in accordance with his own standards. Handing over the company to him would only be the second best alternative. His son is not facing him and his blank expression betrays his feelings.
The situation depicted in this cartoon is not altogether unusual. Many, above all, professionally successful parents, don't have much confidence in their children's abilities and fitness for life's challenges. They may have witnessed their failures at school, their superficial attitude towards values they cherish, their lack of effort and dedication, their weakness of character. They measure their children against their own achievements and find them deficient. What they probably suppress is the memory of their own adolescence. Parents tend to glorify their own past and the brilliance of their present standing. In some cases it may indeed be justified to mistrust one's offspring but as a rule children must be given the chance to fend for themselves and prove their worth – maybe not necessarily in the family business!

III. Translation

Einige Eltern tragen gewaltige Schuldgefühle[1] mit sich herum, weil sie zu wenig Zeit mit ihren Kindern verbringen und versuchen daher, sie dafür mit besonderen Unternehmungen zu entschädigen, wie etwa durch gemeinsame Restaurantbesuche mit der Familie. Solche Eltern tun sich schwer bei praktisch allem, nein zu ihren Kindern zu sagen, und jeder Gedanke[2] an disziplinarische Maßnahmen[3] wird um jeden Preis vermieden. Was die Übernahme von Verantwortung für das Benehmen ihres Kindes angeht, so ist ihnen[4] dies unmöglich.
Wir neigen dazu, uns unsere Kinder als eine Art Spiegelbild unserer selbst vorzustellen. Heutzutage entscheiden wir uns eher bewusst[5] dafür, Kinder zu haben, als dass wir sie zahlreich in die Welt setzen, damit sie uns im Alter versorgen. Deshalb ist es sehr wichtig, dass sie vollkommen sind – etwas, dessen wir uns fast rühmen können.
Einige Eltern tendieren[6] auch dazu, die ‚Freunde' ihrer Kinder sein zu wollen[4], und daher scheuen sie sich, ihrem[7] Verhalten konsequente Grenzen zu setzen. Kinder brauchen nicht noch[4] mehr Freunde, besonders keine älteren[8] – was sie wirklich[4] brauchen sind Eltern.

Anmerkungen

1 Die Menge (*amount*) wird durch den Plural *Schuldgefühle* wiedergegeben.
2 Im Deutschen muss der Singular stehen.
3 auch: streng zu erziehen
4 stilistisch bedingte Einfügungen
5 *bewusst* als Verstärkung von *choose*
6 Die Verbalform als Alternative, hier mit dem Fremdwort, um die Wiederholung von *neigen dazu* (s. o.) zu vermeiden.
7 *ihrem* ist deutlicher als *dem*
8 *alten* ist besetzt durch den Begriff *alte Freunde*

Grundkurs Englisch 2006
Textaufgabe I

A New Irish Migration

Mr. Riley Wells is four years old this summer. His brother, Mr. Liam Wells, is two. They live in Arklow, County Wicklow, about an hour's drive south of Dublin. In Ireland.

The two high points of the summer so far were near-simultaneous visits from two exotic travelling delegations. Tom Duffy's legendary circus pitched its tent in a field outside Arklow for two nights. Uncle Paul[1] and Christina from Ottawa pitched their tent in the guest room of the Wells residence for a little while longer. Tom Duffy's circus came with tigers, prancing llamas and three elephants. After the show one of the elephants wandered through the parking lot, munching distractedly on underbrush, until a circus handler tracked the beast down and scolded it back to its trailer. Paul and Christina came with a plastic dinosaur encased in a toy iceberg. Scale differences notwithstanding, this too was a hit.

Riley and Liam's father, my brother Mark, works these days for a pharmaceutical company. He didn't move to Ireland because our family comes from there. This wasn't a return to cultural roots. It was simple economic migration: Mark moved to good work for good pay in a good place to live.

Which makes him part of a revolution.

Practically everyone has heard of Ireland's economic miracle, which transformed the country from perennial loser to Celtic Tiger[2]. From 1993 to 2001, its economy grew at a staggering annual rate of 8.4 per cent, three times that of the rest of the European Union.

What's less obvious is that success has reversed a historic flow of human traffic. For 100 years after the Irish potato famine of the 1840s, Ireland was a place you left if you possibly could. In 1961, Ireland's population reached its lowest point in modern history, 2.8 million people, less than half its pre-famine tally of 6.5 million in 1841.

For generations, as the former Irish prime minister Garret FitzGerald put it during a recent speech, "no more than half of each age cohort was alive in Ireland at 35. In the early part of the period, they died of TB or some other mortality. And the rest emigrated."

Irish emigration fueled Canadian politics (Brian Mulroney, Jean Charest), US presidential races (Kennedy, Reagan, Clinton), Argentine literature (Juan José Delaney). The Irish found fortune everywhere except Ireland. We visited Kilkenny Castle, which becomes a little less grand when you learn its story: its owner had to auction off all the furniture in 1955 and finally sold the old hulk to the Irish state for £50 12 years later. By 1958, the wreck of Ireland was complete.

So Ireland's leaders asked themselves, "Suppose we do the opposite to everything we're doing so far and see how that works?" Ireland replaced protectionism with a wide-open economy. Ireland joined the European community, cut business taxes sharply, invested heavily and for decades in public education. It took decades for these changes to pay of, but eventually the Irish discovered good luck makes good luck. Irish citizens stopped flooding out of the country in the 1960s. By the 1990s, there weren't enough Irish to do all the work. The work started coming to Ireland.

Ireland's population is only four million, yet by one estimate, from 1995–2000 a quarter of a million people immigrated to Ireland, only half of them returning Irish. Since then the pace has only increased. In May 2004, 10 new countries joined the European Union.

Only Sweden, Britain and Ireland allowed residents of those countries to move in and work right away. In hardly more than a year, 85,000 Eastern Europeans have arrived to work. The woman who checked us into our Dublin hotel was Czech. There's a Polish pub in Limerick, where the local newspaper runs weekly columns in Polish and Chinese.

Dan McLaughlin, chief economist of the Bank of Ireland Group, has predicted that this immigration will fuel a new "Celtic Tiger II" boom: in an economy constrained only by the amount of manpower, every new arrival contributes directly to the nation's bottom line. Ireland was always a good place to visit, but as the Wellses of Arklow have learned, now you want to live there. After giving so much to the world for so long, Ireland is finally ready to take some of the world back.

From an article by Paul Wells in:
Maclean's Canada's Weekly Newsmagazine, 18 August 2005

1 Uncle Paul: Paul Wells, writer of the article
2 Celtic Tiger: term used for the recent economic boom in Ireland

Worksheet:

maximum number of points attainable

I. Questions on the text

Read all the questions first, then answer them in the given order. Use your own words as far as is appropriate.

1. Describe the economic situation of Ireland in the 19th century and its demographic consequences. 10
2. Explain the demographic 'revolution' that has taken place in recent years and analyse its reasons. 20
3. Why does the writer mention the example of Kilkenny Castle? Show how he uses language to prove his point in lines 30 to 33. 10
4. How does the writer see the impact of immigration on host countries? Give precise examples. 20
5. In what ways is the introduction (ll. 1–15) different from the rest of the text? Analyse two characteristic features of each part. 20

II. Composition

Choose *one* of the following topics. Write about 150 to 200 words. 40

1. Migration: a chance and a risk.
2. "The only thing that overcomes hard luck is hard work." (Harry Golden) Discuss.
3. At the end of an exchange year in an English-speaking country you give a farewell speech at a school assembly. Write up the speech, including some of your experiences there.

III. Translation

Translate the following text into German: 40

160

Forget those turn-of-the-century images of Dublin. The prewar city of James Joyce[1] is, of course, long gone. […] Dublin today is the base of an immigration surge that is transforming Ireland at a rate un-paralleled in speed and scale anywhere in Europe. And that has made the Emerald Isle[2] a test case for how Europe will deal one of its greatest dilemmas – the need for, and discomfort with, immigrant labor. […]

Irish laws are still playing catch-up[3] with immigration. And they reflect the conflicting views the Irish have. Even as the country welcomes new workers, it is cracking down on immigration in other ways. Last year lawmakers modified legislation so as to deny automatic citizenship to children born in Ireland. This year the Supreme Court ruled that non-EU immigrant parents of Irish-born children are not automatically entitled to residency. This has […] created a great panic.

From *Ireland's New Force* by Stryker McGuire in:
Newsweek International, 15 December 2003, p. 32f.

1 James Joyce: (1882 – 1941); one of the most important Irish writers, famous for his short stories and novels set in Dublin

2 the Emerald Isle: *dt.* die Grüne Insel

3 to play catch-up: to try to make as much progress as someone or something you are competing with

Lösungsvorschlag

I. Questions on the text

1. *The relevant information is to be found in lines 17 ("Practially everyone ...") to 30 ("... everywhere except Ireland.") You should of course retain some basic facts from your classes.*

   Following the potato famine of the 1840s, Ireland was for a hundred years in a deplorable economic situation. TB and other diseases caused the country to have a very high mortality rate and only 50 per cent of each age group reached the age of 35. Most of those who survived emigrated to the USA and other countries, so that Ireland's population fell from 6.5 million in 1841 to 2.8 million in 1961.

2. *You must first explain what the 'demographic revolution' is, which the writer deals with in lines 20ff. and 41ff. In the second part of your answer you should point out the reasons for this development, which are to be found in lines 34 to 40.*

   Ireland, which was traditionally a country of emigrants, has managed to reverse that flow and has now become a country of immigrants. Half of them are former emigrants who return to the old country, but the other half comes either from Eastern Europe or even from countries of the New World, to which the Irish formerly left, like the Wells family.
   The reason for this 'revolution' is certainly the strong economic performance of the country, with annual growth rates of 8.4 per cent. This in turn was made possible by the country's membership in the European Union and its willingness to introduce free trade policies instead of protectionism. Moreover, Ireland reduced its business taxes and invested heavily in public education, which also contributed to the prolonged economic growth.

3. *Keep in mind: writers often use concrete examples (here in lines 30–33) to illustrate or prove their point. Before you answer, you should look up "hulk" in your dictionary – you will realize that the author compares the state of Ireland to that of a decaying ship.*

   The story of Kilkenny Castle, whose owner first had to sell his furniture at an auction and then gave the whole building to the state for the paltry sum of £ 50, symbolizes the economic decline of Ireland in the late 1950s.
   In order to emphasise his point the author uses the imagery of a decaying ship: he first refers to the castle as an "old hulk" (l. 32), i. e. the body of an abandoned, deteriorating ship. Then he states that the "wreck" (i. e. the destruction) of Ireland was complete in 1958. This choice of words certainly makes Ireland's decline appear even more dramatic.

4. *Throughout the whole text, but especially in the last paragraph, the author sees immigration as a positive factor. Read the text carefully and you will find a lot of passages that confirm this impression.*

   In lines 28/29 the author states that Irish emigration "fueled Canadian politics ..., US presidential races ..., Argentine literature", i. e. he says that the immigrants contributed greatly either to the politics or to the cultures of their new countries. With regard to the impact of immigrants on Ireland, he tells the reader that there "weren't enough Irish to do all the work" (ll. 39/40) and that "Eastern Europeans have arrived to work" (ll. 45/46). The reader can infer that the immigrants keep an economy running.

To emphasise his point at the end of the text the writer quotes the chief economist of the Bank of Ireland, i. e. an indubitable authority, with the words that "every new arrival contributes directly to the nation's bottom line." (ll. 50/51). So immigration is seen as a profit rather than as a burden – nowhere in the text does he mention any negative aspects of it.

5. *Note that the writer uses two different text types in this article: whereas the introduction is mostly* ***narrative*** *and could be the beginning of a short story, the main part is* ***expository*** *and tries to inform the reader about Ireland's economic miracle and its causes. Accordingly, we can find a number of typical devices for each text type.*

   In the introduction the author gives us a humorous account of the Wells brothers' life in Ireland. To get the reader interested he uses a number of stylistic devices, which are only to be found in narrative texts. Not only does he poke fun at his 'heroes' by introducing them as if they were adults ("Mr Riley Wells … Mr Liam Wells …", l. 1), He even reports the events of the summer from the point of view of the two little boys. The arrival of a circus and of relatives are of equal importance to the boys and described with parallelisms ("Tom Duffy's … circus pitched its tent … Uncle Paul and Christina ... pitched their tent …" ll. 4–6) and they both bring something very exciting to the boys: "Tom Duffy's circus came with tigers, llamas, and three elephants. … Paul and Christina came with a plastic dinosaur." (ll. 6/7 and ll. 9/10). He finally states in a humorous way that "this too was a hit." (l. 10/11) Although it contains some subjective interpretation, the main part of the text is mostly a factual report about immigration to Ireland and about its economic boom. Here the tone is serious and the writer uses a lot of technical terms (Celtic Tiger, the potato famine, protectionism). He tries to convince the reader with facts and figures (from 1995–2000 a quarter of a million people immigrated to Ireland; 85,000 Eastern Europeans came in hardly more than a year; the economy grows at an annual rate of 8.4 %; etc.) In order to corroborate his view the author also quotes authorities like the former Irish prime minister Garret FitzGerald (l. 24 f.) and Dan McLaughlin, the chief economist of the Bank of Ireland Group (ll. 48 ff.).

II. Composition

1. *Note that the subject can be seen from the point of view of the migrants as well a from that of the receiving countries. You can of course concentrate on one aspect.*

   All over the world people try to migrate from their mostly poor home countries to the industrialized centers of the West. Millions of Mexicans are trying to make it to the USA every year, where they seek a better life just as hundreds of thousands of Africans do in Europe.
   Of course, they see their journey only as a chance. Most of them are prepared to work hard and in return expect a safe job, decent wages to support their families and a home for themselves and their next of kin in their new surroundings. A lot of migrants have had such positive experiences and their reports incite ever more young people to seek the same.
   What most of them do not know are the risks involved in starting anew in a foreign country. Very often they do not speak the language of the land, which makes them vulnerable. Abusive employers may exploit and cheat them out of money, knowing that they can hardly complain to the authorities. And then there is the native population. Far from being happy about the new workers, many long-time residents see them as unwelcome competitors and react with hostility.
   I think it would be desirable if potential migrants would not only be informed about the opportunities but also about the risks of their enterprise.

2. *It pays to consult your dictionary before you set out to write this composition. You will find that the subject means that only by working hard can you fight and win against something unpleasant that has happened to you by chance.*

At first glance Golden's statement may surprise you. How can a terrible disease that you have contracted be overcome by hard work? Or how can it help you recover from a serious accident? You would rather think you need a good doctor and enough money to pay for your recovery.
But Golden really seems to have a point. If you believe you can achieve things through hard work, you will very probably be successful. He himself managed to overcome a bankruptcy with hard work. But there are also lots of stories in which faith combined with hard work have helped people recover when doctors had given them up. An athlete who has a terrible injury cannot just rely on a therapist to be able to compete again; he or she needs hard work and dedication to be able to be restored to health.
Of course hard work may not be the only thing to overcome bad luck, as Golden suggests. You will also need good doctors or understanding friends and colleagues to get out of such a predicament, but hard work is certainly a key factor.

3. *This is a subject you are likely to choose if you've spent a year at an English or American school. As a guest, you will certainly thank your hosts for their hospitality and for the good time you had. Since experiences differ from person to person, we will concentrate on some of the most obvious differences between the German and English school systems. The student who writes this has spent a year at an English boarding school:*

Mr Headmaster, Ladies and Gentlemen, my dear fellow-students,
thank you very much for giving me the opportunity to address you at the end of my year at your school.
To speak frankly, when I first arrived here a year ago I was very nervous and not so sure that I wanted to stay a whole year. I had never been away from home and now I was to be a boarder in a foreign country. But I soon found that it was very easy to make friends and that those friendships are not superficial but will very possibly last for years to come.
It was also easy to settle in because of the many extracurricular activities your school offers. I had expected some sports groups, but then I really found it hard to choose between sailing, drama, choir, chess, photography, debating and public speaking, to name only a few.
I come from Bavaria, whose schools are supposed to have the most rigorous academic standards in Germany. That may be true, and before I came here I thought that school was mostly about teaching for exams. For the first time did I attend a school where the teachers – at least some of them – lived together with the students and could be asked for help and advice almost any time. I think I will really miss that when I get home. And I will miss you all and I promise that I will never forget you.
Thank you very much.

III. Translation

Vergessen Sie jene Bilder von Dublin um die Jahrhundertwende. Die Stadt der Vorkriegszeit, die Stadt[1] eines James Joyce, gehört natürlich längst der Vergangenheit an. Dublin ist heute das Zentrum einer Einwanderungswelle, die Irland in einer Geschwindigkeit und in einem Maße[2] verändert, welches nirgendwo in Europa seinesgleichen hat. Und das hat die Grüne Insel zu einem Testfall dafür gemacht, wie Europa mit einem seiner größten Probleme umgehen wird – dem Bedarf an und dem Unbehagen über Arbeitsmigranten.[3]
Die irische Gesetzgebung[4] versucht immer noch, mit der Einwanderung Schritt zu halten[5]. Und sie[4] spiegelt die widersprüchlichen Ansichten der Iren wider. Während das

Land einerseits neue Arbeitskräfte willkommen heißt, greift es gleichzeitig in anderer Hinsicht gegen die Zuwanderung hart durch. Letztes Jahr hat der Gesetzgeber[6] das Recht[7] so geändert, dass Kindern, die in Irland geboren werden, die automatische Zuerkennung der irischen[8] Staatsbürgerschaft verweigert wird.
In diesem Jahr hat der Oberste Gerichtshof entschieden, dass Eltern von in Irland geborenen Kindern nicht automatisch[9] Anspruch auf eine Aufenthaltsgenehmigung haben, wenn sie Einwanderer aus einem Nicht-EU-Staat sind[10]. Dies hat große Panik hervorgerufen.

Anmerkungen

1 Die Wiederholung erfolgt hier zur Verdeutlichung. Die wörtliche Übersetzung „Die Vorkriegsstadt von James Joyce" ist im Deutschen missverständlich.

2 "... transforming Ireland at a rate unparalleleled in ... scale ..." Die Schwierigkeit liegt hier darin, dass sowohl *rate* als auch *scale* im Deutschen „Ausmaß" bedeuten können. Hier wurden beide zu „in einem Maße" zusammengefasst.

3 Das Fremdwort „Arbeitsmigranten" trifft hier den Sachverhalt besser als irgendeine deutsche Umschreibung, z. B. „Einwanderer, die Arbeit suchen".

4 *laws* bezieht sich hier nicht auf einzelne Gesetze, sondern auf die Gesetzgebung. Wenn man den Begriff benutzt, muss im folgenden Satz der Singular für *they* stehen.

5 *to play catch-up* ist hier ein Bild, das man nicht wörtlich ins Deutsche übertragen kann. Möglich wäre auch die Übersetzung mit „hinterherhinken", was jedoch negativer als das Original ist.

6 Im Deutschen ist der Singular als Fachausdruck gebräuchlicher.

7 Um die Wiederholung von „Gesetzgeber" – „Gesetz" zu vermeiden, wurde „das Recht" verwendet.

8 Zusatz zur Verdeutlichung

9 Die Wiederholung von „automatisch" ergibt sich aus dem Originaltext.

10 Die englische Fügung *non-EU immigrant parents* lässt sich nur mithilfe eines Nebensatzes ins Deutsche übertragen.

Grundkurs Englisch 2006
Textaufgabe II

From: Charlie Higson, *The Red Line*, 1993

Berto looked up at the Underground map for what seemed like the hundredth time, and still it made no sense to him. Where was Hackney[1]? The map was a jumble of confusing names. The English language seemed to have no rules. Names didn't sound like they were written. That had been made clear to him after Cathy had left the train and he'd tried to ask a man for help. He hadn't been able to make himself understood and in the end the man had simply laughed and shook his head. It had been humiliating. He hadn't found the courage to ask again. Now he was lost, but he wasn't going to let himself get scared. As long as he was moving it was OK … If he just sat here on this train, in this warm carriage, he would eventually work out what to do. As long as he acted sensibly and didn't panic, things would work out.

But London was vast and confusing. Not like Venice. In Venice, when he'd met Cathy, everything had seemed clear and easy. Even though they hadn't been able to talk they had understood each other, and as they'd spent most of their time in bed, talking hadn't been important. So he'd come to England, like she'd said he should … Only it wasn't what he'd expected. For one thing, she had a boyfriend. She hadn't told him that before. She'd tried to talk to him about the boyfriend yesterday in the taxi, on the way to her place from the station, but he wasn't sure he understood. She'd told him about something called a "trial separation" and an "open relationship", and even though he looked the words up, he still didn't understand what they meant. So he nodded and went along with it. To him it all seemed crazy.

She still saw the boyfriend. Last night, his first night in England, they had all had dinner together. Afterwards the boyfriend had kissed Cathy goodnight and gone home. Berto had gone to bed with Cathy and they had started to make love but he could tell that she was tense, that she didn't really want to do it, so he had stopped. All those miles, thinking about her, and now this. If only he'd been able to talk to her about it.

Today had been even stranger. Cathy had been at work, so the boyfriend had shown him around London. Trying very hard to be friendly, telling him about everything they saw, too fast for Berto to understand. That was when Berto realized just how big the city was, how spread out. You couldn't walk, always it had to be buses and what the English called the tubes. So he had no sense of the layout, no internal map.

They had stayed out all day, then met Cathy in a Chinese restaurant. Afterwards they had gone to a party somewhere called Clapham[2]. He hadn't enjoyed the party. Cathy had ignored him, spent the whole time with the boyfriend. Everyone had got drunk, shouting and laughing. He could talk to nobody. He sat on the stairs by himself and people pushed past him all the time as if he didn't exist. He had begun to wonder what he was doing in this country.

Luckily, Cathy wanted to leave early, and luckily the boyfriend didn't come with them. But Cathy hadn't been happy. She said she had had an argument with the boyfriend. Berto tried to talk about this but she only became more upset. They had got on the tube, and Berto had said something which made Cathy angry, he had no idea what. She'd shouted at him – too fast, too many words he didn't understand – and at the next stop she got off the train, swore at him (the few words he did understand) and told him not to follow. And like a fool he didn't.

From: Charlie Higson, *The Red Line*, in: Maria Lexton (ed.), *The Time Out Book of London Short Stories*, London: Penguin Books 1993

1 Hackney: part of London, north-east of the City
2 Clapham: one of the suburbs in the south of London

Worksheet:

	maximum number of points attainable
I. Questions on the text	
Read all the questions first, then answer them in the given order. Use your own words as far as is appropriate.	
1. Describe Berto's situation and state of mind as shown in the first paragraph.	10
2. Analyse Cathy's relationship and behaviour to Berto.	20
3. Outline her relationship to her English boyfriend. How does Berto feel about it?	10
4. Explain the way Berto reacts to London. Show that his view of Venice and London is symbolic of his state of mind.	10
5. What role do language and communication play in Berto's relations to Cathy and her friends?	20
6. Comment on the narrative perspective used in this text and determine its effect on how the reader sees the characters.	10
II. Composition	
Choose *one* of the following topics. Write about 150 to 200 words.	40
1. 'Fun society' – Are we amusing ourselves to death?	
2. The deepest satisfaction a traveller can get is to come to terms with unforeseen problems and difficulties in foreign countries. Do you agree?	
3. A few days after Berto's disappearance. Cathy tries to explain her behaviour and the situation in a letter to him. Write Cathy's letter.	

III. Translation

Translate the following text into German: 40/160

The reasons for London's growth were not simple. Partly, it took place because London's middle-class population was growing so fast, and these people, unable to afford a second home in the country, but able to pay a daily bus or train fare into their City offices, were the ones most likely to choose a suburban existence.

The mixture of town and country had a particular appeal to middle-class Londoners. Perhaps this was because it enabled them to mimic, at modest expense, the country life of the aristocracy. No matter how strongly the suburbs were criticized by moralists and architects for their dull uniformity, for their failure to be either real town or country, they were places in which most middle-class, and many working-class, Londoners chose to live when improving wages, working hours and transport links made it possible. Suburban life, in their view, offered not the worst of both worlds, but the best.

From: Stephen Inwood, *A History of London*. London: Macmillan 1998

Lösungsvorschlag

I. Questions on the text

1. *Make sure to refer both to Berto's situation and his state of mind (only in the first paragraph). It is easier to separate the two aspects in your answer.*

   Berto is lost in the London Underground. After Cathy had walked out on him, he is sitting in a moving train, completely on his own. He cannot find the station he has just passed on the map. A man he asked for help has given up making him understand his explanations.
   He is confused by the weirdness of the tube system (ll. 1 f.) and feels embarrassed and ashamed by his failure to communicate with the man (ll. 6 f.) but forces himself to keep a clear mind and hopes that in the end all will be well.

2. *This is again a double question in connection with the task to analyse both points.*

   Cathy met Berto in Italy. She has a boyfriend in London but started a passionate affair with him all the same. At the end of her holiday, she invited him to see her in London. When Berto actually appears she first tries to do justice to both men but accepts to spend the night with Berto, which turns out to be a disagreeable experience. From then on, she turns a cold shoulder to him, finally insults him and leaves him on the train.
   Her relationship to Berto seems like one of those holiday flirts with a Latin lover, which she forgot once she was back home again. When Berto turned up unexpectedly she felt guilty and at the same time responsible for him. In her confusion, she hoped she could manage the situation somehow by including her boyfriend. But when she took Berto home with her and he tried to renew their romance she probably was ashamed of herself and rejected him (l. 24). As Berto did not understand she behaved more and more rudely to him, before she decided to end their relationship unmistakably, once and for all.

3. *When you are asked to outline something you need not go into detail – but do not forget to comment on Berto's feelings.*

   Cathy had defined her relationship with her boyfriend as an open one (l. 18), in which both partners allow each other some freedom. She had also regarded their separation during her holiday as an experiment to test the depth of their relationship (l. 18). She had been unfaithful to him in Venice and lets Berto stay in her place in London. She also tries to make him accept Berto's presence and has arguments with him in London but they still spend time with each other as good friends. Eventually she cuts her ties with Berto but it is left open whether she loves her boyfriend or not.
   Berto cannot come to terms with the boyfriend's presence and is totally confused about this kind of relationship. He is unable to understand Cathy's behaviour and her explanations (ll. 19 and 41). At some time he regrets having come to London (l. 35 f), and in the end he admits that he acted like a fool (l. 43).

4. *This double question should not present any difficulties. The main evidence is to be found in lines 11f and in the fourth paragraph.*

   A clear reference to Berto's view of London is to be found in line 11: "London was vast and confusing. Not like Venice." It was so 'big' and 'spread out' (l. 28 f.) that you couldn't walk much. Having to move by bus and tube he was unable to picture its layout in his mind.

His image of London is mirrored by his bewilderment at Cathy's weird behaviour. He lost his orientation, both geographically and emotionally. In Venice, on the other hand, everything was "clear and easy" (l. 12). There, unlike in London, he had been happy with Cathy and they had "understood each other" (l. 13).

5. *You will find references to his language and communication problems in the whole text (ll. 3, 5, 13 f., 17, 28, 34, 41). Show how they contribute to the failure of their relationship and do not forget Cathy's friends.*

   Berto's mastery of the English language is rather limited. English "seems to have no rules" (l. 3). In Venice, this did not present any problems: their love did not rely on language, they "had understood each other" and "talking hadn't been important" (ll. 13 f.). In London, however, Berto couldn't comprehend Cathy's explanations (l. 17), and the dictionary wasn't of much help, either. After the party, when he tried to discuss her feelings and behaviour, they failed miserably to communicate. He recognized a few swearwords and realized that their love had come to an end.
   As to Cathy's friends, only her boyfriend forces himself to talk to Berto – too fast for him (l. 27 f.). The people at the party don't even bother, they ignore him completely. Thus it is evident that only Cathy really tried to communicate with him but due to his linguistic shortcomings he can neither adequately react to the increasing complication of their relationship nor explain his own feelings, and loses her "like a fool" (l. 43).

6. *See also 'Tips for Questions on the Text' (perspective). The point-of view used here is a third person narrator's, in reported thought. Its effects on the reader are similar to those of a first person narrative*

   The perspective used in this text is the reported thought of a third person narrator (e. g. "Where was Hackney?", l. 2; "… it wasn't what he expected", l. 14 f.; "To him all seemed crazy", l. 20), in which the reader sees the events through Berto's eyes and shares his feelings and observations. The effect is that he identifies more with Berto than with the other characters. This device, on the other hand, limits his insight – he can only speculate about the motives of the other persons and remains ignorant of how far Berto himself is responsible for the reaction of the others.

II. Composition

1. *The topic alludes to Neil Postman's book 'Amusing ourselves to death' (1986) in which he criticises the so-called fun society. If you haven't heard of it, you can also open your essay with a short explanation of how you understand the topical question.*

   Neil Postman's book 'Amusing ourselves to death' has been widely discussed in the intellectual community but left no mark among the members of the 'fun society' – who might be too busy amusing themselves with more trivial matters.
   Modern entertainment facilities like TV, pop music, or computer games have an overwhelming attraction for especially the younger generations. Millions of people in affluent societies spend several hours every day watching trash programmes or films on private TV channels, MTV, or DVD players, leading endless campaigns on their play stations and are hooked up to their iPods. When they are done with it they go partying, which normally includes deafening music, excessive drinking and the consumption of all kinds of drugs. Work and cultural activities are considered boring; all that counts is having fun.
   The consequences are that people live in second-hand realities. They deliberately close their eyes to issues that really determine the fate of mankind. Guided by their search for cheap thrills and numbed by a daily flood of pictures they lose their ability to un-

derstand what is relevant. They find it difficult to concentrate, think and speak coherently; their conversation topics are mostly based on the trivialities of the media while meaningful exchanges are rare. Apart from the social effects, risks that are more personal are noticeable as well: exaggerated individualism, aggression, psychosomatic disturbances and serious health problems caused by noise overdoses and drug consumption.
Postman's observations are truly disturbing. I agree that our civilisation has taken an unhealthy direction and my only hope is that people will increasingly become aware of this and a movement will set in to correct this development.

2. *It will help you to collect a few possible unforeseen problems before you start writing your composition. If you are an adventurous spirit, you can agree with the proposition but it is quite all right to defend the perfectly uneventful trip.*

   No doubt, Columbus returned to Spain as a deeply satisfied person. Since then travel has become as easy as a walk in the park. Tourists can choose in catalogues from family package tours to individual trekking in the Himalayas. Once you are on your way, there is, however, always the chance of unforeseen obstacles, which may mess up your holiday. Whereas the common tourists will furiously complain to their travel agencies if they did not get their money's worth of beach, sun, and booze, the true traveller enjoys the unexpected twists of fortune where he can prove his courage and resourcefulness. Let him get stranded in the middle of nowhere and he will follow the stars to reach civilisation; let him be arrested or even held hostage by uncomprehending natives and he will talk his way out of the dilemma or escape from the dungeon. If foul weather turns into sandstorm or hurricane, he will be a model of level-headedness and lead his willing followers out of harm's way. He will laugh in the mugger's face and outrun him, and he will even find a way to escape from marrying the village chief's daughter. He will regard all these adversities as welcome challenges and return triumphant.
   How can anyone not agree with the proposition of the topic?

3. *This is a very personal letter. You should not use 'dearest' or 'my dear' in your opening, nor 'love' as signature – unless Cathy is still in love with him and wants to win him back! No address or date are necessary here. You may want to do justice to the personal character of the letter by writing in a more colloquial style (contractions, vocabulary). Your main task is to explain her behaviour, which should not be too difficult.*
   As it is not very realistic to expect Cathy to write to someone who barely speaks English, we have added a postscript.

   Dear Berto,

   I'm pretty sure that I have deeply hurt your feelings. You came to London because I more or less invited you and then I only made you suffer.
   Since we parted, I've had time to think about what happened. I now know I should never have allowed myself to start an affair with you in Venice. I'd left Angus in a quarrel and you were very sweet and romantic. When I asked you to come, I really meant it but, you see, Angus and I've long since made it up and we know we love each other more than ever. So, when you actually arrived I was rather shocked. In the beginning, I forced myself to be hospitable and friendly with you. I still admire you for the sensitivity with which you felt that I didn't want to sleep with you – but after that night I was ashamed of myself and decided that this couldn't go on. I tried to behave to you in a way that should make it easier for you to break with me but you didn't seem

to understand – so I exploded rather rudely. I really should have made more of an effort to explain myself but then you still don't understand English well enough, do you? Can you forgive me? Please do because I don't want you to have hard feelings! I will always remember our time in Venice but it is a closed chapter in my life.

Kindest regards,

Cathy

P.S. I hope you found someone to translate this letter for you!

III. Translation

Die Ursachen für das Wachstum Londons waren eher vielschichtig.[1] Zum Teil vollzog es sich, weil die mittelständische Bevölkerung Londons so stark im Zunehmen begriffen war[2]. Diese Menschen konnten sich zwar[3] keinen Zweitwohnsitz auf dem Lande leisten, waren aber durchaus[3] in der Lage, eine tägliche Bus- oder Zugfahrt zu ihren Büros in der Innenstadt[4] zu bezahlen[5]. Sie[6] kamen am ehesten dafür infrage, sich für ein Leben in der Vorstadt zu entscheiden. Die Mischung aus Stadt und Land war von besonderem Reiz für die Londoner Mittelklasse. Dies hatte möglicherweise damit zu tun, dass sie so[3] das Landleben des Adels mit bescheidenem Aufwand imitieren konnten. Wie heftig auch die Vorstädte von Moralisten[7] und Architekten kritisiert wurden, wegen ihrer öden Einheitlichkeit und weil es ihnen nicht gelang, entweder wirklich städtisch oder ländlich zu sein, so waren sie doch[3] Orte, in denen die meisten Londoner aus der Mittelschicht und viele aus der Arbeiterklasse leben wollten, wenn Verbesserungen bei Löhnen, Arbeitszeiten und Verkehrsverbindungen ihnen[3] dies ermöglichten. Das Leben in den Vororten bot ihnen aus ihrer Sicht nicht die schlechteste von zwei Welten, sondern die beste.

Anmerkungen

1 Es klingt oft besser, wenn man ein verneintes Adjektiv mit seinem Gegenteil übersetzt.

2 Um den Aspekt (progressive form) wiederzugeben: ‚*Im … begriffen war*'. ‚*Zunehmen*' wurde gewählt, um nicht noch einmal ‚*Wachsen*' zu benutzen. An dieser Stelle kann man auch problemlos einen neuen Satz beginnen.

3 Stilistisch bedingte Einfügungen

4 *City* großgeschrieben meint eigentlich die ‚*City of London*', das historische Zentrum und der selbstständige Verwaltungsbezirk – man könnte auch einfach ‚*City*' stehen lassen.

5 *fare* ist das Fahrgeld, wird aber durch ‚*Fahrt bezahlen*' hinreichend wiedergegeben.

6 Es ist besser, wenn man den langen Satz unterbricht.

7 Die Bedeutung von ‚*moralists*' wird aus dem Kontext nicht klar, sodass das vage Fremdwort ‚*Moralisten*' gewählt wurde (statt z. B. ‚*Moralapostel*').

Leerseiten verbilligen in diesem Fall die Herstellung des Buches!

Grundkurs Englisch 2007
Textaufgabe I

Fill Notebooks, And Then A Few Bellies

JOHANNESBURG – I recently bought an elaborate dinner for some of my sources. Given the jaundiced eye some people train on journalists these days that may sound tawdry, if not downright corrupt.

So be it. These particular sources live outside Lusaka, the capital of Zambia. They are stone-crushers, a class of laborers who cling to the lowest social rung even in this, one of the world's poorest nations. Mostly women and children, they live by reducing boulders to gravel and powder, which are sold to local construction workers at starvation-level prices. Their lives are as miserable as those of almost any group I have seen in three years in Africa.

So after a few hours of interviews about their struggle to survive, I left them and drove to a grocery. There I bought about $75 worth of food: cornmeal, cooking oil, rice, orange concentrate, bread, milk, a big bag of candy. Then I returned and unloaded it, to undiluted pandemonium – mothers' riotous joy,. youngsters mobbing for sweets: actual dancing in the street; for 30 people, a real live Christmas in July.

They were that hungry.

No Westerner can travel the less developed world, at least outside the lobbies of the three- and four-star hotels that now populate most major cities, and not be struck by the immense gulf between their own personal wealth and the utter destitution of the masses around them.

How to respond to it is a moral dilemma that lurks in the background of many interviews. Reputable journalists are indoctrinated with the notion that they are observers – that their job is to tell a story, not to influence it. So what to do when an anguished girl tells a compelling story about her young brother, lying emaciated on a reed mat, dying for lack of money to buy anti-AIDS drugs? Is it moral to take the story and leave when a comparatively small gift of money would keep him alive? If morality compels a gift, what about the dying mother in the hut next door who missed out on an interview by pure chance?

In reputable journalism, paying for information is a major sin, the notion being that a source who will talk only for money is likely to say anything to earn his payment. So what to do when a penniless father asks why he should open his life free to an outsider when he needs money for food?

Sometimes, an article moves generous readers to contribute their own money toward bettering the situation of a source, or his family, or even an entire village. Two years ago, after my fellow correspondent and wife Sharon LaFraniere and I profiled a Swaziland town hit hard by AIDS, readers of *The New York Times* offered about $10,000 to give its residents lifesaving access to antiretroviral[1] drugs.

But here, too, there are hurdles. How can money be funneled[2] securely to villages without banks? Even if the money can be transferred, can people to whom $10,000 is a vast fortune be trusted to spend it wisely? What if money is misused or goes for naught? Have readers been misled?

Most wrenching[3] of all, what happens when the money runs out? Outsiders' gifts are balms, but many needs – for food, AIDS drugs, tuition – are chronic. In passing out small amounts of money, is it right to raise hopes that are destined to be dashed?

Even skeptical journalists are occasionally misled. Playing on the compassion – or guilt – of outsiders is a basic survival tactic among some of the poor.

There are few fixed rules to cover such situations. My own code is simple: I never give people money in advance of an interview. I argue that the value of educating the world about their problems is reason enough to talk. When I am personally moved by an individual's situation, I sometimes offer help after completing an interview, and tell myself that I cannot also help all his neighbors and friends without impoverishing myself.

Those rules are no panacea. But better to light one candle, so to speak.

That said, it can be haunting to realize that it is in fact usually just one candle, and usually in places where bonfires are needed.

From: "Fill Notebooks, And Then a Few Bellies" by Michael Wines, New York Times, August 27, 2006, Copyright © 2006 by New York Times Co. Reprinted with permission

1 antiretroviral: used to treat HIV
2 funneled: *here:* transferred, sent
3 wrenching: *here:* saddening

Worksheet:

maximum number of points attainable

I. Questions on the text

Read all the questions first, then answer them in the given order.
Use your own words as far as is appropriate.

1. What did Michael Wines experience in Zambia and how did he react? Refer to lines 4 to 20. — 10
2. Analyse the moral dilemma he and many of his colleagues find themselves in. — 20
3. What personal journalistic "code" (l. 46) has Wines developed to find a way out of his dilemma? — 10
4. How effective, according to Wines, are money donations? — 20
5. What is the function of the very first sentence of the text? — 10
6. Analyse two rhetorical devices the writer uses to appeal to the reader and to make his article interesting. — 10

II. Composition

Choose *one* of the following topics. Write about 150 to 200 words. — 40

1. By helping others we also help ourselves. Discuss.
2. Write a newspaper leader entitled "Poverty in the USA/Britain today".
3. You have seen a shocking picture in a newspaper. Write a letter to the editor pointing out why you find this particular picture so appalling.

III. Translation

Translate the following text into German: — 40

160

No one is likely to adopt Hermia. At 14 she is too old and she also has a younger brother. So, because their father disappeared some years ago and their mother died last year at 32, probably of AIDS, the pair rely on the generosity of others. The family next door has taken them under their wing, making sure they go to school.

While Madonna's controversial adoption of a 13-month-old boy from a Malawi children's home has focused attention on Africa's orphans, Hermia's plight is more typical of that of millions of children across sub-Saharan Africa orphaned by AIDS, malaria or conflicts.

Adoptions by foreigners are welcomed by many Africans working with distressed children, despite concerns about plucking youngsters from their own culture. But foreigners almost always want to adopt babies, overlooking the older children and that for every child taken overseas, hundreds of thousands remain in institutions or grapple to survive on their own.

From: *The Guardian*, October 18th 2006

Lösungsvorschlag

I. Questions on the text

1. *Here you must answer two questions; the reference to the lines shows that you should concentrate on the mere facts!*

   Michael Wines is a journalist working in Africa where he has been confronted again and again with the shocking discrepancy between a small wealthy upper class and the mass of people living in dismal conditions. From Lusaka, Zambia, he reported on the abominable working and living conditions of stone-crushers (l. 5), mostly women and children, who are paid so little for their physically demanding work that they can just about survive (ll. 7/8).
   Deeply appalled at what he had seen, he went and bought $ 75 worth of basic food (ll. 11/12), which he distributed among them, thus giving them the time of their lives. He himself must have felt like Santa Claus in the middle of summer.

2. On the one hand there is Michael Wines, the journalist, who is expected to give neutral, unbiased accounts on what he sees and finds: he must be the observer (l. 21) whose job it is "to tell a story, not to influence it" (l. 22). Following this ethos, he is not to pay his sources: there is too great a danger his informants might furnish him with false or exaggerated information just to get money (l. 29).
   On the other hand, there is Michael Wines, the sensitive human being, who has to face poverty, hunger, disease, misery, injustice. He feels it is his duty to do something to improve these conditions. So he finds himself stuck between either committing the "major sin" (l. 28) of paying his informants – thus betraying a basic principle of his professional ethos – or committing the moral sin of not helping where help is badly needed.
   On top of that, taking sides a journalist may find himself in the additional trouble of not being able to help all the cases he is confronted with, simply because there are too many (ll. 25–27).

3. Michael Wines has found his personal way to solve the said dilemma. As a journalist he sees his main duty is to inform people on sufferings and injustices: he educates the world about problems (ll. 47/48), and that in itself may arouse interest and sympathy, it may even move his readers to take up action and help. When he is personally touched by an "individual's situation" (ll. 48/49) he himself offers help – but always only after an interview is finished, never beforehand. Thus he keeps his reputation of being a serious journalist while at the same time he soothes his conscience in the face of misery and suffering.

4. *Even though examples of donations are scattered all over the text, the main information can be found in the section from line 32 to line 45.*

   Besides telling us the story of spending $ 75 worth on food, sweets etc. at the beginning, Michael Wines gives one example where one of his reports in the NYT – co-written with his wife – moved its readers to donate about $ 10,000 to residents of a "Swaziland town hit hard by AIDS" (ll. 34/35), a very personalised and specific action where donators knew who would benefit from the money and how (giving AIDS victims "access to antiretroviral drugs"; l. 36).
   Other than that, he has a number of reservations about how effective these donations may be. There are practical "hurdles" (l. 37) like missing infrastructure: how can you transfer money when there is no bank (ll. 37/38)? Personal weaknesses come in the

way: can someone living below the povertyline resist the temptation of misusing at least some of the money? And some victims might even exaggerate their miserable conditions (ll. 44/45).
Furthermore, anyone familiar with the problems knows that in the end all these gifts are only "balms" (l. 42), i.e. they only help to cure some of the symptoms superficially without really healing the causes. And above all, there is simply too much misery and injustice in the world: helping in *one* case is like "lighting one candle" (l. 51) knowing that actually "bonfires are needed" (l. 53).

5. Michael Wines shocks his readers by saying he "recently bought an elaborate dinner for some of [his] sources" (l. 1). This sounds like a confession one would not expect from a journalist writing in a serious newspaper like the NYT. Speaking of an "elaborate dinner", the writer gives the impression that he tried to bribe some important people in an African country – just the sort of thing many readers expect to be normal working conditions for a journalist on the black continent. But the reader is misled. The "sources" turn out to be poor people living at the bottom of their society, and the "elaborate dinner" did not include lobster, caviar and champagne but food that meets the basic needs of the poorest of the poor.

6. *The text contains a number of rhetorical devices. We will write about a few from which you can choose any two.*

One of the most vivid rhetorical devices are **metaphors**. At the end of his article, the author uses the positive imagery of light to illustrate what one does when giving money and donations to solve problems in a Third World country: he calls it "lighting a candle" (l. 51), i.e. he makes people's lives brighter. He picks up the imagery of light in the last sentence when he speaks of "bonfires" (l. 53) which are necessary, thus making a **contrast** between the little a single action can achieve and the huge task of actually solving the entire problem.
Personifications are another very common rhetorical device. We find a very effective one when he speaks of a dilemma that "lurks in the background" (l. 20): the verb gives the word 'dilemma' the quality of a dangerous animal hiding in the dark, waiting to attack any moment.
Looking at sentence structure, we find two very **short sentences** which contrast strikingly with the rather complicated long sentences we usually find in this text. "So be it." (l. 4): having misled the reader into thinking that journalism is "tawdry" (l. 2) and "corrupt" (l. 3), Michael Wines can easily act as if he is going to confirm this concept knowing the turn his article is going to take. The sentence "They were that hungry." (l. 15) underlines in its laconic shortness the extent of the poverty and contrasts with the joy mentioned just before.
The text contains a number of questions, but only a few of them are **rethorical** (ll. 29–31), most are **real** questions: the writer turns to the reader to show that he can't come up with a model answer to any of them, i. e. he openly shows the dilemma he writes about (e.g., ll. 22–27).

II. Composition

1. *A look at the text you just wrote about can give you ideas as can examples from your own experience.*

   Helping others is one of the values on which our society is based. On the other hand, today's political credo tells us to think of our own well-being first. Both ideas, obviously, seem to contradict or even exclude each other.
   I have always been very good at maths, and consequently classmates who were rather weak at this subject would turn to me for advice. Sometimes we would sit down together before an important test and work through some of the difficulties. I have always found that these occasions have helped me, too, to understand a mathematical problem more thoroughly. Generally, I have found that pupils who share their knowledge with others can also benefit in a more general sense from their helpfulness because they are accepted in class better than swots who keep all their expertise to themselves. And what is true for an individual or a small group, also goes without saying for a whole society: if we spend money on those who are on the brink of dropping out because they have no job, no money, little education, we will save a lot more money than what the taxpayer will have to pay in the end if he does not help in the first place.
   So, I think it is always in our own interest, too, if we help others.

2. *This sounds like an interesting topic to write about – but: what do you do when you have no access to books or the Internet, no one to ask for information …? So, why not again take a more personal approach?*

   Our son Larry, 16, has an exchange student from Europe – Germany, to be exact – who arrived here only a week ago. Daniel, also 16, is going to stay here for a year. Of course, Daniel had heard all about Hollywood, the Walk of Fame, the villas of Malibu. So last Friday, when I picked the two boys up from school, I thought we might take a detour through *nuevo los angeles.*
   There it was: overcrowded and underdeveloped housing areas, bashed up cars in littered streets, shabby small shops, unemployed people hanging around. At a certain point he asked very naively if we couldn't "just walk around a bit". I told him that this wasn't such a good idea.
   And I felt ashamed.
   There was this Old World kid in God's own rich country – who had no idea about the poverty, the desolation, the crime in our city …
   And, of course: there is all this glitter and glamor, there are our success stories, there is our shiny modern highly civilised metropolis. Yes, it is all there. But going to the Hispanic part of LA is always like going to a different city – a city in the Third World. We must not forget that there is still a long way to go before we have arrived in the 21st century.

3. *Before you start, you must have a very precise idea about the shocking picture. It can be anything from violence or poverty to environmental issues.*

   Dear Sir or Madam,

   There was this picture of a dead seagull all covered in crude oil from the wrecked Panamanian oil tanker, washed ashore off the coast of Malaga last week. We were deeply shocked. This is where my husband and I spent our holidays for twenty-seven years while we were working. And now being retired, we go down there twice a year because for us this is the most beautiful part of the world.

We are both appalled that miles and miles of such a magnificent coastline has now been ruined by ruthless business people who are obviously only interested in making as much profit as possible by ignoring all safety regulations on their ships.
Moreover, we are great bird-lovers, and bird-watching is one of our favourite pastimes. We are shocked that thousands and thousands of these innocent and beautiful creatures have fallen victim again to criminal ship-owning companies who violate the most simple rules of international shipping.
We really hope that pictures like that will arouse people all over the world to think about increasing oil consumption. Even my husband and I are thinking about cancelling future flights to Spain, in the hope of contributing, albeit in a small way, to the reduction of oil consumption.

Yours sincerely,
Miranda Richardson

III. Translation

Wahrscheinlich wird niemand Hermia adoptieren. Sie ist 14 und damit[1] zu alt; außerdem hat sie einen kleineren Bruder. Und weil ihr Vater vor einigen Jahren verschwunden und ihre Mutter im letzten Jahr im Alter von 32 gestorben ist – wahrscheinlich an AIDS –, deswegen also[1] sind die beiden angewiesen auf die Großzügigkeit anderer Leute. Die Nachbarfamilie hat sie unter ihre Fittiche[2] genommen und kümmert sich darum[3], dass sie zur Schule gehen.

Während Madonnas umstrittene Adoption eines 13 Monate alten Jungen aus einem Kinderheim in Malawi die Aufmerksamkeit der Welt[1] auf die Waisenkinder Afrikas gelenkt hat, ist die Notlage von Hermia typischer für die Situation[1] von Millionen von Kindern im ganzen[4] Afrika südlich der Sahara[5], die durch AIDS, Malaria oder bewaffnete[1] Konflikte zu Waisen geworden sind.

Adoptionen durch Ausländer werden von vielen Afrikanern befürwortet, die mit Not[6] leidenden Kindern arbeiten, obwohl es natürlich Bedenken gibt, ob man Kinder aus ihrer eigenen Kultur herausreißen soll. Aber Ausländer wollen fast immer nur Babys adoptieren und übersehen dabei die älteren Kinder und die Tatsache, dass für jedes Kind, das nach Übersee gebracht wird, Hunderttausende in öffentlichen Einrichtungen verbleiben oder sich abkämpfen allein zu überleben.

Anmerkungen

1 stilistisch bedingte Einfügung(en)
2 wem der ornithologische Fachbegriff nicht einfällt, der kann auch „unter ihre Obhut" übersetzen
3 *making sure:* wörtlicher „um sicher zu stellen, um sicher zu gehen, um zu garantieren"
4 *across:* hier in der Bedeutung *all over*
5 *sub-Saharan Africa* auch als „Schwarzafrika" zu übersetzen
6 *distress(ed)* kann auch stärker mit „Elend" übersetzt werden

A couple of years after 9/11 Oskar, a boy living in New York City, is still haunted by the events of that day.

After forever, I got out of bed and went to the closet where I kept the phone. I hadn't taken it out since the worst day. It just wasn't possible. A lot of the time I think about those four and a half minutes between when I came home and when Dad called.

I opened the apartment door, put down my bag, and took off my shoes, like everything was wonderful, because I didn't know that in reality everything was actually horrible, because how could I? I went to the phone to check the messages and listened to them one after another.

MESSAGE ONE: 8:52 A.M.
MESSAGE TWO: 9:12 A.M.
MESSAGE THREE: 9:31 A.M.
MESSAGE FOUR: 9:46 A.M.
MESSAGE FIVE: 10:04 A.M.

© ullstein bild – Reuters

I thought about calling Mom. I thought about grabbing my walkie-talkie and paging Grandma. I went back to the first message and listened to them all again. I thought about running away and never talking to anyone again. I thought about hiding under my bed. I thought about rushing downtown to see if I could somehow rescue him myself. And then the phone rang. I looked at my watch. It was 10:22:27.

I knew I could never let Mom hear the messages, because protecting her is one of my most important raisons d'être, *so what I did was I took Dad's emergency money from on top of his dresser, and went to the Radio Shack on Amsterdam*[1]*. It was on a TV there that I saw that the first building had fallen. I bought the exact same phone and ran home and recorded our greeting from the first phone onto it. I wrapped up the old phone, and put that in a grocery bag, and I put that in a box, and I put that in another box, and I put that under a bunch of stuff in my closet.*

That night I really needed to hear him.

I was extremely careful not to make any noise as I took the phone out of all its protections. Even though the volume was way down, so Dad's voice wouldn't wake Mom, he still filled the room, like how a light fills a room even when it's dim.

MESSAGE TWO. 9:12 A.M. IT'S ME AGAIN. ARE YOU THERE? HELLO? SORRY IF. IT'S GETTING A BIT SMOKY. I WAS HOPING YOU WOULD. BE. HOME. I DON'T KNOW IF YOU'VE HEARD ABOUT WHAT'S HAPPENED. BUT. I. JUST WANTED YOU TO KNOW THAT I'M OK. EVERYTHING. IS. FINE. WHEN YOU GET THIS, GIVE GRANDMA A CALL. LET HER KNOW THAT I'M OK. I'LL CALL AGAIN IN A FEW MINUTES. HOPEFULLY THE FIREMEN WILL BE. UP HERE BY THEN. I'LL CALL.

I stared at the fake stars forever.
I invented.
I gave myself a bruise.
I invented.

I got out of bed, went over to the window, and picked up the walkie-talkie. “Grandma? Grandma, do you read me? Grandma? Grandma?” “Oskar?” “I’m OK. Over.” “It’s late. What’s happened? Over.” “Did I wake you up? Over.” “No. Over.” “What were you doing? Over.” “I was talking to the renter.”

The renter had been living with Grandma since Dad died, and even though I was at her apartment basically every day, I still hadn’t met him. He was constantly running errands, or taking a nap, or in the shower, even when I didn’t hear any water. Mom told me, “It probably gets pretty lonely to be Grandma, don’t you think? Maybe she needs an imaginary friend. There’s nothing wrong with someone needing a friend.” “Are you actually talking about Ron now?” “No, I’m talking about Grandma.” “Except actually you’re talking about Ron.” “No, Oskar, I’m not. And I don’t appreciate that tone.” “I wasn’t using a tone.” “You were using your accusatory tone.” “I don’t even know what ‘accusatory’ means, so how could that be my tone?” “You were trying to make me feel badly[2] for having a friend.” “No I wasn’t.” She put her hand with the ring on it in her hair and said, “You know, I actually *was* talking about Grandma, Oskar, but it’s true, I need friends, too. What’s wrong with that?” I shrugged my shoulders. “Don’t you think Dad would want me to have friends?”

Excerpt from EXTREMELY LOUD AND INCREDIBLY CLOSE*: A novel by Jonathan Safran Foer. Copyright © 2005 by Jonathan Safran Foer. Reprinted by permission of Haughtan Mifflin Company. All rights reserved*

1 Amsterdam: street name
2 feel badly [sic]: feel bad

Worksheet:

maximum number
of points attainable

I. Questions on the text

Read all the questions first, then answer them in the given order. Use your own words as far as is appropriate.

1. Sum up what happens on the day Oskar's father dies and what Oskar, alone in his room, does a couple of years later. 20

2. Examine Oskar's father's message. What do the message and its language tell you about the situation he finds himself in and about his feelings? 20

3. Analyse Oskar's relationship with his mother and his grandmother. To what extent does his behaviour towards these two people characterize him? 20

4. Examine the protagonists' strategies of coping with the loss of a father, a son or a husband. 10

5. How does the author use language to convey Oskar's distress? 10

II. Composition

Choose *one* of the following topics. Write about 150 to 200 words. 40

1. A real friend is one who walks in when the rest of the world walks out.

2. Security versus individual liberties – have the measures taken since 9/11 gone too far?

3. Describe the cartoon as precisely as you can.
   Sum up what you regard as its intention.

   FDNY: New York City
   Fire Department

© Copyright 2004 Daryl Cale –
All rights reserved

III. Translation

Translate the following text into German: 40/160

That September 11th changed America dramatically is hardly open to debate: George Bush's presidency has been about little else since then. But some of the changes have been unexpected. Who would have guessed, as a shocked country rallied round the flag, that five years later partisan divisions would be deeper than ever? Who would have guessed, as the president pledged that "the people who knocked these buildings down will hear all of us soon," that five years later Mr bin Laden would still be at liberty?
The attacks brought an abrupt end to the "holiday from history" that followed the fall of the Soviet Union. They also brought an abrupt end to America's sense of invulnerability: for all its military might, the country was wide open to attack from fanatics living in caves in Afghanistan.
All this produced a mood of soul-searching. It also produced something more visceral: a desire for revenge.

From: *The Economist*, September 2nd 2006

Lösungsvorschlag

I. Questions on the text

1. *The events of September 11 are printed in italics and are framed by the later ones, in ordinary print. You are not supposed to comment on Oskar's feelings and thoughts, so stick to the events.*

   In the morning of September 11 Oskar returns to his home and innocently opens the messages on the answering machine of the family phone. There are five, all from his father, who is trapped in one of the Twin Towers after the first terrorist attack and is trying to contact his family. Oskar first considers calling his mother and grandmother but then listens to his father's words again. He is completely confused about what to do and when the phone rings again he does not dare to answer it. Instead, he grabs his dad's 'emergency money' (l. 27) and goes to buy an identical phone from an electronics shop where he sees the collapse of the first Tower on TV. Back home he copies the old greeting message to the new phone and hides it in his wardrobe.
   One night a few years later, he feels the need to listen to his father again. He plays the painful messages, with the volume turned low, so as not to wake his mother. Then he contacts his grandmother on his walkie-talkie.

2. *Here you are to analyze the content and language of message 2 to explain the circumstances and his father's feelings. Give evidence from the text!*

   His father mentions that something has happened, that there is smoke in the building, which could also explain his difficulty in speaking, (l. 38 f.) and that he is waiting for the firemen (l. 41). His sentence structure betrays his anxiety – there are stops within the sentences (But I. just, l. 39) which are short and often incomplete (Sorry if, l. 37). On the other hand, he makes efforts not to upset his family by using understatement (a bit smoky, l. 38), and telling them not to worry, that he is alright and everything is fine (l. 39). He also expresses the hope that the firemen will arrive soon (l. 40).

3. *You will find evidence for your answer in both parts of the text.*

   Oskar cares a lot about his mother: She is the first person that comes to his mind after listening to his father's words. It is of the highest importance to him to protect her (l. 27) and he knows that the messages will break her heart – so he keeps the tape hidden from her in the following years. Later we learn that he still has not come to terms with the fact that a new boyfriend has come between him and her.
   He sees his grandmother almost every day (l. 50 f.) and seems to contact her frequently on their private walkie-talkie line. She also is a very important person in his life and the second one he thinks of calling after listening to the messages. He is confused about her obviously imaginary 'renter' who satisfies her need for friendship, as his mother tells him.
   Oskar behaves like a substitute father, which is unusual for a child – he wants to protect his mother from emotional shock and does not want to share her or his grandmother with someone else. Even several years later he tries to make his mother feel guilty about taking a boyfriend ("your accusatory tone", l. 57).

4. *Don't overlook the plural in 'protagonists'!*

   Oskar does not accept his father's death ("It just wasn't possible", l. 6). He has his messages locked up in his closet as his personal memento. He thinks a lot about them (l. 6 f.) but tries to live on as if nothing had happened, only – years later – he needs to listen to them again.

Oskar's grandmother has invented a 'renter' to overcome her loneliness after the loss of her son. His mother is the most realistic person of the family – she accepts the inevitable and has found someone new to keep her company.

5. *Don't bring in narrative techniques like point-of-view here – only language is to be considered. You should, however, mention the frequent use of 'I'.*

   Short sentences and repetitions (e.g. l. 20), as well as the frequent use of the personal pronoun I, show that Oskar is highly affected by the events and his own helplessness. This is also noticeable in his exact indication of the times when his father called. The comparison 'how a light fills the room' (l. 36) emphasizes the importance of his father for him and how he misses him even after all those years.

II. Composition

1. *Even when you take the trouble to look up a simple word like 'friend' in you dictionary you will get useful ideas, from expressions related to 'friend' and 'friendship', and a proverb you can use in this context: A friend in need is a friend indeed.*

   The word friend has come to be used rather indiscriminately nowadays. It stands for people you know and like. Their number can run up to hundreds and even may include people that 'walk in' from certain Internet sites.
   It is rather easy to have people around you whom you consider your friends. They will talk to you when you meet, accept your invitations to parties and spend some of their free time with you. When you, however, find yourself in a critical situation, a lot of these 'friends' will walk out on you. If, for example, the general opinion about you changes dramatically, because of unjust or even justified accusations, not many will stand up for you. If you desperately need a large sum of money to escape from some serious difficulty, most will turn away from you rather than help you out. Should you develop a psychological problem that makes you unacceptable for society – who would still stand by you?
   These are moments, when you discover who your true friends are – the ones that 'walk in' – because a friend in need is a friend indeed.

2. *First you should make a list of such security measures to provide some examples for your essay. You can use one of them in your introduction. Avoid being too general.*

   In the wake of 9/11 thousands of travelers are forced to part with seemingly harmless objects of personal hygiene. Security guards at international airport check-ins will mercilessly confiscate your nail file and your shampoo bottle.
   In many areas of life security has tightened considerably. Observation by video cameras is omnipresent, tapping of phones and electronic messages are common practice. People are treated as potential criminals, especially if they look Islamic. Arrests are made far too quickly, without careful previous investigation. The most spectacular infringement of individual liberties is taking place at Guantánamo, where suspects have been unlawfully imprisoned for years, without formal indictment – even torture is not excluded! German authorities as well cannot resist the temptation to introduce measures which run counter to some articles in our Basic Law, which protect private homes, correspondence and the right to peaceful assembly.
   Despite the public discussion about the justification for these measures, people seem to be willing to accept them, as long as they lower the risk of terrorist attacks. It is a small inconvenience to suffer lengthy checks of persons and baggage, if it becomes less likely that your flight will end in disaster. When it, however, comes to massive viola-

tions of civil liberties, only few will applaud. It has been a long and painful process for mankind to establish respect for individual liberties and they should not lightly be tampered with, not even in times like these.

3. *The description of the cartoon should not be too difficult. Don't, however, overdo it, as you have only a limited number of words for the whole essay and the second, equally important part asks you to comment on the artist's intention. Don't forget to refer to the details in the picture, which lead you to your opinion. The verb aspect of description is the present progressive tense.*

The cartoon, which was published on the 2nd anniversary of 9/11, shows a little girl who is parading on her clothes various references to this event. The front of her cap presents the motto 'I remember 911', her T-shirt design refers to the heroes of the New York City Fire Department, set into the smoke from the burning Twin Towers, with Miss Liberty sitting on her pedestal in disbelief. Her left hand is holding a pennant with the bald-headed eagle on top and the famous words of the rescue team – let's roll! The girl is drinking from a '911 Spirit Big Gulp' cup and wearing 911 loafers. The number 911 is the most prominent element in the picture, besides the stars and stripes of the American flag.
The cartoon shows the way in which some Americans deal with 9/11 and criticizes it at the same time. The girl's extremely exaggerated outfit expresses the artist's dislike for the hype which has developed in the aftermath of the catastrophe, especially its commercial exploitation (cap, sunglasses, shoes, shirt, bag, cup). This girl cannot possibly understand the implications of the tragedy and stands for the superficial and nationalistic attitude taken by many US citizens in order to cope with it.

III. Translation

Dass der 11. September Amerika auf dramatische Weise verändert hat, steht kaum zur Diskussion[1]: die Präsidentschaft George Bushs dreht sich seitdem fast um nichts anderes[2]. Aber einige der Veränderungen waren unerwartet. Wer hätte geahnt, als ein geschocktes Land sich um seine Flagge scharte, dass fünf Jahre später die Parteien[3] tiefer zerstritten sein würden als jemals zuvor? Wer hätte in dem Moment[4], als der Präsident gelobte, dass „die Leute, die diese Gebäude zum Einsturz brachten, bald von uns hören werden[5]", vermutet, dass fünf Jahre später Herr Bin Laden noch auf freiem Fuß wäre?
Die Terrorattacken[6] beendeten jäh die „Ferien von der Geschichte", welche dem Untergang der Sowjetunion folgten. Sie beendeten ebenso plötzlich Amerikas Gefühl der Unverwundbarkeit – bei[7] all seiner militärischen Stärke war das Land den Attacken von Fanatikern, die in Höhlen in Afghanistan lebten, schutzlos ausgesetzt.
Dies alles führte zu einer Stimmung der kollektiven[4] Gewissensforschung. Es erzeugte auch etwas Emotionaleres – ein Verlangen nach Rache.

Anmerkungen

1 Auch: „lässt sich kaum bestreiten". „Diskussion" liegt näher bei *debate*
2 *To be about sth.* wörtlich: „handeln von, darum gehen".
3 *Partisan divisions*: *partisan* ist das Adjektiv zu „Partei", *divisions* sind hier „Meinungsverschiedenheiten". Vgl. auch: *bipartisan politics* („die gemeinsame Politik der beiden amerikanischen Parteien")
4 Stilistisch bedingte Einfügungen
5 *Will hear all of us* – so hat er es gesagt! Hier wurde das *all* ignoriert, weil die Aussage dann sinnvoller erscheint
6 Ein häufiger in diesem Zusammenhang gebrauchter Ausdruck
7 Die Bedeutungsvariante von *for* ist hier natürlich „trotz" oder „bei"

Grundkurs Englisch 2008
Textaufgabe I

Minding about the gap

For a people who pride themselves on ignoring social class, Americans are suddenly remarkably interested in it. The country's two leading newspapers are winding up blockbuster series on the subject. The *New York Times's,* in ten parts, is called, simply enough, "Class matters". The *Wall Street Journal's* offering is ostensibly about social mobility. But the series' conclusion is that social mobility has failed to keep up with widening social divisions: in other words, that class does indeed matter.

America has always prided itself on the assumption that talented people are free to rise to their natural level. The country's favourite heroes have been Benjamin Franklin types who made something out of nothing. (The 15th child of a candle-and-soap-maker, Franklin retired a wealthy man at 42.) And its favourite villains have usually been Paris Hilton types, who combine inherited wealth with an obvious lack of talent. "The mass of mankind has not been born with saddles on their backs", said Thomas Jefferson, "nor a favoured few booted and spurred, ready to ride them."

There was more to this than self-flattery. Foreigners have also been struck by America's social fluidity. In the 1830s, Alexis de Tocqueville[1] noted the average American's "hatred" of the "smallest privileges". In the 1860s, Karl Marx remarked that "the position of wage labourer is for a very large part of the American people but a probational[2] state, which they are sure to leave within a longer or shorter term". Joseph Ferrie[3] has crunched[4] the census numbers from 1850 to 1920 and discovered that there was something to all this: more than 80 % of unskilled men in America moved to higher-paying occupations, compared with less than 51 % in Britain.

Today's America gives every impression of being more classless than ever. But beneath this bland surface, social divisions are getting wider. There is little doubt that the social ladder is getting higher. In 1980–2002 the share of total income earned by the top 0.1 % of earners more than doubled. But there is also growing evidence that the ladder is getting stickier: that intergenerational mobility is no longer increasing, as it did during the long post-war boom, and may well be decreasing.

These days the biggest determinant of how far you go in life is how far you go in education. The gap in income between the college-educated and the non-college-educated rose from 31 % in 1979 to 66 % in 1997. But access to college is increasingly determined by social class. The proportion of students from upper-income families at the country's elite colleges is growing once again, having declined dramatically after the second world war. Only 3 % of students in the most selective universities come from the bottom income quartile[5], and only 10 % come from the bottom half of the income scale.

The obvious way to deal with this is to use the education system to guarantee a level playing field. Improve educational opportunities for the poorest Americans, make sure that nobody is turned away from university on grounds of financial need, and you will progressively weaken the link between background and educational success. Alas, there are at least three big problems with this.

The first is that the schools the poorest Americans attend have been getting worse. This is partly a problem of resources, to be sure. But it is even more a problem of bad ideas. The American educational establishment's weakness for airy-fairy notions about the evils of standards and competition is particularly damaging to poor children who have few educational resources of their own to fall back on.

The second is the politics of education reform. The Democrats are too closely tied to the teachers' unions to push for sensible reforms, such as testing and school choice. Their notions of improvement seem limited to pouring in more money.

The third reason is the most powerful of all: that the educated classes still do such a superb job of consolidating and transmitting their privileges. The *New York Times* has supported its series on class with editorials condemning Mr Bush's tax cuts[6]. But even if the paper's argument is correct, it ignores the basic fact that so many people have become so good at passing their educational privileges on to their children. That is not something that is going to go away with a mere tweak of tax policy; after all, they are only doing what comes naturally.

From: The Economist, *June 11th 2005*

1 Alexis de Tocqueville: (1805–1859) French political thinker and historian, well-known for his *Democracy in America,* which was published in 1835 and 1840 after his travels in the United States
2 probational: probationary
3 Joseph Ferrie: an economic historian at Northwestern University
4 crunched: to crunch numbers: to do a lot of calculations in order to find an answer
5 bottom income quartile: *here:* the 25 % of the population with the lowest income
6 Mr Bush's tax cuts: Mr Bush has repeatedly reduced taxes for higher income groups

Worksheet:

maximum number of points attainable

I. Questions on the text

Read all the questions first, then answer them in the given order.
Use your own words as far as is appropriate.

1. Analyse how the writer supports the idea that class was not too important to America. Refer to lines 1 to 21. — 20
2. What do the facts and figures given in the text indicate about the meaning of class in American society today? — 20
3. How should the problem of widening social divisions be dealt with and what difficulties does the writer see with this approach? — 20
4. What is meant by the "gap" and how do Americans feel about it? Refer to the title and the first paragraph. — 10
5. What type of text is this and what kind of reader is it intended for? Justify your answer. — 10

II. Composition

Choose *one* of the following topics. Write about 150 to 200 words. — 40

1. Is money the only attribute that defines social status?
2. Write a review about a film or a book dealing with the American Dream for an Internet forum.

3. Comment on the cartoon.

"I expect you all to be independent, innovative critical thinkers who will do exactly as I say!"

From: http://www.eriding.net

III. Translation

Translate the following text into German: 40 / 160

A man's world?

Few things have been more true than that women get the rough end of life in poor countries. They bear the burden of child-rearing and a disproportionate share of the work of running the household, and rarely have real equality before the law.

Yet the sexual balance of power in the world is changing, slowly but surely. The most obvious changes are in education. The number of countries in which the gap between the sexes has more or less disappeared has risen by a fifth since 1991.

Better educated women help countries move into higher-tech businesses, as is happening in India. Female education is closely correlated with smaller family size, so the growth in the world's population should continue to slow. More wives will also have a better education and possibly a higher income than their husbands, which is likely to change family roles profoundly.

From: *The Economist,* November 1st 2007

Lösungsvorschlag

I. Questions on the text

1. *Even though you are asked to refer to lines 1 to 21, most answers to this question are found in paragraphs two and three (ll. 7–21).*

   The writer starts out by saying that Americans have always prided themselves on "ignoring social class" (l. 1). He supports this idea by stating the example of Founding Father Benjamin Franklin, who rose from rags to riches, and illustrates his career by giving details from his life. On the other hand, he mentions Paris Hilton who, though being born into a wealthy family, is notorious for her "obvious lack of talent" (l. 11) and therefore disliked by the public.
   Next, the author gives some quotations to prove his point: The first is by Thomas Jefferson who stresses the idea that every man has equal possibilities. In the 19th century, even foreigners like Alexis de Tocqueville or Karl Marx attested that America offered her citizens an easy climb up the social ladder and upward mobility.
   Finally, the writer says that the statistics actually give evidence that from "1850 to 1920" an American workman had a greater chance of moving up in society than his British counterpart.

2. Contrary to what the text says in the first part about the past, the figures given in the rest of the text indicate that today "class indeed does matter" (l. 6) and that "social divisions are getting wider" (l. 23). First of all, the income gap has widened: within little more than twenty years, the top 0.1 % of earners have doubled their share of total income (ll. 24/25). But even more important, education makes all the difference: in 1997, people with a college education earned 66 % more than those without (a gap twice as big as that of not even twenty years ago). What makes things worse is the fact that access to top universities is determined by family income: only 3 % of the students at prestigious colleges come from the bottom income bracket, only 10 % from its lower half. To sum up, social mobility from one generation to the next has become stagnant: in the author's words, the social "ladder is getting stickier" (ll. 25/26).

3. *There are two questions put into one both referring to the last part of the text (from l. 35 to the end); it is very useful in answering part two of this question that the article is so clearly structured here (The first …; the second …; the third reason …).*

   Since education has become the decisive factor in creating social equality – or rather: inequality – equal opportunities in education should be offered to all Americans regardless of their income.
   But this is easier said than done and meets with a number of obstacles: the standards of the schools attended by America's poor have become worse. "Pouring in more money" (l. 47) as the Democrats suggest, may help; but on the other hand, there is also the "problem of bad ideas" (l. 41): the author says that American teachers – and especially their unions – are not convinced by ideas like standards and competition; therefore "sensible reforms" (l. 46) which might help especially the poor children, are unlikely to come into effect. Last but not least, the educated classes are interested in passing on their privileges only to their own children, and will continue to do so which is the obvious thing to do for parents since "they are only doing what comes naturally" (ll. 53/54).

4. In this context the word "gap" means the "social divisions" (ll. 5/6) within the USA today. The first paragraph says that Americans tend to think of themselves as a classless society, i.e. class distinction does not exist in their country. On the other hand, it seems to be a subject which is attracting more and more attention to the point where two of the country's leading newspapers have come up with a series on the subject, both of which have come to the conclusion that "class matters" (l. 4).

5. *Whereas part one of this question can be answered precisely, you can only guess when it comes to answering part two. Giving evidence, therefore, becomes very important!*

   The text is a non-fictional article from a leading English magazine which presents both argumentative and informative parts (e. g. background information stated in percentages). It is intended for an educated and politically interested reader: the text contains a number of sociological and political terms (e. g. "social fluidity", l. 15; "income quartile", ll. 33/34; "consolidating and transmitting their privileges", l. 49), it refers to a wide range of personalities like Benjamin Franklin, Karl Marx and Paris Hilton, and current political issues like "Mr Bush's tax cuts" (l. 50) or the close ties of the Democrats to the teachers' unions (ll. 45/46), on the assumption that the readers are familiar with these terms.

II. Composition

1. Being rich is something most people dream of, not only because money makes life a lot easier but also because rich people usually enjoy high social status in our society. And there are certainly people who admire and envy the rich, simply for the only reason that they are rich, regardless of how they obtained their wealth.
   But I think there are other things which define someone's social status as well. This is true for certain professions. Doctors, for example, need not necessarily make a fortune, but still they are highly thought of because their job involves a high degree of responsibility, along with personal commitment and is regarded as socially useful.
   And it is not only an academic training that brings high social status. In general, being educated and cultivated are two other prestigious qualities. The rich and powerful have always liked to be seen as friends of artists, musicians or intellectuals because there seems to be something glorious, something special about them, which money cannot buy.
   To sum up, the fact that celebrities like Paris Hilton are sneered at because they only inherited the wealth they do not really deserve, is proof enough that however much people might adore money it is not the only attribute that defines social status.

2. *There are a countless number of books and films which deal with the American Dream. One of the books, which is widely read at school, is F. Scott Fitzgerald's classic* The Great Gatsby. *Even though it has a rather critical view of the American Dream it is an excellent choice to write about. (See also: 2008-10)*

   Published more than 80 years ago, F. Scott Fitzgerald's novel *The Great Gatsby* has lost nothing of its magic and power for the modern reader, mainly because of its hero, the ambiguous and mysterious Jay Gatsby.

Coming from a very humble background in the Midwest, Gatsby has managed to accumulate enormous wealth within a few years. His is the typical rags-to-riches-tale which lies at the basis of the American Dream: anyone who uses his talents and tries hard enough can make it to the top.
Even though Gatsby seems to live extravagantly in his chateau-like house, he never actually joins in his parties, nor does he drink or indulge in any other frivolous pleasures. But the fact that the reader is never really told how he acquired all his wealth (there are only rumours, and his few "friends" are crooks and gangsters) makes him suspicious. On the other hand, there is the world of Old Money, the world of the Buchanans, including Daisy, but they are shallow and selfish and sneer at newcomers like Gatsby.
In the end, after Gatsby's death, the disillusioned narrator packs up and leaves the glitzy, but corrupt, superficial world of New York in the 1920s, to go back to the more modest, but healthier life in the Midwest from where he came.

3. The cartoon shows a scene in a classroom: a teacher is standing in front of a class where you can see a few pupils looking at him attentively, curiously, some even timidly. Behind the teacher there is a blackboard covered with illegible writing. The teacher addresses his pupils saying, "I expect you all to be independent, innovative critical thinkers who will do exactly as I say!"
The cartoon is funny because of the obvious contradiction between the teacher's words and the situation. On the one hand, he voices the creed of today's education: its main objective is supposed to create young people who are ready to meet the demands of our society's requirements, like being cooperative and creative. On the other hand, it is obvious that this teacher fails to fulfill his own pedagogical objectives: the way he looks at the pupils and the exclamation mark at the end of his sentence show that he will tolerate no questioning of his authority.
The cartoon becomes less funny when you realize that it actually reflects the reality in most classrooms today. Most teaching is dominated by rather traditional methods and in particular by a staff who expect pupils "to do exactly as they say".
But – come to think of it, does our society really want independent critical thinkers?

III. Translation

Eine Männerwelt[1]?

Kaum etwas ist wahrer[2] als die Tatsache, dass Frauen in den armen Ländern im Leben den Kürzeren ziehen. Sie tragen die Bürde der Kindererziehung ebenso[3] wie einen unverhältnismäßig hohen Anteil an der Haushaltsführung[4] und nur selten sind sie vor dem Gesetz wirklich gleichgestellt.

Dennoch ändert sich langsam aber sicher das Gleichgewicht der Kräfte der Geschlechter[5] in der Welt. Die offensichtlichsten Veränderungen gehen im Bereich der Bildung vor sich[6]. Die Anzahl der Länder, in denen die Kluft zwischen den Geschlechtern mehr oder weniger verschwunden ist, hat sich seit 1991 um ein Fünftel erhöht.

Besser ausgebildete Frauen helfen ihren Ländern, sich auf höher technisierte Geschäftsbereiche umzustellen[7], wie es derzeit in Indien geschieht. Die Ausbildung der Frauen steht in enger Wechselbeziehung zu kleineren Familien[8], weshalb sich das Wachstum der Weltbevölkerung wohl weiterhin verlangsamen dürfte. Mehr Ehefrauen werden auch eine bessere Ausbildung genießen und damit auch möglicherweise ein höheres Einkommen als ihre Männer[9], was die Rollenverteilung in der Familie wahrscheinlich tiefgreifend ändern wird.

Anmerkungen

1 *Eine Welt für Männer* ist ebenso möglich wie Übersetzungen, die *man* im Singular belassen
2 Freier wäre möglich: *Es ist eine Binsenweisheit, dass …*
3 Stilistisch bedingte Einfügung
4 *Running the household* meint im Zusammenhang dieses Textes mehr als nur Abwaschen oder Fensterputzen
5 Wem die Aufeinanderfolge zweier Genitive nicht gefällt: die Übersetzung *das Kräfteverhältnis der Geschlechter* gibt den Sinn ebenfalls wieder
6 *Are* lässt sich aus stilistischen Gründen freier handhaben (z. B. auch *findet man*)
7 *Move into high-tech businesses*: hier muss eine freiere Übersetzung gefunden werden; andere Möglichkeiten wären z.B. *umstellen auf* für *move into* oder *Industriezweige* für *businesses*
8 *Size* kann weggelassen werden
9 *Wives/husbands*: es reicht aus, wenn im Deutschen einmal auf die Ehe hingewiesen wird

Grundkurs Englisch 2008
Textaufgabe II

The Locked Room by Paul Auster

One incident is particularly vivid to me. It concerns a birthday party that Fanshawe and I were invited to in the first or second grade, which means that it falls at the very beginning of the period I am able to talk about with any precision. It was a Saturday afternoon in spring, and we walked to the party with another boy, a friend of ours named Dennis Walden. Dennis had a much harder life than either of us did: an alcoholic mother, an overworked father, innumerable brothers and sisters. I had been to his house two or three times – a great, dark ruin of a place – and I can remember being frightened by his mother, who made me think of a fairy-tale witch. She would spend the whole day behind the closed door of her room, always in her bathrobe, her pale face a nightmare of wrinkles, poking her head out every now and then to scream something at the children. On the day of the party, Fanshawe and I had been duly equipped with presents to give the birthday boy, all wrapped in colored paper and tied with ribbons. Dennis, however, had nothing, and he felt bad about it. I can remember trying to console him with some empty phrase or other: it didn't matter, no one really cared, in all the confusion it wouldn't be noticed. But Dennis did care, and that was what Fanshawe immediately understood. Without any explanation, he turned to Dennis and handed him his present. Here, he said, take this one – I'll tell them I left mine at home. My first reaction was to think that Dennis would resent the gesture, that he would feel insulted by Fanshawe's pity. But I was wrong. He hesitated for a moment, trying to absorb this sudden change of fortune, and then nodded his head, as if acknowledging the wisdom of what Fanshawe had done. It was not an act of charity so much as an act of justice, and for that reason Dennis was able to accept it without humiliating himself. The one thing had been turned into the other. It was a piece of magic, a combination of off-handedness and total conviction, and I doubt that anyone but Fanshawe could have pulled it of.

After the party, I went back with Fanshawe to his house. His mother was there, sitting in the kitchen, and she asked us about the party and whether the birthday boy had liked the present she had bought for him. Before Fanshawe had a chance to say anything, I blurted out the story of what he had done. I had no intention of getting him into trouble, but it was impossible for me to keep it to myself. Fanshawe's gesture had opened up a whole new world for me: the way someone could enter the feelings of another and take them on so completely that his own were no longer important. It was the first truly moral act I had witnessed, and nothing else seemed worth talking about. Fanshawe's mother was not so enthusiastic, however. Yes, she said, that was a kind and generous thing to do, but it was also wrong. The present had cost her money, and by giving it away Fanshawe had in some sense stolen that money from her. On top of that, Fanshawe had acted impolitely by showing up without a present – which reflected badly on her, since she was the one responsible for his actions. Fanshawe listened carefully to his mother and did not say a word. After she was finished, he still did not speak, and she asked him if he understood. Yes, he said, he understood. It probably would have ended there, but then, after a short pause, Fanshawe went on to say that he still thought he was right. It didn't matter to him how she felt, he would do the same thing again the next time. A scene followed this little exchange. Mrs Fanshawe became angry at his impertinence, but Fanshawe stuck to his guns, refusing to budge under the barrage of her reprimands. Eventually, he was ordered to his room and I was told to leave the house. I was appalled by his mother's unfairness, but when I tried to speak up in his defense, Fanshawe waved me off. Rather than protest any more, he took his punishment silently and disappeared into his room.

From: Paul Auster, The Locked Room *in:* The New York Trilogy, *Collected Novels Vol. 1, London 2004*

Worksheet:

maximum number of points attainable

I. Questions on the text

Read all the questions first, then answer them in the given order. Use your own words as far as is appropriate.

1. Describe the three boys' social backgrounds and the relationship between them. — 20
2. Dennis feels bad about not having a present. Compare the narrator's and Fanshawe's reactions to this situation. How does the narrator judge Fanshawe's behaviour? — 20
3. What does the scene at Fanshawe's house reveal about the personalities of the three main characters (the narrator, Fanshawe and his mother)? — 20
4. Analyse the imagery used in lines 42/43. How does it reflect the outcome of this scene? — 10
5. Examine the narrator's perspective and choice of language. What effect do they have on the reader? — 10

II. Composition

Choose *one* of the following topics. Write about 150 to 200 words. — 40

1. Childhood determines the rest of your life.
2. Write a review of a film dealing with parent-child relationships for an Internet forum.

3. Comment on the cartoon.

From: http://www.cartoonstock.com

III. Translation

Translate the following text into German: 40/160

The text is an excerpt from Paul Auster's acceptance speech for the Prince of Asturias Prize for Letters, which he received in October 2006.

Fiction exists in a somewhat different realm from the other arts. Its medium is language, and language is something we share with others. From the moment we learn to talk, we begin to develop a hunger for stories. Those of us who can remember our childhoods will recall how ardently we relished the moment of the bedtime story, when our mother or father would sit down beside us in the semi-dark and read from a book of fairy tales.

Those of us who are parents will have no trouble conjuring up the rapt attention in the eyes of our children when we read to them. Why this intense desire to listen? Fairy tales are often cruel and violent. One would think this material would be too frightening for a young child, but what these stories allow the child to experience is precisely an encounter with his own fears in a perfectly safe and protected environment.

From: *The Observer,* November 5th 2006

Lösungsvorschlag

I. Questions on the text

1. Though there is not much information in the text we can assume that Fanshawe's and the narrator's parents have no problems in affording the birthday presents for the "birthday boy" (ll. 11/12) and wrapping them nicely, in "colored paper and … ribbons" (l. 12). Dennis, however, lives in a family of many children. His father has to work hard to make ends meet, his mother is an alcoholic, a "witch" who screams at her children. Their house is a "ruin of a place" (l. 7) and there seems to be no money for a birthday present.
   Fanshawe and the narrator are obviously good friends – after all, the narrator accompanies Fanshawe to his home after the party. Dennis is probably not one of their close friends, as he is described as just "another boy" (l. 4).

2. *This question, like the first one, is also a double question.*

   The narrator misjudges the extent of Dennis' embarrassment and tries to make light of the situation by suggesting it wasn't really important to bring a present, and nobody would notice it anyway. Fanshawe, however, understands the boy's dilemma at once and reacts in a more practical and selfless way – he gives him his own present. The narrator at first doesn't appreciate Fanshawe's gesture. He thinks it might humiliate Dennis. When he sees that Dennis accepts it as "an act of justice" (l. 21) he admires Fanshawe for his "truly moral act" (l. 31) and realises that nobody else could have resolved the situation in a better way.

3. The narrator is deeply impressed by Fanshawe's gallantry and can't contain himself in front of his mother. He is an innocent and impulsive character who means well and, again, shows himself as a poor judge of situations. He proves to be a good friend of Fanshawe's.
   Fanshawe's mother doesn't come off well in the discussion. Far from being "not so enthusiastic" (l. 32 f.) she emphasises that on the one hand her son had "cost her money" (l. 34) and wasted it, on the other hand she would make a bad impression on others for not providing a present. She is shown as a materialistic, heartless and unfair person who worries more about what people might think of her instead of appreciating her son's generous attitude.
   Fanshawe doesn't defend himself much and firmly stands up to his act even if he listened attentively to his mother's telling-off – he would do the same thing again. This makes him appear as a mature personality who sticks to his moral standards, even under pressure.

4. The author uses metaphors with a military connotation. Someone who sticks to his guns and takes the barrage of enemy fire without retreating is a hero and deserves a medal of honor. These images reflect the hostility of the situation and Fanshawe's bravery in front of his mother's accusations and her attempts to make him admit that his conduct was a mistake. When he finally has to retreat he does so as the moral winner of this verbal combat.

5. *Be careful to answer the three points in the question. For 'perspective' see also 'Tips for Questions on the Text'/Analyse the perspective/point of view.*

   The text is written in a limited first-person perspective. It is seen through the eyes of an adult who remembers an episode from his childhood. This is reflected in the language. The narrator's vocabulary and style is sometimes more sophisticated than a child's could be. Some examples are: 'vivid' (l. 1), 'innumerable' (l. 6), 'console' (l. 13), 'humiliating' (l. 22), or 'barrage of … reprimands' (l. 43).
   The effect on the reader is that he sympathises with the narrator and tends to share his views. A more critical and pedantic reader might ask himself how a child could possibly evaluate the situation so precisely.

II. Composition

1. *Take a few minutes to think about childhood conditions which may play a decisive role in a person's future life. It is widely recognized in science that childhood does have a great influence (you could use this in your introduction), so there is no need to discuss the pros and cons much, as long as you mention the genetic factor. As always, you can also describe personal experiences, or treat the matter lightly, for example by tracing the childhood feats of a computer wizard and his rise to saviour of mankind.*

   Many a famous footballer is known to have started kicking the ball around in his backyard as soon as he could walk. Now he is making millions as a professional and may well serve as an example for the theory that childhood determines the rest of your life. It is true that there is no break between childhood and adulthood. Nobody wakes up on the day of his 18th birthday to find he is a changed person.
   What we are biologically is determined by our genes from the beginning, whereas our personality and our future status in life may well be affected by a child's social background. It makes quite a difference whether we are born into a poor or wealthy family. This accident of birth may decide on what kind of education we can expect to receive and influences the chances for a future career. The attention a child gets from his parents also has a very significant impact. It is well known that children who were mistreated at home are often seriously damaged in their emotional and social development for the rest of their lives. Affectionate parents and family members are the best role models in a child's development. Other children you socialise with in kindergarten and in school also shape to a great extent your personality. As the example of the football player indicates one's early interests play an important role as well.
   Growing up and living your life is a permanent process of formation but I have no doubt that essential foundations are laid down in your childhood.

2. *As you probably know an Internet forum is a website where you can place your opinions anonymously or as a registered participant on specific subjects, to be read by other users. Unlike in a chat room you are not online simultaneously with others. The contributions are rather short and, depending on the intellectual level of the forum, are often written in pretty colloquial language, are careless of mistakes (which is, of course, not a valid excuse in exam conditions), full of Internet slang, are subjective or even provocative, and often try to be funny. It remains to be seen if this new kind of Abitur task will have a future, as it is very difficult to evaluate.*
   If you write to a serious forum try to stick to formal categories: introduce the film, summarise it briefly and comment on the aspect of parent-child relationships. You do not have to choose a film you have seen in class (which makes it more difficult for the corrector).

*We picked a movie you should be familiar with (*The Dead Poets Society*) as it is a classic in the teaching of English and not a film based on a book (the book appeared later and is only half as good!). We decided to write in a colloquial style which is typical of young people, even if many blogs are also quite formal.*

Hi there, I'd like to have my say in the discussion of DPS and bring up the parent-child relationship in it. Sure, I agree that the movie is basically about stuff like 'freedom of thought and individuality' and the teaching of such at schools, but hey! – the story of Neil Perry and how his creepy parents deal with him really knocked me out, and I'm not the only one, believe me! OK, his mother is a poor soul and totally henpecked by her man. But: Who says she can't show a bit of the old affection for her son, if necessary behind the bully's back? Anyway, she isn't a terribly good mom, as you can see by the thoughtless birthday present she sent (!) him. It's a load of rubbish he never wanted in the first place and gets rid of as soon as he can.
And old man Perry – he is in no way interested in what goes on in Neil. All he wants is for him to have a great career, no fun and no play – big deal! But listen, what's wrong with a guy who loves poetry and acting? This joke of a father doesn't give a damn what playing Puck means to his son. All he feels is blind fury at his 'insubordination'. And then – punishing him by removing him from his school and friends and sending him off to a military academy of all places! Can anybody not understand why this had to push Neil to the limit? When I first saw the movie I was still hoping for a happy ending, but no – Neil went on to kill himself – some hero! A completely stupid sacrifice, all because of insane family relationships. Hopefully, this movie will teach some parents a lesson!

3. *Keep your description of the picture short – it is really irrelevant, and it is hardly possible to squeeze much detail out of it. First try to discover what the cartoon wants to say – in this case it seems to criticize the stupidity of people who make inconsiderate gifts – and then proceed to comment on this kind of behaviour. If you like you can include examples of people you know and experiences you had. In our composition we decided not to take the topic too seriously – which is always an alternative, especially when you don't like the topic.*

In the cartoon a man is entering a shop with the name or motto 'It is the thought that counts!' In the window an assortment of ridiculous nondescript objects are advertised as 'totally useless gifts!'. The humour of it lies in the stupidity of the idea that anyone would be pleased with such a present.
Let us assume you are invited to a birthday party. It is perfectly clear that the pleasure of your company alone will, under ordinary circumstances, not be enough to please your host – unless you wrap yourself in gift paper and make a few appropriate promises. So you better decide to bring something. The choice of your gift will express the degree of your appreciation of the birthday boy or girl: something you know they have always wanted but never expected to get, or something that shows by its sheer value how precious the recipient is to you. But alas – you are a thrifty or careless person and don't care about the host's feelings and the sneers of the other guests! So why not bring a totally useless gift from the shop, or one that has clearly changed hands a couple of times because everybody wanted to get rid of it? As a precaution against criticism or disappointment you could defend yourself by insisting that it is the thought that counts. Another strategy could be to give it all a humorous twist, emphasize the absurdity of the gift and refer to the host's fantastic sense of humour whose tastes go far beyond the useful and common. Wait and see what you will get in return one day.

III. Translation

Die erzählende Literatur[1] herrscht in einem etwas anderen Reich[2] als die übrigen Künste. Ihr Medium ist die Sprache, und Sprache ist etwas was wir mit anderen Menschen[3] gemein haben. Von dem Augenblick an, in dem wir sprechen lernen, beginnen wir auch[3] einen Hunger nach Geschichten zu entwickeln. Diejenigen von uns, die sich an ihre Kindheit erinnern können, werden daran zurückdenken, mit welch glühender Begeisterung[4] wir die Zeit[5] der Gutenachtgeschichte genossen, wenn Mutter oder Vater sich wie so oft[6] im Halbdunkel neben uns setzten und aus einem Märchenbuch vorlasen.
Die Eltern unter uns werden sich ohne weiteres[7] an die hingerissene Aufmerksamkeit in den Augen unserer Kinder beim Vorlesen erinnern[8] können. Woher kommt dieses intensive Bedürfnis zuzuhören? Märchen sind oft grausam und gewalttätig. Man möchte meinen, dass diese Stoffe[9] ein kleines Kind zu sehr erschrecken würden, aber was diese Geschichten dem Kind an Erfahrung ermöglichen, ist eben[3] genau eine Konfrontation10 mit seinen eigenen Ängsten in einer vollkommen sicheren und behüteten Umgebung.

Anmerkungen

1 *Fiction* ist, genau genommen, nur die erzählende Literatur, beinhaltet zum Beispiel keine Sachtexte. *Literatur* wird wohl auch akzeptiert werden
2 *Herrschen* statt *existieren* wurde verwendet, um den Begriff *realm* (Reich, Königreich) mit einzubeziehen
3 Stilistisch bedingte Einfügungen
4 *Ardently* (leidenschaftlich, glühend)
5 *Zeit* ist logischer als *Moment.*
6 *Would sit down* als Ausdruck einer immer wiederkehrenden Tätigkeit in der Vergangenheit. Möglich auch: *pflegten sich zu uns zu setzen*
7 *No trouble*: wörtlich *mühelos*
8 Dieser Satz kann auch präsentisch übersetzt werden *(... werden sich vorstellen können ... vorlesen)*
9 Der Plural ist hier logischer
10 Auch: *Begegnung*

Leerseiten verbilligen in diesem Fall die Herstellung des Buches!

Grundkurs Englisch 2009
Textaufgabe I

Britons are leaving the gym

A world without the gym: a glorious Utopia, or the road to (yet more) national slothfulness[1]? Whichever your view, the death of the treadmill has arrived. For the first time since gyms muscled their way into the public consciousness in the Eighties, there has been a sharp decline in the number of people joining them.

Open a copy of *Grazia* or *heat*[2], and you will find confirmation. A decade ago we were bombarded with images of celebs on their way to and from the gym. Now we are more likely to learn about Geri Halliwell's love of swinging kettleballs[3] in the park.

Five years ago, where gyms and health clubs were at the peak of their popularity, 8.7 million of us in Britain were members. But statistics reveal that 54,000 fewer people took out gym memberships during 2007 than they had 18 months previously. And there is worse to come, according to business analysts.

Thanks partly to changed lifestyle choices and partly to the economy, the gym's heyday has come and gone. Just as Jane Fonda[4] and her legwarmers were superseded by the treadmill in the late Eighties, so in the new millennium the gym has been elbowed aside by yoga, Pilates and outdoor programmes such as park circuits.

Besides, we have realized that gyms don't work. Research last year at the University of Leicester confirmed that the fitness-industry boom has had little impact on the nation's girth. Sociologist Dr Jennifer Smith Maguire, the study's author, says: "Many Western countries have experienced this strange situation, with fitness and exercise industries expanding alongside problems of inactivity."

There is a growing realization, too, that gyms are sterile environments, and that their clinical approach to working out becomes simply boring after a while. This may help to explain why, alongside the gym's demise, alternative forms of exercise are flourishing. It has become obvious to consumers that there are other, more appealing, means of burning calories.

According to Dr Smith Maguire, gyms focus on "image rather than health", which tends to mean that their customers' commitment is sustained for only a limited period. Psychologists are convinced that the ploys used by the fitness industry to attract new members will have short-lived health benefits, if any, for those they attract. "Gyms feed into people's insecurities about their weight and appearance, and get them to join in the belief that they can change those things," says Martin Hagger, a social and health psychologist at the University of Nottingham. "Yet it has been shown time and again in studies that extrinsic motivational factors – such as improving the way you look, or losing weight – are unlikely to achieve the desired results."

"If people exercise simply to shed fat, not because they enjoy it, they will either give up before they achieve their goal or will think 'job done' when it is finally reached, then revert to their old habits of inactivity."

What has been lost, it seems, is an accurate perception of what activity means. "People think you need to join a gym to get fitter, but activity doesn't have to be done in a single 60 to 90-minute session," says Dr Colin Waine, chairman of the NOF[5]. "The real key is to build exercise into your daily life. You can become much more active without spending anything."

Dr Beckie Lang, of the Association for the Study of Obesity, agrees. "Consistency is what matters – and that means that activity must become a habit." Many studies have linked moderate daily activity to more significant and longer-lasting improvements in health than the occasional gut-busting session at a gym.

Dr Waine says that the fitness industry has complicated exercise so much that we make absurd attempts to achieve what could easily be integrated into our day. "People drive to fitness centres, and gyms have installed escalators and lifts to save people walking," he says. "They just need to be more active each day and obesity levels would drop."

Activity need not be done in a single burst. Current government recommendations suggest that 30 minutes of moderate exercise is enough to make an impact on health, but more is obviously better. "This eliminates the common excuses of not having the time or money to exercise," says Dr Lang. "Do whatever you enjoy and you are likely to want to do more – gardening, walking, cycling to work, playing football with the kids. Just get moving."

From: Bee Peta, *The Times,* March 4, 2008

1 slothfulness: unwillingness to work or move
2 *Grazia, heat:* entertainment magazines
3 kettleball: iron ball with a handle, used for fitness training
4 Jane Fonda: American actress; her workout videos made aerobic popular in the 80s
5 NOF: National Obesity Forum

Worksheet: Britons are leaving the gym

maximum number of points attainable

I. Questions on the text

Read all the questions first, then answer them in the given order. Use your own words as far as is appropriate.

1. Describe how the attitude to British gyms has changed. What reasons are given in the text? — 20
2. Outline the theories of psychologists and sociologists concerning the effectiveness of physical exercise in the gym. — 20
3. What are the two contrasting ways of getting fit? Show that the article favours one of them. Refer to lines 38–56. — 20
4. Analyse three stylistic devices the writer uses to make the text interesting. — 20

II. Composition

Choose *one* of the following topics. Write about 150 to 200 words. — 40

1. "The most important thing in the Olympic Games is not winning but taking part; the essential thing in life is not conquering but fighting well." (Pierre de Coubertin)
   Discuss.
2. British public schools place great importance on sport, because they are convinced that 'sport builds character'. Is their conviction justified?

3. Analyse the cartoon and discuss its intended message.

http://obesitymyths.com/myth4.3.htm

III. Translation

Translate the following text into German: 40/160

A more effective way of combating child obesity

The World Health Organisation's report on health inequalities is a stark reminder that tackling the growing gap between rich and poor is not only a moral imperative, but an economic one.

The report concludes a "toxic combination of bad policies, economics and politics is in large measure responsible for the fact that a majority of people in the world do not enjoy the good health that is biologically possible. Social injustice is killing on a grand scale." Those from affluent areas tend to enjoy longer, healthier lives than those from more deprived neighbourhoods.

While governments of any political persuasion are in a position to do something about many of the causes of poor health – the report concludes education and bad housing need particular attention – tackling others requires citizens to change their lifestyle. That will be easier said than done. But failure could prove costly.

From: www.guardian.co.uk/society/joepublic/2008/Aug/29/Health.Children; The Guardian Blog, Bawden Anna, August 29, 2008

Lösungsvorschlag

I. Questions on the text

1. *Questions 1, 2 and 3 basically all point in the same direction: changing attitudes towards the modern health cult and reasons for that change. This may make it difficult to keep the three answers separate. So when answering question 1, be careful to concentrate on the ordinary British man or woman, i. e. to ll. 1 to 25.*

   After gyms had begun to enter Britain's everyday life in the Eighties, they became a well-established entity of entertainment magazines ten years ago, reaching the "peak of their popularity" (l. 8) five years ago. Today, the most obvious sign of a changing attitude towards the gym among Britons is decreasing membership figures: even though a decline of less than one percent within one and a half years can hardly be called "sharp" (l. 4), business analysts fear that there is "worse to come" (l. 11).
   This change is due to a number of different factors. One reason can be found in "changed lifestyle choices" (l. 12), another in the "economy" (l. 12). Furthermore, the fact that many people have realized that gyms did not have the effect they had hoped for has made Britons turn to other forms of activity. Last, the text mentions that "gyms are sterile environments" (l. 21): they lose their appeal after a while and become "boring" (l. 22), and that is why customers are turning away from them.

2. *Here now you are to turn to evidence given by sociologists and psychologists. The text quotes four different experts; but looking ahead at question 3, which expressly refers to ll. 38 to 56, you must concentrate here on ll. 16–37.*

   One of the experts, Dr. Smith Maguire, blames gyms for focusing on "image rather than health" (l. 26), i. e. rather than attracting customers for health benefits gyms appeal to people who are self-consciously concerned about their appearance and their weight (ll. 29–31), as Martin Hagger, another expert explains. People believe that "to shed fat" (l. 35) will make them look better. Once they have achieved that aim – or, even worse, when they find they cannot achieve it – they will drop the activity immediately, especially when they do not "enjoy it" (l. 35), after which, very often, they return to their former lifestyle (they "revert to their old habits of inactivity", ll. 36/37). Consequently, the effects of working out are "short-lived" (l. 29) if anything.

3. Two contrasting ways of getting fit are mentioned in the text. On the one hand, there is the concept of a "single 60 to 90-minute session" (ll. 39/40), perhaps done only once a week ("occasional", l. 46). People tend to think that this will do, especially when they work out very hard ("gut-busting", l. 46). On the other hand, there is the concept of building "exercise into your daily life" (l. 41). "Consistency" (l. 43) is the keyword for a "moderate daily activity" (l. 45) which must be integrated into a person's daily routine and which is even free ("without spending anything", ll. 41/42).
   The text clearly favours the latter. First of all, all the experts quoted – including "government recommendations" (l. 51) – unanimously share that attitude. There is not one single opinion which speaks in favour of health clubs. Secondly, there are sentences without any quotation marks which show that the author has actually internalized the views mentioned (e. g.: "Activity need not be done in a single burst", l. 51). Moreover, the author uses a number of negative words in the context of gyms. They are called "treadmills" (l. 2) right from the beginning, they are "sterile", "boring", their clients have lost "an accurate perception of what activity means" (l. 38) and make "absurd attempts to achieve" (l. 48) their aims. You cannot be more explicit!

4. *We will give you more than just three stylistic devices from which you can choose the ones you find most striking.*

In the opening question (ll. 1–2), we find a good example of *exaggeration* since both "glorious Utopia" as well as "national slothfulness" are expressions far too strong for a rather low-key topic – but they will not fail to attract the attention of both opponents or advocates of the gym.
Two very apt *personifications* can be found in the expressions "gyms muscled their way" (l. 3) and "the gym has been elbowed aside" (l. 14). In both cases, the verbs are taken from parts of the human body, and interest in their physical well-being is just why people go to the gym.
We can also find a number of *metaphors* in this text. The expression "bombarded with images of celebs" (l. 6) is a very obvious one, and the negative image that comes with it fits very well with the writer's intention. The adjectives "sterile" and "clinical" (ll. 21/22) which are used to describe the atmosphere in a gym evoke images of hospitals, surgery and illness rather than of health and joy.
One can also find a number of *alliterations*, e. g. "peak of popularity" (l. 8), "customers' commitment" (l. 27) or "absurd attempts" (l. 48). These alliterations make the text more colourful and attractive.
There is also a constant use of *first-person pronouns* like "we" (l. 5, l. 6, l. 16) or "us" (l. 9), and sometimes the reader is *directly addressed* ("Whichever your view", l. 2; "Open a copy … and you will find", l. 5). Thus, the author tries to establish a sense of community between himself and the reader and convince us of his views.

II. Composition

1. *Both topics 1 and 2 are very similar; so we have chosen two very different ways of looking at the subject, the first being very critical, the second rather positive.*

Pierre de Coubertin, founder of the modern Olympic Games, coined that famous phrase that "not winning but taking part" was the most important thing about them; and he transferred his view to life in general by saying that there "the essential thing … is not conquering but fighting well".
When it comes to sports one can only say that this idea is wishful thinking. In today's sport business, the only thing that counts is winning. Being the first, the fastest, the strongest has become so important that athletes seem to be willing to do almost anything to achieve that aim: they take drugs that build up their muscles, they take risks that might cost their health – and sometimes even their lives – just to come in first. Nobody takes any notice of you if you are only second. And since a lot of money is involved in sports today as well, I fear the situation will only get worse.
Things might still be different in "real" life. But even at school, I have found a growing tendency to fight for ever better marks among my classmates in the last two years. Competition is not yet so important, and it is still thought a flaw in your character if you are considered a swot. But as the final exams have drawn nearer and nearer and admission to university or applying for a job at a bank or at an airline have grown more imminent, I have found that conquering has become more important for all of us rather than just fighting well.

2. *Instead of rephrasing the topic as an introduction we suggest you simply rewrite the title and start straight away with your essay.*

For the last two years, I have been enrolled in an advanced course in PE (i. e. Leistungskurs Sport), and besides improving a number of my skills I think I have learned a lot of other things, from which I hope to benefit in the years to come.
First, I learned that self-discipline can actually be very wholesome. I have become less

self-pitying when it comes to little complaints; on the other hand I have become much more aware of looking after my own health – among other things, I actually gave up smoking which I had started when I was sixteen. And I am convinced that not only my physical health has benefited from giving up some bad habits.
Second, you work in a team much more often than in any other course. That goes without saying for team sports like volleyball or football, but it is also true when it comes to single achievements like doing the long jump or throwing the javelin. You always do things which are immediately and openly discussed by everyone else. And of course, you can only be successful at games like football when you play with your team, not against it.
Third, it is very difficult to cheat when you do sport at school because everyone watches you. So you just don't do it.
To sum up, I can only agree with the view that sport builds character – and if you do it properly, it will build your character well.

3. The cartoon shows a couple sitting on their sofa in their living-room watching television. The man who is smoking and who is rather slumped on his sofa than sitting upright has a remote control in his hand and says to his wife, "I'm thin so I must be healthy."
The man's whole appearance, the way he looks, his posture, all this makes him seem unhealthy – and the only sport he does seems to be flicking around from one TV channel to another. Obviously he must have come across those health programmes which tell people that you are healthy when you are thin. And for many people in our society this equation works. Becoming, being or staying thin, losing weight, attaining the ideal weight have developed into an obsession, up to the point where emulating these images of super-thin super-models may actually become life-threatening. And I have even heard people say that smoking can help lose a few pounds!
I think that the cartoon, without advocating obesity, has just this narrow-minded and short-sighted cult of thinness in mind and criticizes it. People should not forget that leading a healthy life involves much more than just having the ideal weight – like enjoying a good meal with friends or going for a walk every day to develop a strong immune system.

III. Translation

Ein wirksamerer Weg zur Bekämpfung der Fettleibigkeit bei Kindern

Der Bericht der Weltgesundheitsorganisation über Ungleichheiten im Gesundheitsbereich[1] ist eine ernst zu nehmende[2] Erinnerung daran, dass die Überwindung[3] der wachsenden Kluft zwischen Arm und Reich nicht nur eine moralische Verpflichtung[4] sondern auch eine wirtschaftliche ist.

Der Report kommt zu dem Schluss, dass eine „tödliche[5] Verkettung von schlechten Verhaltensweisen, wirtschaftlichen und politischen Verhältnissen in großem Ausmaß dafür verantwortlich ist, dass die Mehrzahl der Menschheit[6] sich nicht der guten Gesundheit erfreut, die biologisch möglich ist. Soziale Ungerechtigkeit bringt die Leute[7] in großem Stil um." Menschen aus wohlhabenden Gegenden erfreuen sich gewöhnlich eines längeren und gesünderen Lebens als solche aus sozial benachteiligteren Vierteln.

Während jedoch Regierungen jeglicher politischer Richtung[8] in der Lage sind, gegen viele der Ursachen schlechter Gesundheit etwas zu unternehmen – der Bericht kommt zu dem Schluss, dass besonderes Augenmerk gerichtet werden muss auf Erziehung und schlechte Wohnverhältnisse[9] –, so verlangt die Bewältigung anderer, dass die Bürger ihren Lebensstil ändern. Das ist leichter gesagt als getan. Aber ein Scheitern kann sich als teuer herausstellen.

Anmerkungen

1 *health* kann Gesundheit, aber auch Gesundheitsvorsorge, -zustand, -system bedeuten
2 *auch:* unmissverständlich, deutlich
3 *to tackle* heißt eigentlich nur „ein Problem angehen“; hier ist wohl auch die Lösung des Problems gemeint
4 *auch:* Erfordernis
5 *toxic*: nicht jedes Gift tötet; hier ist aber wohl eher an die medizinische Bedeutung von „toxisch“ gedacht
6 *wörtlich:* der Menschen auf der Erde
7 stilistische Ergänzung
8 *auch:* Couleur; Überzeugung
9 *wörtlicher:* „Erziehung und schlechte Wohnverhältnisse bedürfen besonderer Beachtung“

Tis – A Memoir
by Frank McCourt

Frank McCourt was born in 1930 in New York to Irish immigrant parents, grew up in Limerick, and returned to America at the age of nineteen. This excerpt is taken from his second autobiographic novel.

The bad days in the lobby are Thursday and Friday when the girls and boys meet and sit and drink and laugh, nothing on their minds but college and romance, sailing around in the summer, skiing in the winter, and marrying each other so that they'll have children who will come to the Biltmore[1] and do the same, I know they don't even see me in my houseman's uniform with my dustpan and broom and I'm glad because there are days my eyes are so red[2] they look bloody and I dread it when a girl might say, excuse me, where is the restroom? It's hard to point with your dustpan and say, over there beyond the elevators, and keep your face turned away at the same time. I tried that with one girl but she went to the maitre d'[3] and complained I was rude and now I have to look at everyone who asks a question and when they stare at me I blush so hard I'm sure my skin matches my eyes in the redness department. Sometimes, I blush out of pure anger and I want to snarl at the people who stare but if I did I'd be fired on the spot.

They shouldn't stare. They should know better the way their mothers and fathers are spending fortunes to make them educated and what's the use of all that education if you're so ignorant you stare at people just off the boat with red eyes? You'd think the professors would be standing in front of their classes telling them that if you go to the Biltmore Hotel lobby or any other lobby you're not to be staring at people with red eyes or one leg or any class of a disfigurement.

The girls stare anyway and the boys are worse the way they look at me and smile and nudge and pass remarks that make everyone laugh and I'd like to break my dustpan and broom over their heads till blood spurted and they begged me to stop and promise they'll never again pass remarks on anyone's sore eyes.

One day there's a yelp from a college girl, and the maitre d' rushes over. She's crying and he's moving things around on the table before her and looking under it, shaking his head. He calls across the lobby, McCourt, get over here right now. Did you clean up around this table?

I think I did.

You think you did? Goddammit, excuse me, miss, don't you know?

I did, sir.

Did you remove a paper napkin?

I cleaned up. I emptied the ash trays.

Paper napkin that was here. Did you take it?

I don't know.

Well, lemme tell you something, McCourt. This young lady here is the daughter of the President of the Traffic Club that rents a huge space in this hotel and she had a paper napkin with a phone number from a Princeton boy and if you don't find that piece of paper your ass is in hot water, excuse me, miss. Now what did you do with the trash you took away?

It's gone down to the big garbage bins near the kitchen.

All right. Go down there and search for that paper napkin and don't come back without it.

The girl who lost the napkin sobs and tells me her father has a lotta influence here and she wouldn't want to be me if I don't find that piece of paper. Her friends are looking at me and I feel my face is on fire with my eyes.

The maitre d' snaps at me. Go get it, McCourt, and report back here.

The garbage bins by the kitchen are overflowing and I don't know how I'm going to find a small piece of paper lost in all that waste, coffee grounds, bits of toast, fishbones, egg-shells, grapefruit skins. I'm on my knees poking and separating with a fork from the kitchen where the Puerto Ricans[4] are singing and laughing and banging on pots and that makes me wonder what I'm doing on my knees.

So I get up and go into the kitchen saying nothing to the Puerto Ricans calling to me, Frankie, Frankie, Irish boy, we teach you Sponish. I find a clean paper napkin, write a made-up phone number on it, stain it with coffee, hand it to the maitre d' who hands it to the girl with her friends cheering on all sides. She thanks the maitre d' and passes him a tip, a whole dollar, and my only sorrow is that I won't be there when she calls that number.

Excerpt from "Tis – A Memoir" by Frank McCourt, 1999

1 Biltmore: name of a hotel in New York City

2 red eyes: his eyes are red due to an eye infection

3 maitre d': headwaiter

4 Puerto Ricans: they work there as dishwashers

Worksheet: Frank McCourt, "Tis – A Memoir"

maximum number of points attainable

I. Questions on the text

Read all the questions first, then answer them in the given order. Use your own words as far as is appropriate.

1. Describe Frank's job at the hotel and the guests he encounters there. Analyse the way they treat him. — 20
2. Sum up the incident with the college girl from Frank's point of view. What solution does he find to the problem? — 20
3. Show how the other employees of the hotel behave towards Frank. — 10
4. Analyse Frank's personality before the incident. How does this experience change him? — 20
5. Identify the narrative perspective. What impact does this perspective have on the reader? — 10

II. Composition

Choose *one* of the following topics. Write about 150 to 200 words. — 40

1. Comment on the following quotation: "When life knocks you down, you have two choices – stay down or get up."
2. Courage. Write a review of a film or book which deals with this topic.

3. Comment on the cartoon.

Society hates bullies, son ... Except for grown-up ones with money. For some reason they are okay.

III. Translation

Translate the following text into German: 40/160

Mobility is the promise that lies at the heart of the American dream. It is supposed to take the sting out of the widening gulf between the have-mores and the have-nots. There are poor and rich in the United States, but as long as one can become the other, as long as there is something close to equality of opportunity, the differences between them do not add up to class barriers.

But class is still a powerful force in American life. Over the past three decades, it has come to play a greater, not lesser, role in important ways. At a time when education matters more than ever, success in school remains linked tightly to class. At a time when the country is increasingly integrated racially, the rich are isolating themselves more and more. At a time of extraordinary advances in medicine, class differences in health and lifespan are wide and appear to be widening.

From: *The New York Times,* May 15, 2005

Lösungsvorschlag

I. Questions on the text

1. *Mind the triple task: the description of Frank's job, of the guests and the analysis of the way he is treated. It will help the corrector if you separate the three parts clearly. If you can't guess what a houseman is, look it up in your dictionary (a person employed to do general jobs in a … hotel; OALD)*

   Frank is employed as a houseman and is supposed to do general jobs in the hotel, like dusting and cleaning up around the lobby and removing the garbage. Naturally he is also expected to attend to the guests' requests. It is an inferior and precarious position, which he had to accept being an immigrant "just off the boat" (l. 15).
   The guests he has to deal with are college kids, children of wealthy parents, who spend their free time on Thursdays and Fridays in the lobby of the stylish Biltmore Hotel, drinking, laughing and chatting about topics like college life, romance, and the typical pastimes of their class, such as sailing and skiing. They play with the idea of marrying each other and expect their children to frequent the Biltmore in the same way one day.
   To them, Frank is a nobody, an insignificant servant they mostly ignore. They take it for granted that he has to minister to their wishes at any time. They stare at him and make fun of his infected eyes. When they are not satisfied with him, they immediately complain to the headwaiter, as in the case when Frank is too ashamed to look at a girl when she asks him something.

2. *Here you have two aspects to consider (incident and his solution). Don't worry about the detail "from Frank's point-of-view" – the text is autobiographical and told from his perspective anyway.*

   One day Frank is angrily summoned by the headwaiter. A girl can't find a paper napkin on which a Princeton boy has noted his telephone number for her. Frank is held responsible for actually having done his job to tidy up and remove the waste, which probably contained the napkin. Both the student and the maitre d' threaten him with dire consequences should he not be able to retrieve it from the big garbage can near the kitchen.
   He rummages through all kinds of disgusting waste and tries hard to locate the napkin. When the kitchen helpers start mocking him noisily he becomes ashamed of his ignoble activity and decides on a different course. He takes a new napkin, gives it a used look, scribbles a fake phone number on it and hands it over to the relieved girl – who, instead of thanking him, tips the headwaiter generously.

3. *The other employees are the headwaiter and the Puerto Rican dishwashers.*

   The maitre d' openly expresses his superiority to Frank. He orders him around – "McCourt, get over here right now." (l. 25), humiliates him in front of the college kids with his dictatorial attitude and rude language ("Goddammit", l. 28; "your ass is in hot water", l. 37), for which he feels he has to apologize to the girl, and openly threatens him ("… don't come back without it", ll. 40/41).
   The Puerto Rican dishwashers are even lower in the hotel hierarchy than Frank. As a group they obviously enjoy making fun of Frank, as in the scene when he searches the garbage. They tease him by singing and banging their pots and calling him "Frankie, Frankie, Irish boy" and offering to teach him "Sponish" (l. 52).
   Both Frank's superiors and inferiors are used to treating him without respect.

4. *The first three paragraphs give evidence for Frank's humility and resignation. After the incident he fights back.*

   In the beginning Frank is portrayed as a shy person. He is ashamed of his bloodshot eyes and doesn't dare to face the guests. When the college kids look at him he blushes and always suppresses his anger to avoid being fired. Only inwardly he complains about the arrogant students' lack of education and has violent fantasies of hurting them when they sneer at him. His status as a recently arrived and vulnerable immigrant on his first job prevents him from standing up against their bullying.
   During the incident he first behaves in his usual, humble way and does what he is told. When, however, the jolly dishwashers begin to tease him while he is on his knees sorting through the garbage, he realizes how miserable his behaviour is and revolts for the first time. He takes revenge on the headwaiter and the students by faking a phone number.
   Although he will continue to behave as he is expected to, he has found a way to keep his self-esteem, which will help him deal with his role as an immigrant in the future.

5. *The excerpt is from an autobiographical novel, in which the author tells his own story and is part of the action himself. This, of course, makes it a first- person- narrative.*

   Frank McCourt tells his own experiences as an Irish immigrant to the United States. So, needless to say, he uses himself as a first-person-narrator who is personally involved in the action. With this perspective he is limited to present what he himself remembers. He gives his own interpretation of the other characters' reactions and behaviour which induces his readers to identify with him. They will tend to share his emotions and to accept his observations and conclusions, and will take his side, of course.

II. Composition

1. *Here you have a rather simplistic topic to write about. Our best advice is to take up the boxing image and find some examples of desperate experiences.*

   "Seven, eight, nine …" and the boxer on the floor has lost his fight, his opponent's last punch has truly knocked him down. Boxers, however, nearly almost recover and prepare for their next challenge.
   The boxing metaphor of the topical quotation is often used to comment on strokes of fate and is based on the concept of life as a permanent struggle with ups and downs. Everybody has experienced events which have 'knocked them down' in utter defeat, when it seems impossible that one will get back on one's feet again. You may have lost a person dear to you in an accident, the great love of your life has left you for good, or a financial manoeuvre has caused your complete ruin. Naturally most people will be devastated at first and despair of their lives and their future. Yet, if these 'knockouts' don't kill you, time will invariably heal your wounds. The choice you have is whether you "take arms against a sea of troubles", as Hamlet says in his famous soliloquy, or to carry on in resignation. What course you take is a question of character. If you have a courageous mind you will struggle to 'get up' and probably will be your own self again soon. The knocked-out boxer will either shake off his defeat and go for the next fight, or he will give up his career. In both cases he will survive.

2. *Even though the topic of courage plays a prominent part especially in children's literature, historical and military novels or films, you will find examples in most other genres as well. Mind that German sources are not explicitly ruled out.*
   Books that come to mind and which you might know are Lord of the Flies, 1984, Fahrenheit 451, Lord of the Rings, *or the* Harry Potter *volumes. Movies that contain brav-*

ery are, for example, Braveheart, Hero, Patriot Games, *or* Men of Honour. *Recent and suitable German films in which moral courage is demonstrated are* Sophie Scholl *or* Das Leben der Anderen. *The format of a review expects you to first summarize the plot and then allows you to present praise and criticism of your own choice. In the assignment at hand you will have to concentrate on the issue of courage, though.*
We decided to base our review on the film Cry Freedom.

The movie *Cry Freedom* is set at the time of apartheid in South Africa. It is based on the true story of Steve Biko, a black leader who fights for the rights of the suppressed majority. The editor of a liberal newspaper, Donald Woods, becomes interested in Biko and his politics. Both men show enormous courage in the face of persecution by the security police. Biko, who has already been banned, is prohibited to write or publish and to leave a designated area. Due to his character and the responsibility he feels for the black community he bravely ignores these restrictions, is arrested and eventually killed while in police custody. The journalist, who has become a close friend of Biko's, continues the fight. Though warned more than once and terrorized by the authorities he goes on writing to denounce the role of the police in Biko's death. One can imagine how, above all, the targeting of his wife and children hurts Woods, and it speaks for his moral courage that he won't give in to the injustice and brutality of the security forces. He finally succeeds in escaping from South Africa and publishing his book.
The two protagonists show extraordinary courage for a noble cause, risking their lives and the safety of people they love.

3. *As always in these tasks you should first describe the cartoon and then comment on it.*

The cartoon shows a little boy and an elderly man, possibly his grandfather, talking on an old-fashioned sofa. The setting is a lower middle class one, with a potted plant and a painting of a sunset on a seascape, and frills on the furniture. Maybe the boy has come across a bully and asks his grandpa's advice. The old man, from his experience, comments on society's attitude towards bullies: it hates them, unless they are adults belonging to the moneyed class.
Bullying among children is not uncommon. It usually consists of efforts to exclude someone weak from a group by picking on him and making him an outsider, or takes the form of threatening a child to hand over his or her money, sandwiches or cell phone. For the little boy his grandpa's words of wisdom may hold some comfort, if he or friends of his are suffering from a bully – he learns that society, his parents or teachers are on his side after all. When he grows up, however, he may have to face different kinds of bullies, like employers or superiors who allow themselves to intimidate and humiliate people dependent on them with no regard to human decency. He will have to find out for himself whether to share his grandfather's resignation or to try and assert himself against the 'ones with money'.

III. Translation

Die Verheißung von (gesellschaftlicher) Mobilität[1] liegt im Wesen des Amerikanischen Traums.[2] Sie soll eigentlich der zunehmenden Kluft zwischen den Besitzenden und Habenichtsen die Schärfe[3] nehmen. Es gibt Arme und Reiche in den Vereinigten Staaten, aber solange die Einen zu den Anderen werden können, und solange es etwas Ähnliches wie Chancengleichheit gibt[4], laufen die Unterschiede zwischen den beiden Gruppen[5] nicht auf eine Erhöhung der Klassenschranken hinaus.

Dennoch übt die Klassenzugehörigkeit[6] weiterhin einen starken Einfluss im Leben der Amerikaner aus.[7] Während der letzten drei Jahrzehnte ist ihre Rolle in wichtigen Belangen eher[8] größer als kleiner geworden. In einer Zeit, in der Ausbildung mehr als je von Belang ist, bleibt der schulische Erfolg[9] eng an die Klassenzugehörigkeit gebunden[10]. In einer Zeit zunehmender Rassenintegration im Land grenzen sich die Reichen immer mehr ab. In einer Zeit außergewöhnlicher medizinischer Fortschritte sind Klassenunterschiede bei der Gesundheit und Lebenserwartung immer noch[8] groß und scheinen sich sogar[8] noch zu vergrößern.

Anmerkungen

1 Auch: *Freizügigkeit, Bewegungsfreiheit.*
2 Auch möglich ist*: liegt zugrunde, gehört wesentlich zum*
3 Auch: *den Stachel*
4 Auch: *etwas gibt, was der Chancengleichheit nahe kommt*
5 Oder: *beitragen zu, summieren sich zu*
6 *Klasse* allein würde man im Deutschen nicht benutzen
7 Oder: *stellt einen machtvollen Faktor dar*
8 Stilistisch bedingte Einfügungen
9 Oder: *das Abschneiden in der Schule*
10 Auch: *verknüpft mit*

Grundkurs Englisch 2010
Textaufgabe I

Caterpillars and Cookie Dough

Growing up on a farm near Yamhill, Oregon, I quickly learned to appreciate the difference between fresh, home-grown foods and the commercial versions in the supermarket.

Store-bought lettuce was always green and pristine, and thus vastly preferable to lettuce from my Mom's vegetable garden (organic before we called it that). Her lettuce kept me watchful, because a caterpillar might come crawling out of my salad.

We ate beef from steers raised on our own pasture, but "grass-fed" had no allure[1] for me. I longed for delicious, wholesome food that my friends in town ate. Like hot dogs.

Over the years, though, I've become nostalgic for an occasional bug in my salad, for an apple that feels as if it were designed by God rather than by a committee. More broadly, it has become clear that the same factors that impelled[2] me toward factory-produced meat and vegetables – cheap, predictable food – also resulted in a profoundly unhealthy American diet.

I've often criticized America's health care system, and I hope that we're going to see a public insurance option this year. But one reason for our health problems is our industrialized agriculture system, and that should be under scrutiny as well.

A terrific new documentary, "Food, Inc.", offers a powerful and largely persuasive diagnosis of American agriculture. Go see it, but be warned that you may not want to eat for a week afterward.

(It was particularly unnerving to see leftover animal bits ground into "hamburger filler".)

"The way we eat has changed more in the last 50 years than in the previous 10,000," Michael Pollan, the food writer, declares in the film.

What's even more eerie[3] is the way animals are being re-engineered. For example, most Americans prefer light meat to dark, so chickens have been redesigned to produce more white meat by growing massive breasts that make them lopsided[4].

"When they grow from a chick and in seven weeks you've got a five-and-a-half pound chicken, their bones and their internal organs can't keep up with the rapid growth," explained Carole Morison, a Maryland chicken farmer who allowed the film crew into her barns. "A lot of these chickens here, they can take a few steps and then they plop down. It's because they can't keep up with all the weight that they're carrying."

Huge confinement operations for livestock and poultry[5] produce very cheap meat and eggs. But at what cost?

The documentary introduces us to Barbara Kowalcyk, whose two-and-a-half-year-old child, Kevin, went from healthy to dead in 12 days, after he ate a hamburger tainted with E. coli bacteria. Even after his death, it took weeks for the tainted meat to be re-called.

"Sometimes it seems that industry was more protected than my son," Ms. Kowalcyk complains.

She has a point. Agribusiness companies exercise huge political influence, and industry leaders often fill regulatory posts. The F.D.A.[6] consequently dozed, and the number of food safety inspections plunged[7].

There is some evidence that pathogens[8], including E. coli, become much more common in factory farming operations. Move cattle out to a pasture for five days, and they will lose 80 percent of the E. coli in their gut[9], the film says. And the massive routine feeding of antibiotics to farm animals is a disgrace that reduces the effectiveness of antibiotics in treating sick humans.

Pathogens are now seeping into the unlikeliest foods. On June 19, the F.D.A. advised consumers not to eat Nestlé cookie dough – cookie dough! – because of concerns about E. coli contamination, after reports of illness in 28 states.

American agribusiness is wondrous. When I moved back to the United States from China, I remember visiting a supermarket and feeling a near-religious awe. Yet one consequence of this wondrous system is that unhealthy calories are cheaper than nutritious ones.

The solutions aren't simple, and may involve paying more for what we eat, although we may save some of that in reduced health costs for diabetes and heart disease. In any case, "Food, Inc." notes that we as consumers do have power. "You can vote to change the system," it declares, "three times a day."

From: Nicholas D. Kristof: "Caterpillars and Cookie Dough" from The New York Times, © 20 June 2009. The New York Times. All rights reserved. Used by permission and protected by the Copyright Laws of the United States. The printing, copying, redistribution, or retransmission of the material without express written permission is prohibited.

1 allure: attraction
2 impelled: *here:* drove
3 eerie: scary, frightening
4 make them lopsided: *here:* make them unable to keep their balance
5 confinement operations for livestock and poultry: *Massentierhaltung von Vieh und Geflügel*
6 F.D.A.: Food and Drug Administration: US government agency responsible for food safety
7 plunge: decrease rapidly
8 pathogen: bacteria causing disease, e. g. E. coli
9 gut: *Eingeweide*

Worksheet: Caterpillars and Cookie Dough

maximum number of points attainable

I. Questions on the text

Read all the questions first, then answer them in the given order. Use your own words as far as is appropriate.

1. Examine the development of the writer's eating habits. — 10
2. "The way we eat has changed more in the last 50 years than in the previous 10,000" (l. 20). Examine this development and its consequences. — 20
3. What is "Food, Inc." (l. 16) and why does the writer recommend it to his readers? — 10
4. Who is responsible for the current development in the food industry and what can be done to reverse the trend? — 20
5. Show how the author uses language and style to express his criticism. Analyse three examples. — 20

II. Composition

Choose *one* of the following topics. Write about 150 to 200 words. 40

1. You work in a fair-trade shop. Write an article for your school-magazine, in which you try to convince your fellow students to buy such products.
2. Can cooking shows change our eating habits for the better?
3. Describe the cartoon and comment on it.

© Copyright 2009 David Fitzsimmons
All Rights Reserved

III. Translation

Translate the following text into German: 40

160

The chef Jamie Oliver deserves everyone's thanks for tackling a problem that politicians have ignored for too long: the discgraceful quality of the country's fat-ridden, salt-sodden school meals. This is a national problem for two reasons. First, more nutritious food would lead to better-behaved pupils, more willing to learn. Secondly, if nothing is done, not only will educational standards fall, but the health service could be burdened with the cost of an increasingly obese nation. If present trends continue, the younger generation could, for the first time, have a shorter lifespan than their parents.

Viewers watching Jamie's School Dinners[1] have been treated to a riveting piece of reality TV[2] with a strong social message. Observing how the chef was able to convince children – so addicted to junk food[3] that they cannot even give names to fresh vegetables they were shown – that healthy food was also tasty was a joy to watch.

From: http://www.guardian.co.uk/society/2005/mar/09/publichealth.schoolmeals

1 Jamie's School Dinners: a UK documentary series by Jamie Oliver; *do not translate*

2 reality TV: *do not translate*

3 junk food: *do not translate*

Lösungsvorschlag

I. Questions on the text

1. The writer grew up on a farm in Oregon, and when he was a child he would eat food which today is known as "organic": home-grown salad from his mother's garden or meat from animals that they raised on their own land. But he did not like it because it very often contained insects like caterpillars; moreover, the food which came from the supermarkets looked much better and therefore seemed to be much more attractive to him. Besides, he always envied his friends in town who were allowed to eat tasty food like hot-dogs.
   Now as a grown-up, being aware of how food is produced in the US and knowing about the health risks that come with some of it, the author has become very critical of meat and vegetables produced in factories. So he would like to go back to his childhood days and eat the food he hated then. He even longs for a bug in his salad now and then.

2. *Be careful: the phrase "examine this development" in the task refers to the last 50 years only. You are not supposed to give an outline of man's eating habits in the previous 10,000 years – simply because the text does not contain any information about that.*

   The amount of food on offer today, and its variety, has become overwhelming: when the author enters an American supermarket for the first time after returning from a stay in China, he feels a "near-religious awe" (l. 49). Modern consumers also demand food that is cheap and perfect-looking (l. 11; l. 30; "green and pristine", l. 3); for example, they "prefer light meat to dark" (l. 23).
   In order to meet this demand, animals are being "re-engineered" and "redesigned" (ll. 22, 23) so that chickens, for example, grow huge breasts, providing more of the preferred white meat (ll. 23/24). Also, American agribusiness has developed strategies for the mass production of meat and vegetables. Thus, chickens are kept in "huge confinement operations" (l. 30). As a consequence, animals are more easily infected by bacteria, as is shown by the example of the E. coli bacteria, which seem to be much less common in cattle which are raised outdoors on open pastures (ll. 40–42). In order to prevent this, animals which are kept inside only are treated with massive doses of antibiotics, which in turn reduces their effectiveness in treating sick people (ll. 43/44).
   Lastly, industrial food production has contributed greatly to the fact that people eat too much of the wrong things because "unhealthy calories are cheaper than nutritious ones" (ll. 50/51). This is obviously one of the reasons why health costs for treating heart disease and diabetes are rising. (l. 53).

3. "Food, Inc." is a documentary offering a "diagnosis of American agriculture" (ll. 16/17). It is very critical of American agribusiness by showing examples of the mass production of meat in the US and of its dangerous – and sometimes even fatal (as in the case of two-and-a-half-year-old Kevin, ll. 32–34) – consequences. Obviously, the film also gives examples of how much healthier organic food can be (ll. 40–44). Furthermore, it aims to encourage its viewers to change this system and become more health-conscious in choosing their food, by showing off-putting and even disgusting scenes (ll. 17–19) and appealing to the consumers to use their power and influence (ll. 54/55).

4. According to the text, there are three groups who share responsibility for the current development. First of all, the author puts the blame on the "agribusiness companies," one of which is even mentioned in the text (Nestlé; l. 46). They are only interested in profit and even seem to be using delay tactics at the expense of the consumer when it

comes to re-call products from the market (l. 34). The next blame can be found in political institutions like the F.D.A. Instead of controlling food safety in the interests of the American citizen, the author claims that they are heavily influenced by lobbying from companies, whose leaders even "fill regulatory posts" (l. 38) in these government agencies. As a consequence, these public organisations have become too slack and careless in fulfilling their duty, and companies have been inspected on food safety less often. Lastly, the writer states that customers are also responsible, because they are obviously only interested in buying as much food as possible as cheaply as possible and care more about the way food looks than about its nutritional value.
Because of all that, it will not be easy to reverse the trend ("solutions aren't simple" l. 52). The writer says that the most significant impulse must come from the consumers: if they are willing to pay more for healthier and more nutritious food they can change the whole "industrialized agriculture system" (ll. 14/15) because they "do have power" (l. 54), a power which the author compares, at the end of his text, to the basic democratic power of voting.

5. *The writer's attitude towards his subject is obviously very critical; and the text contains quite a number of examples where he uses language to express his criticism, so we will give you more than just three examples from which you can choose.*

It is quite obvious that the writer is very critical of the "wondrous" American agribusiness (l. 48). He expresses his opinion openly by using either negative or positive terms: the way animals are kept and fed is "eerie" (l. 22) and a "disgrace" (l. 43); scenes in the documentary are "unnerving" (l. 19); the average American's diet is "profoundly unhealthy" (l. 11). On the other hand, the film is called "terrific," "powerful," "largely persuasive" (l. 16).
As another stylistic device the writer applies imagery to live animals which would normally be associated with inanimate things: meat and vegetables are "factory-produced" (l. 10), animals are "re-engineered" (l. 22) and "redesigned" (l. 23) like machinery, and they are kept in "factory farming operations" (l. 41). In this way the author stresses the artificial way in which food is produced. The repetition of the word "cookie dough" (l. 46) stresses the fact that even the "unlikeliest foods" (l. 45) are now affected; the effect is heightened by adding an exclamation mark.
At times the author makes use of quotations to underline his own position, and to make the text more vivid. He also uses short matter-of-fact phrases to make clear that there is no possible contradiction to what he says: "She has a point." (l. 37); "Kevin went from healthy to dead in 12 days" (l. 33). The same can be said about the rhetorical question "But at what cost?" (l. 31).
Throughout the text the author uses comparatively simple language which can be easily understood by the average reader, since he is writing about an everyday topic affecting the everyday consumer. The reader is sometimes directly addressed, even called upon to take action: "Go see [the film]" (l. 17); "we as consumers do have power" (l. 54). In the title the author uses two strongly contrasting words to attract the reader's attention: whereas we all love something sweet like cookies, we probably all find caterpillars rather disgusting. The contrast is even heightened by using alliteration.
Irony can be found when the writer describes hot dogs that his friends in town were allowed to eat as "wholesome" (l. 7). Since he was a child then, this irony also implies that the preference for this eating habit is somewhat childish. The tone of the text is quite humorous and entertaining overall.
The article concludes with a *metaphor* in which the private act of buying food is compared to the political action of voting (ll. 54/55).

II. Composition

1. Hi folks,
   A lot of you know me from playing the trumpet in our school jazz band, but only a few know that I spend quite a lot of my free time working in the fair-trade shop only some five hundred yards down the road from our school, close to the small shopping centre. I see lots of you passing by and entering the supermarkets opposite – and I wonder why so few of you ever bother to come in and at least have a look at what we have to offer.
   Certainly, the things we sell – snacks, tea, coffee, fabrics, clothes, bags etc. – might be a little more expensive than in the shops on the other side. But then, what costs more is usually also more valuable, isn't it? That means we will treat it with more respect and care – and so it will last longer.
   Lots of the things we offer were made in the same countries as those in the more fashionable boutiques with their well-known brand names: shirts, scarves, and sandals from Malaysia, India or somewhere in South America. But we only sell products which are produced under healthy and humane working conditions: no children under twelve, regular working hours, health care for the workers, decent payment. Besides, the food we sell is much healthier for you than the stuff you get in the supermarket. And we also make a great effort that our goods are produced environmentally friendly, which is not only good for the region where they come from, but also for the people who buy them here.
   So, next time you are looking for a pencil for school, writing paper, a new T-shirt or some bananas: why don't you just drop in and have a look? I'm sure you will find just what you are looking for!

2. Almost every evening, millions of Germans watch at least one cooking show on television. Have these shows turned us into innovative and creative cooks? Or have they at least changed our eating habits?
   Quite frankly, I doubt that very much. First of all, most people watch these shows only because of the participants: either famous chefs who everyone knows from cookery books or magazines, or celebrities from TV, music or politics. Viewers are more interested in learning minor details of their private lives, and anecdotes that might give them some insight into their everyday lives, rather than in their cooking skills. Secondly, the act of cooking seems terribly easy in all these shows: the food is lying there on the work surface, all clean and ready to cook, the dishes and all the kitchen utensils are there at their disposal, the kitchens are equipped with the latest cooking facilities, and afterwards no one ever has to clean up the mess – everyone just leaves. As soon as you start cooking yourself, you realise what hard work it is and how much time it actually requires – and you do not even bother to start. And lastly, the meals which are prepared in these cooking shows are usually rather complicated, with the ingredients hard to get or really expensive, and the way the food is presented is quite sophisticated, which puts a lot of people off trying themselves.
   To sum up, even though the odd person now and then will get some inspiration from one of these cooking shows, the majority of people have not changed their eating habits through them. As far as I can see, my friends still prefer a pizza or a Big Mac and a bottle of beer in front of the TV while watching these programmes.

3. The cartoon shows a scene from Halloween. Two children – a boy disguised as a zombie and a girl disguised as a witch – are about to set off on their trick-or-treat-tour into the night: each of them is holding a bag, in which they expect to collect as many sweets and cookies as they can get. Their parents are standing opposite: the father is taking a picture of them both, while their mother is warning them: "Have fun but be careful.

There are some sick evil people out there who might be handing out treats laced with trans-fats and sugar."

I think the cartoon makes fun of the hysteria of many modern parents who have become over-anxious because of all the reports in the media telling them about children eating too much sugar and fat.

The joke and criticism can be found in the expression "sick evil people" which the mother applies to people who give out sweets and other titbits to children, following in all innocence a century-old tradition: these grown-ups are now compared to the witches, ghosts and evil spirits who were supposed to have been banned in the old days when the Halloween rites originated. They vanished a long time ago. But their obnoxious and destructive powers were replaced by the dangers of today's food, as modern dietary scientists turned harmless delicacies into poison. The parents in the cartoon are obviously keeping quite a lot of treats inside an emptied pumpkin by the door for the children who turn up on their doorstep during the evening. Maybe they will treat their neighbours' kids to apples and carrots instead of chocolates and lollipops?

III. Translation

Der Starkoch[1] Jamie Oliver verdient Jedermanns[2] Dank dafür, dass er ein Problem angegangen ist[3], das die Politiker nur allzu lange ignoriert[4] haben: die schändliche[5] Qualität der vor Fett triefenden, total versalzenen Schulessen im Lande. Dieses Problem geht das ganze Land aus zwei Gründen an. Erstens würde nahrhafteres Essen[6] dazu führen, dass die Schüler sich besser aufführen würden, also[7] bereitwilliger lernen würden. Und zweitens: wenn nichts unternommen wird, sinken nicht nur die erzieherischen Maßstäbe[8], sondern das Gesundheitswesen könnte mit den Kosten für ein zunehmend fettleibiger werdendes Volk belastet werden. Wenn sich der gegenwärtige Trend[9] fortsetzt, könnte die heutige Jugend zum ersten Mal eine kürzere Lebenserwartung haben[10] als ihre Eltern.

Den Zuschauern von Jamie's School Dinners wurde ein fesselndes Stück Reality-TV mit einer deutlichen[11] gesellschaftlichen Botschaft serviert. Zuzusehen[12] wie der Starkoch Kinder, die so sehr an Junkfood gewöhnt[13] sind, dass sie nicht einmal die Namen der frischen Gemüsesorten kennen, die ihnen gezeigt wurden, davon überzeugen konnte, dass gesundes Essen auch schmeckt[14], war eine Augenweide[15].

Anmerkungen

1 Englisch *chef* ist mehr als nur ein einfacher Koch; auch *Küchenchef* oder *Sternekoch* möglich
2 Auch: *unser aller*
3 Auch: *angepackt hat*
4 Auch: *links liegen gelassen haben*
5 Auch: *schäbig; beklagenswert*
6 Auch: *Lebensmittel*
7 Stilistische Ergänzung
8 Auch: *Standards*; auch Einzahl möglich: *das erzieherische Niveau*
9 Auch Plural möglich
10 Wörtlicher: *weniger lang leben*
11 Auch: *klaren; überzeugenden*
12 Auch: *Zeuge zu werden; zu beobachten*
13 Auch: *von Junk Food abhängig*
14 Auch Präteritum möglich
15 Auch: *eine große/echte/reine Freude*

The Uncommon Reader

The Queen has lately taken up a new hobby …

As a girl, one of her greatest thrills had been on VE[1] night, when she and her sister had slipped out of the gates and mingled unrecognised with the crowds. There was something of that, she felt, to reading. It was anonymous; it was shared; it was common. And she who had led a life apart now found that she craved it. Here in these pages and between these covers she could go unrecognised.

One of the Queen's recurrent royal responsibilities was to open Parliament, an obligation she had never previously found particularly burdensome and actually rather enjoyed: to be driven down the Mall[2] on a bright autumn morning even after fifty years was something of a treat. But not any more. She was dreading the two hours the whole thing was due to take, though fortunately they were in the coach, not the open carriage, so she could take along her book. She'd got quite good at reading and waving, the trick being to keep the book below the level of the window and to keep focused on it and not on the crowds. The duke didn't like it one bit, of course, but goodness it helped.

Which was all very well, except it was only when she was actually in the coach, with the procession drawn up in the palace forecourt and ready for the off, that, as she put on her glasses, she realised she'd forgotten the book. And while the duke fumes in the corner and the postillions[3] fidget, the horses shift and the harness clinks, Norman is rung on the mobile. The Guardsmen stand at ease and the procession waits. The officer in charge looks at his watch. Two minutes late. Knowing nothing displeases Her Majesty more and knowing nothing of the book, he does not look forward to the repercussions that must inevitably follow. But here is Norman, skittering across the gravel with the book thoughtfully hidden in a shawl, and off they go.

Still, it is an ill-tempered royal couple that is driven down the Mall, the duke waving viciously from his side, the Queen listlessly from hers, and at some speed, too, as the procession tries to pick up the two minutes that have been lost.

At Westminster she popped the offending book behind a cushion in the carriage ready for the journey back, mindful as she sat on the throne and embarked on her speech of how tedious was the twaddle she was called on to deliver and that this was actually the only occasion when she got to read aloud to the nation. 'My government will do this … my government will do that.' It was so barbarously phrased and wholly devoid of style or interest that she felt it demeaned the very act of reading itself, with this year's performance even more garbled than usual as she, too, tried to pick up the missing couple of minutes.

It was with some relief that she got back into the coach and reached behind the cushion for her book. It was not there. Steadfastly waving as they rumbled along, she surreptitiously felt behind the other cushions.

'You're not sitting on it?'

'Sitting on what?'

'My book.'

'No, I am not. Some British Legion[4] people here, and wheelchairs. Wave, for God's sake.'

When they arrived at the palace she had a word with Grant, the young footman in charge, who said that while ma'am had been in the Lords the sniffer dogs had been round and security had confiscated the book. He thought it had probably been exploded.

'Exploded?' said the Queen. 'But it was Anita Brookner[5].'

The young man, who seemed remarkably undeferential, said security may have thought it was a device.

The Queen said: 'Yes. That is exactly what it is. A book is a device to ignite the imagination.' The footman said: 'Yes, ma'am.'

It was as if he was talking to his grandmother, and not for the first time the Queen was made unpleasantly aware of the hostility her reading seemed to arouse.

'Very well,' she said. 'Then you should inform security that I shall expect to find another copy of the same book, vetted and explosive-free, waiting on my desk tomorrow morning. And another thing. The carriage cushions are filthy. Look at my gloves.' Her Majesty departed. 'Fuck,' said the footman, fishing out the book from where he had been told to hide it down the front of his breeches.

From: Alan Bennet, The Uncommon Reader, Faber & Faber, London 2007

1 VE: Victory in Europe Day (May 8, 1945)

2 the Mall: wide avenue leading from Buckingham Palace to Trafalgar Square used for royal parades

3 postillion: person in charge of a horse-drawn carriage

4 British Legion: charity providing (financial, social and emotional) support to people serving in the British Armed Forces and their families

5 Anita Brookner: English novelist

Worksheet: The Uncommon Reader

maximum number of points attainable

I. Questions on the text

Read all the questions first, then answer them in the given order. Use your own words as far as is appropriate.

1. How has the Queen's attitude towards her "royal responsibilities" (l. 6) changed? What is the reason for this change?	10
2. Examine to what extent the Queen's actual thoughts and behaviour on her way to Westminster and in Parliament reveal this change in attitude.	20
3. Why is the book gone when the Queen returns to her carriage? Compare Grant's version of its disappearance with what has really happened.	10
4. In the first paragraph, the Queen tries to explain her fascination with reading. What is her explanation and how does it relate to the title of the novel?	20
5. Choose two examples of how the writer uses humour to ridicule people's lack of understanding for the Queen and explain precisely how they work.	10
6. Analyse the language and style used by the writer in lines 14–22 and determine their effect on the reader.	10

II. Composition

Choose *one* of the following topics. Write about 150 to 200 words. 40

1. The Queen is looking for new books to read and has asked schools to come forward with suitable suggestions. Write an email recommending one of your favourite books.
2. Libraries – institutions of the past?
3. Describe the cartoon and comment on it.

"180 quid that Nintendo wii cost me! And you're reading a bloody book!"

© Clive Goddard, www.CartoonStock.com

III. Translation

Translate the following text into German: 40

160

The Future of Reading: Pick Books You Like

Fans of reading workshops say that assigning* books leaves many children bored or unable to understand the texts. Letting students choose their own books can help to build a lifelong love of reading.

Critics of the approach question whether teachers can really keep up with a roomful of children reading different books. Even more important is the loss of a common body of knowledge based on the literary classics – often difficult books that children are unlikely to choose for themselves.

However, some previously staunch advocates of a rigid curriculum have moderated their views. "I actually used to be a high-culture kind of person who would want to stick to Dickens," said Mark Bauerlein, professor of English. "But now I think if they read Harry Potter, that's good. We just need to preserve book habits among the kids as much as we possibly can."

From: Motoko Rich: "The Future of Reading" from The New York Times,
© 29 August 2009. The New York Times. All rights reserved.
Used by permission and protected by the Copyright Laws of the United States. The printing, copying, redistribution, or retransmission of the material without express written permission is prohibited.

* to assign a book: to make a book compulsory reading for a whole class

Lösungsvorschlag

I. Questions on the text

A general remark: even though the text is comparatively easy to read, it helps if you are familiar with certain aspects of political life in Britain: the role of the sovereign, the ceremony of the State Opening of Parliament; the Royal Family; the Lords ...

1. In the past, the Queen had "actually rather enjoyed" (l. 7) her royal responsibilities; the narrator describes her pleasure at being driven down the Mall for the opening of Parliament in almost naive, child-like terms ("something of a treat" ll. 8/9). Today, she does not enjoy these duties any more: they are a burden she is "dreading" (l. 9). The reason for this change is the simple fact that the Queen has found a new hobby: she loves reading. And all her public obligations keep her from her new-found private passion.

2. Of course, the Queen knows that she cannot show open disrespect for her responsibilities: she uses a trick and keeps "the book below the level of the window" (l. 12), so she can go on reading unnoticed while at the same time waving at the crowd outside.
   But there are more hints in this scene which show that she has very little interest in fulfilling her duties. When she finds out that she has forgotten her book, she stops the whole procession until it is finally brought to her, "thoughtfully hidden in a shawl" (ll. 21/22), so that no one notices the reason for the delay.
   On the way to Parliament, her attention is on her book instead of on the crowds (l. 12); and on the way back she even has to be reminded by her husband to wave at a group of her obviously important subjects: "Some British legion people here, and wheelchairs. Wave, for God's sake" (ll. 40/41).
   In Parliament, her thoughts not only reveal her displeasure at delivering the annual speech of her majesty's government, pre-written by her Prime Minister; she even shows that she can now apply literary criticism to the text she has to read out: she thinks it is boring "twaddle" (l. 28), phrased very roughly and without style (l. 30). This year, her performance is even worse ("more garbled than usual" l. 32) because she hurries up to try to make up for the time she lost when looking for her book at the beginning of the procession. The Queen feels that the whole ceremony is a disgrace to "the very act of reading itself" (l. 31).

3. Grant, a young footman, says that the Queen's book was confiscated after the dogs had found it. Since they thought it "was a device" (l. 47) the book has probably been destroyed. Grant knows that he is lying when he tells the Queen all that, because in reality someone had ordered him to remove the book and hide it from the Queen by sticking it into his trousers.

4. When she was a young woman, the Queen once secretly left the royal grounds on VE night to mix "unrecognised with the crowds" (l. 2). Doing something "anonymous," something "shared" (l. 3) then, was very exciting. Today she has the same feeling of doing something both forbidden and ordinary when she reads a book. Nobody is supposed to know anything of the new passion that makes her a person like everybody else. The covers of the books she reads protect her from being recognised as someone special (l. 5), someone "apart" (l. 4). Reading is not a privilege of the sovereign but an activity she has in common with millions of ordinary people. So she actually could be a "common reader," and she does yearn to be ordinary for a change.
   The title suggests, however, that her reading is not such a common activity after all.

As is shown later in the text, she is not like everybody else: she is Head of State – and not only of Great Britain; she is the one who opens Parliament; everybody waits for her when she calls for a delay; everyone is pleased when she waves at the crowds. So, in fact, she is an uncommon person and therefore an "uncommon" reader, as the title says.

5. *The question suggests that there are more than just two examples. So we have chosen four from which you could have picked any two.*

   The Queen's husband shows his dislike of his wife's new hobby very clearly when he loses his temper and shouts at his wife, "Wave, for God's sake" (ll. 40/41). This domestic scene inside the coach, which depicts the royal couple as an ordinary couple quarrelling over something quite insignificant, contrasts sharply with the solemnity of the occasion outside.
   The fact that a simple book is mistaken for a terrorist bomb shows the overreaction of the people surrounding the Queen, who are very critical of Her Majesty's new hobby.
   Grant, the footman, has no understanding for the Queen's new hobby at all. Instead, when she comes up with the metaphor that a book is a "device to ignite the imagination" (ll. 48/49), he answers rather patronizingly, "Yes, ma'am," as if the queen was old and slightly deranged.
   Grant provides another instance of ridiculous behaviour when he hides the book "down the front of his breeches" (l. 56), meaning in his trousers, which is a most unsuitable place and which shows that he has no sensitivity towards what reading means to the Queen.

6. The passage begins with a relatively long narrative sentence in the past tense in which the reader is informed that the Queen has forgotten her book. This is followed by a series of short sentences in the simple present tense which convey a sense of hectic activity: several different actions are taking place at the same time performed by different people. The duke, the postillions, the Guardsmen, the officer in charge, and even the horses are mentioned. The use of the present simple tense – instead of the progressive form – also shows how the course of events is interrupted and brought to a standstill, and is then resumed with Norman bringing the book. The last few words pick up the action again: "and off they go" (l. 22). These four words convey the routine with which this annual event is swiftly carried out. The reader gets a very clear image of the formality of the procession lining up in the forecourt, its importance underlined by the officer already worrying about possible "repercussions" (l. 20) because of a few minutes' delay. This image is interrupted, however, by the description of the guards standing at ease and, most of all, by Norman "skittering" across the yard (l. 21) – a word and image you would not expect at such a stately occasion at all.

II. Composition

1. *Since the idea of schoolchildren suggesting suitable new books for the Queen is so far from any reality, this gives you a good chance to use your imagination. So what about adopting the role of a child who might address the Queen very naively?*

   Your Majesty,

   You have invited pupils to come up with suggestions for further reading. My name is Jamie and I attend Fulham North Comprehensive School. My favourite books are the Harry Potter novels, of which I have already read the first three.
   Harry Potter is the main character. He is an orphan. When he is eleven (that is my age, too), he discovers that he is a wizard (I sometimes wish I could be one, too). He is sent

to a boarding school, Hogwarts School of Witchcraft and Wizardry, where he is supposed to learn everything that will make him the perfect wizard. At Hogwarts, he meets Ron and Hermione, and they become really good friends. Since you were entirely tutored at home, it might be interesting for you to read something about life at a boarding school. There are a number of funny teachers there (I wish I had at least one or two like that), but there is also a lot of bullying. The greatest danger, though, comes from evil Lord Voldemort, who is into black magic and tries everything to become ruler of the world.
The books are very well written and are an exciting read. Even though the Harry Potter novels are supposedly written for children, I know many grown-ups who enjoy reading them. I am sure that you especially will like them, because you are certainly familiar with the situation: you are a good queen and must fight against all the evil in the world.

Your book-friend
Jamie

PS. Make sure you begin with "Harry Potter and the Philosopher's Stone," because there are now seven volumes of Harry Potter and this is the first one.

2. When I was a child, my mother would take me to our local library, where she would borrow some novels, and I would always find some picture books to take home with me, too. When I wrote my "Facharbeit" for my advanced course in biology a few months ago, I hardly used any books for reference but found most of the sources on internet websites at home. What has happened in these ten years? Have libraries become institutions of the past?
I am afraid the answer to this question is basically, "yes". Only two years ago, the most important encyclopaedia publisher in Germany decided to publish its volumes online only. The latest articles from science magazines or prestigious institutes from all over the world can be found on the internet, as well. There is no need to go to a library any longer and perhaps wait for a book or a magazine to be given back by somebody else who has borrowed them. Most of the printed material one might want to read is put on computers in libraries, too, and must be viewed on a screen. But you are not supposed to talk to others but keep silent when you are in a library so as not to disturb anyone – so you might as well work at home on your own anyway.
The only reason why I sometimes still go to a library is when I find the time to read literary works, which I still like doing – in my holidays. Instead of buying books which I will probably read only once, I borrow them from our local library, which is still quite busy when I go there; with mothers and their children, mostly.

3. The cartoon shows a boy's room: a desk with a TV and probably a Playstation on top, as well as some posters on the wall. The boy is sitting on his bed reading a volume of Harry Potter. The boy's mother is standing in front of him. She is apparently very annoyed at her son's activity, as the expression on her face shows, and she is complaining: "180 quid that Nintendo wii cost me! And you're reading a bloody book!" says the caption underneath the cartoon.
The fun in this cartoon comes from the fact that normally we expect parents and teachers and the rest of literate society, too, to complain about young people not reading books but spending all their free time in front of their computers playing games or watching music videos on TV. Here it is just the other way round. I think the artist wants to draw our attention to the fact that many young people still read – as the success of J. K. Rowling, Stephen King, Stephenie Meyer and a lot of other authors shows; writers who are particularly popular among the younger generation.

There is no need to worry about a new generation growing up without books. Reading still holds a great attraction for those of us who love thrilling and romantic stories. I am convinced that young people who love books will not stop reading because of video and online games. On the other hand, perhaps the odd young non-reader who only loves surfing the internet might one day find something there to motivate them to open a proper book.

III. Translation

Die Zukunft des Lesens: Such dir die Bücher aus, die dir gefallen

Fans[1] von Literaturkursen[2] sagen, bei der verpflichtenden Lektüre von Büchern seien viele Kinder gelangweilt oder unfähig die Texte zu verstehen[3]. Schüler ihre eigenen Bücher auswählen zu lassen, kann hingegen[4] helfen, eine lebenslange Liebe zum Lesen aufzubauen.

Kritiker dieser Methode[5] sagen, es sei fraglich, ob Lehrer wirklich mit einem Raum voller Kinder, die alle verschiedene Bücher lesen, fertig werden können. Noch schwerer wiegt der Verlust eines gemeinsamen Kanons von klassischen literarischen Werken – oft sind dies[6] schwierige Bücher, die Kinder wahrscheinlich nicht selbst als Lektüre[7] auswählen würden.

Einige ehemals standhafte[8] Verteidiger eines starren Lehrplans[9] haben jedoch ihre Ansichten gemäßigt. „Eigentlich war ich ein Vertreter der Hochkultur, der unbedingt an Dickens festhalten wollte", sagte Mark Bauerlein, Professor für Englisch. „Aber jetzt denke ich, wenn jemand Harry Potter liest, dann ist das gut. Wir müssen bei den Kindern einfach die Gewohnheit, sich mit Büchern zu beschäftigen, so weit wie möglich aufrecht erhalten."

Anmerkungen

1 Auch: *Freunde*

2 Der Text bezieht sich offensichtlich auf eine Schulsituation mit verpflichtenden Lektüren, also ist die wörtliche Übersetzung *Lesewerkstatt/-workshop* eher zu unverbindlich.

3 Die Konstruktion *leaves children bored* ... sollte nicht wörtlich übersetzt werden.

4 Stilistische Ergänzung

5 Auch: *Vorgehensweise*

6 Stilistische Ergänzung

7 Stilistische Ergänzung

8 Auch: *überzeugte*

9 Auch: *eines Kodex/Kanons verpflichtend zu lesender Werke*

Ihre Meinung ist uns wichtig!

Ihre Anregungen sind uns immer willkommen. Bitte informieren Sie uns mit diesem Schein über Ihre Verbesserungsvorschläge!

Titel-Nr.	Seite	Vorschlag

Bitte hier abtrennen

Lernen • Wissen • Zukunft
STARK

Bitte hier abtrennen

Zutreffendes bitte ankreuzen!

Die Absenderin/der Absender ist:

- ☐ Lehrer/in in den Klassenstufen: ____
- ☐ Fachbetreuer/in
  Fächer: ____
- ☐ Seminarlehrer/in
  Fächer: ____
- ☐ Regierungsfachberater/in
  Fächer: ____
- ☐ Oberstufenbetreuer/in
- ☐ Schulleiter/in
- ☐ Referendar/in, Termin 2. Staatsexamen: ____
- ☐ Leiter/in Lehrerbibliothek
- ☐ Leiter/in Schülerbibliothek
- ☐ Sekretariat
- ☐ Eltern
- ☐ Schüler/in, Klasse: ____
- ☐ Sonstiges: ____

Unterrichtsfächer: (Bei Lehrkräften!)

____

Kennen Sie Ihre Kundennummer?
Bitte hier eintragen.

Absender (Bitte in Druckbuchstaben!)

Name/Vorname

Straße/Nr.

PLZ/Ort/Ortsteil

Telefon privat

Geburtsjahr

E-Mail

Schule/Schulstempel (Bitte immer angeben!)

20-VD9

Bitte ausfüllen und im frankierten Umschlag an uns einsenden. Für Fensterkuverts geeignet.

STARK Verlag
Postfach 1852
85318 Freising

Sicher durch das G9 Abitur!

Klare Fakten, systematische Methoden, prägnante Beispiele, Übungs- sowie Abitur-Prüfungsaufgaben mit erklärenden Lösungen zur Selbstkontrolle.

Deutsch

Gedichte analysieren und interpretieren .... Best.-Nr. 944091
Dramen analysieren und interpretieren .... Best.-Nr. 944092
Epische Texte analysieren und interpretieren .... Best.-Nr. 944093
Erörtern und Sachtexte analysieren .... Best.-Nr. 944094
Abitur-Wissen Prüfungswissen Oberstufe .... Best.-Nr. 94400
Abitur-Wissen Deutsche Literaturgeschichte ..... Best.-Nr. 94405
Abitur-Wissen Textinterpretation
Lyrik, Drama, Epik .... Best.-Nr. 944061
Abitur-Wissen Erörtern u. Sachtexte analysieren Best.-Nr. 944064
Kompakt-Wissen Rechtschreibung .... Best.-Nr. 944065

Englisch

Themenwortschatz .... Best.-Nr. 82451
Grammatikübung .... Best.-Nr. 82452
Übersetzung .... Best.-Nr. 82454
Grundlagen, Arbeitstechniken und
Methoden mit Audio-CD .... Best.-Nr. 944601
Sprechfertigkeit mit Audio-CD .... Best.-Nr. 94467
Sprachmittlung .... Best.-Nr. 94469
Klausuren Englisch Oberstufe .... Best.-Nr. 905113
Abitur-Wissen Landeskunde Großbritannien ..... Best.-Nr. 94461
Abitur-Wissen Landeskunde USA .... Best.-Nr. 94463
Abitur-Wissen Englische Literaturgeschichte ...... Best.-Nr. 94465
Kompakt-Wissen Kurzgrammatik .... Best.-Nr. 90461
Kompakt-Wissen Abitur Themenwortschatz .... Best.-Nr. 90462
Kompakt-Wissen Abitur Landeskunde/Literatur . Best.-Nr. 90463

Französisch

Sprachmittlung · Übersetzung .... Best.-Nr. 94512
Landeskunde Frankreich .... Best.-Nr. 94501
Literatur .... Best.-Nr. 94502
Themenwortschatz .... Best.-Nr. 94503
Textarbeit Oberstufe .... Best.-Nr. 94504
Abitur-Wissen Französische Literaturgeschichte .. Best.-Nr. 94506
Arbeitsheft Französisch 10./11. Klasse
Gymnasium · Gesamtschule
mit Audi-CD (G8) .... Best.-Nr. 955013
ohne Audio-CD (G8) .... Best.-Nr. 955011
Kompakt-Wissen Kurzgrammatik .... Best.-Nr. 945011
Kompakt-Wissen Abitur Themenwortschatz .... Best.-Nr. 945010

Spanisch

Kompakt-Wissen Abitur Themenwortschatz .... Best.-Nr. 945401

Latein

Abitur-Wissen
Lateinische Literaturgeschichte .... Best.-Nr. 94602
Abitur-Wissen Römische Philosophie .... Best.-Nr. 94604
Abitur-Wissen Prüfungswissen Latinum .... Best.-Nr. 94608
Kompakt-Wissen Kurzgrammatik .... Best.-Nr. 906011

Religion

Katholische Religion 1 – gk .... Best.-Nr. 84991
Katholische Religion 2 – gk .... Best.-Nr. 84992
Abitur-Wissen GK ev. Religion
Der Mensch zwischen Gott und Welt .... Best.-Nr. 94973
Abitur-Wissen GK ev. Religion
Die Verantwortung des Christen in der Welt .... Best.-Nr. 94974
Abitur-Wissen Glaube und Naturwissenschaft ..... Best.-Nr. 94977
Abitur-Wissen Jesus Christus .... Best.-Nr. 94978
Abitur-Wissen Die Frage nach dem Menschen .... Best.-Nr. 94990
Abitur-Wissen Die Bibel .... Best.-Nr. 94992
Abitur-Wissen Christliche Ethik .... Best.-Nr. 94993

Ethik

Ethische Positionen
in historischer Entwicklung – gk .... Best.-Nr. 94951
Abitur-Wissen Philosophische Ethik .... Best.-Nr. 94952
Abitur-Wissen Glück und Sinnerfüllung .... Best.-Nr. 94953
Abitur-Wissen Freiheit und Determination .... Best.-Nr. 94954
Abitur-Wissen Recht und Gerechtigkeit .... Best.-Nr. 94955
Abitur-Wissen Religion und Weltanschauungen Best.-Nr. 94956
Abitur-Wissen Wissen · Technik · Verantwortung Best.-Nr. 94957

Wirtschaft/Recht

Betriebswirtschaft ....Best.-Nr. 94851
Abitur-Wissen Volkswirtschaft ....Best.-Nr. 94881
Abitur-Wissen Rechtslehre ....Best.-Nr. 94882
Kompakt-Wissen Abitur Volkswirtschaft (G8) .....Best.-Nr. 948501
Kompakt-Wissen Abitur Betriebswirtschaft.........Best.-Nr. 924801

Kunst

Abitur-Wissen Malerei, Plastik, Architektur (G8)...Best.-Nr. 949618
Abitur-Wissen Malerei ....Best.-Nr. 94961
Abitur-Wissen Analyse und Interpretation .... Best.-Nr. 94962
Kompakt-Wissen Abitur Kunst ....Best.-Nr. 949601

Sport

Bewegungslehre · Sportpsychologie ....Best.-Nr. 94981
Trainingslehre ....Best.-Nr. 94982
Arbeitsheft Sport Trainingslehre (G8) ....Best.-Nr. 9559803

(Bitte blättern Sie um)

Geschichte

Geschichte 1	Best.-Nr. 94781
Geschichte 2	Best.-Nr. 94782
Methodentraining Geschichte	Best.-Nr. 94789
Abitur-Wissen Die Antike	Best.-Nr. 94783
Abitur-Wissen Das Mittelalter	Best.-Nr. 94788
Abitur-Wissen Französische Revolution (G8)	Best.-Nr. 947812
Abitur-Wissen Die Ära Bismarck: Entstehung und Entwicklung des deutschen Nationalstaats	Best.-Nr. 94784
Abitur-Wissen Imperialismus und Erster Weltkrieg	Best.-Nr. 94785
Abitur-Wissen Die Weimarer Republik	Best.-Nr. 47815
Abitur-Wissen Nationalsozialismus und Zweiter Weltkrieg	Best.-Nr. 94786
Abitur Wissen Deutschland von 1945 bis zur Gegenwart	Best.-Nr. 947811
Abitur Wissen USA (G8)	Best.-Nr. 947813
Abitur Wissen Naher Osten (G8)	Best.-Nr. 947814
Kompakt-Wissen Abitur Geschichte Oberstufe (G8)	Best.-Nr. 947601

Sozialkunde

Abitur-Wissen Demokratie	Best.-Nr. 94803
Abitur-Wissen Sozialpolitik	Best.-Nr. 94804
Abitur-Wissen Die Europäische Einigung	Best.-Nr. 94805
Abitur-Wissen Politische Theorie	Best.-Nr. 94806
Abitur-Wissen Internationale Beziehungen	Best.-Nr. 94807
Kompakt-Wissen Abitur Politik/Sozialkunde (G8)	Best.-Nr. 948001

Geographie/Erdkunde

Geographie 1 – 11. Klasse (G8)	Best.-Nr. 94911
Geographie 2 – 12. Klasse (G8)	Best.-Nr. 94912
Abitur-Wissen Entwicklungsländer	Best.-Nr. 94902
Abitur-Wissen Die USA	Best.-Nr. 94903
Abitur-Wissen Europa	Best.-Nr. 94905
Abitur-Wissen Der asiatisch-pazifische Raum	Best.-Nr. 94906
Abitur-Wissen GUS-Staaten/Russland	Best.-Nr. 94908
Kompakt-Wissen Erdkunde	Best.-Nr. 949010

Erziehungswissenschaft/Psychologie

Erziehungswissenschaft	Best.-Nr. 94941
Grundwissen Pädagogik	Best.-Nr. 92480
Grundwissen Psychologie	Best.-Nr. 92481

G9 Abiturprüfung 2011

Viele Jahrgänge der zentral gestellten Abitur-Prüfungsaufgaben an Gymnasien in Bayern, einschließlich des **aktuellen Jahrgangs**. Mit **vollständigen Lösungen**.

G9 Abitur Mathematik – LK Bayern	Best.-Nr. 95000
G9 Abitur Mathematik – gk Bayern	Best.-Nr. 95100
G9 Abitur Physik – LK Bayern	Best.-Nr. 95300
G9 Abitur Physik – gk Bayern	Best.-Nr. 95320
G9 Abitur Biologie – LK Bayern	Best.-Nr. 95700
G9 Abitur Biologie – gk Bayern	Best.-Nr. 95710
G9 Abitur Chemie – LK Bayern	Best.-Nr. 95730
G9 Abitur Chemie – gk Bayern	Best.-Nr. 95740
G9 Abitur Geschichte – LK Bayern	Best.-Nr. 95760
G9 Abitur Geschichte – gk Bayern	Best.-Nr. 95780
G9 Abitur Sozialkunde – gk/LK Bayern	Best.-Nr. 95800
G9 Abitur Geographie – LK Bayern	Best.-Nr. 95900
G9 Abitur Geographie – gk Bayern	Best.-Nr. 95930
G9 Abitur Wirtschaft/Recht – LK Bayern	Best.-Nr. 95850
G9 Abitur Wirtschaft/Recht – gk Bayern	Best.-Nr. 95880
G9 Abitur Deutsch – LK Bayern	Best.-Nr. 95400
G9 Abitur Deutsch – gk Bayern	Best.-Nr. 95410
G9 Abitur Deutsch Colloquium – gk BY	Best.-Nr. 95411
G9 Abitur Englisch – LK Bayern	Best.-Nr. 95460
G9 Abitur Englisch – gk Bayern	Best.-Nr. 95470
G9 Abitur Französisch – gk/LK Bayern	Best.-Nr. 95500
G9 Abitur Latein – gk/LK Bayern	Best.-Nr. 95600
G9 Abitur Religion r.-k. – gk Bayern	Best.-Nr. 95990
G9 Abitur Religion ev. – gk Bayern	Best.-Nr. 95970
G9 Abitur Ethik – gk Bayern	Best.-Nr. 95950
G9 Abitur Sport – LK Bayern	Best.-Nr. 95980
G9 Abitur Kunst – LK Bayern	Best.-Nr. 95960

Fachübergreifend

Richtig Lernen Tipps und Lernstrategien – Oberstufe	Best.-Nr. 10483
Referate und Facharbeiten – Oberstufe	Best.-Nr. 10484
Training Methoden Meinungen äußern, Ergebnisse präsentieren	Best.-Nr. 10486

Natürlich führen wir noch mehr Titel für alle Schularten. Wir informieren Sie gerne!

Telefon: 0180 3 179000* **www.stark-verlag.de**

Telefax: 0180 3 179001* **E-Mail: info@stark-verlag.de**

Bestellungen bitte direkt an:
STARK Verlagsgesellschaft mbH & Co. KG · Postfach 1852 · 85318 Freising
Tel. 0180 3 179000* · Fax 0180 3 179001* · www.stark-verlag.de · info@stark-verlag.de
*9 Cent pro Min. aus dem deutschen Festnetz, Mobilfunk bis 42 Cent pro Min.
Aus dem Mobilfunknetz wählen Sie die Festnetznummer: 08167 9573-0

Lernen • Wissen • Zukunft
STARK

20-VD9